Harry Waugh's Wine Diary

VOLUME NINE

'Le Degustation' by L. Boillot (1825) brought up to date by Harry Waugh and the team from Jackson's, Piccadilly.
Clockwise: Mr Hancock – the general manager, Julian Cotterell – managing director, Mr. Jarvis who sold the wines, with Harry Waugh.

Harry Waugh's Wine Diary

VOLUME NINE: 1978–1981

Christie's Wine Publications: 1981

Christie's Wine Publications
8 King Street, St James's, London SW1, England
Editor-in-Chief, Michael Broadbent, MW
Consultant Editor, Patrick Matthews
Editorial Adviser, Edmund Penning-Rowsell

By the same author:
Bacchus on the Wing (1966)
The Changing Face of Wine (1968)
Pick of the Bunch (1970)
Diary of a Winetaster (1972)
Winetaster's Choice (1973)
Harry Waugh's Wine Diary, Volumes Six (1975), Seven (1976),
    and Eight (1978)

ISBN 0-903432-24-2

design/print in England by
Eyre & Spottiswoode Ltd, Queen's Printers,
Grosvenor Press, Portsmouth

Contents

List of illustrations

Foreword

It is not surprising that Harry has a great following. I am only sorry that the very many people who have written to us saying 'when is the next edition of the Wine Diary being published?' have been kept waiting. At least, with this, his latest book, Waugh afficionados will have their fill.

Since Volume 8 was published three years ago, a lot of wine has flowed under the Waugh bridge and a lot of mileage has been covered, or more appropriately, flown, by England's ambassador of wine.

For many of us, being as open, indeed as transparent, as Harry would reveal not a few flaws. So in Harry one sees nothing but appealing traits, amongst the more obvious and endearing being kindness and enthusiasm. And it comes out in his writing. Perhaps writing is not exactly the word, for I think it is pertinent for the reader to know that these diaries or travel journals are basically the result of Prue typing what Harry dictates daily into a pocket tape recorder after every tasting, dinner and journey. The result is fresh, idiosyncratic, pure Waugh. The written page is Harry talking directly to us.

I must confess that in editing the typescripts which became volumes 6, 7 and 8, I tended to wield the editorial scissors and paste fairly rigorously, partly out of sheer necessity, as twice as much material was produced for the book size and format which, in turn, was necessitated by mundane factors such as number of pages, the fiendish cost of setting and printing, and even weight (for most of Christie's Wine Publications are sold to an exclusive and loyal group of readers by direct mail). In short, cost and selling price. Rightly or wrongly I felt that our readers would be interested principally in Harry's tasting notes and assessments, rather than in his observation of developments in wine areas, and recollections of gourmet evenings. Incidentally, the importance of the latter is not just to titillate our palates but to provide salutary lessons in gracious living, imaginative menus and combinations of wines – and, sometimes, how *not* to do all these things. For if I have any criticism at all of the otherwise engagingly warm hospitality of our American friends, it is that their *largesse* is sometimes a little *too* large: a dinner party or tasting is planned as though it is the last they or anyone else will ever attend, often with rather too many courses, too many wines. If it seems rather ungrateful to mention this I would gently draw attention to the most civilised gourmets and wine lovers, the towering survivors, who managed to enjoy life to the full but not the *over*full, and whose motto is, or was, consciously or unconsciously, 'moderation in all things'. André Simon, one of the greatest of all times, lived until well into his 90s. He put this down to appreciation of the finer things in life, in moderation – and his liveliness and longevity to a half-bottle of champagne every morning of his life! The late Pierre Lanson, again a nonegenarian, when asked about his long life ascribed it to a daily dose of his own champagne – and this remark was not just a specious publicity stunt. Harry Waugh – we will not talk about his age, but his brightness and sprightliness deny it – is another. And whoever saw André, Harry or any of their peers the worse for drink? This brings me to the last point which, more than their connection with food and wine, makes these people interesting and rewarding to know. It is what I mentioned earlier: enthusiasm, plus an unquenchable interest in what is going on around them, and in people.

Without wishing to detain the reader further – indeed I am sure most of you have delved straight into the heart of the book – I must thank Patrick Matthews, our editorial consultant, for putting the whole of this volume into shape. I am sure Patrick has not used my scissors and paste; he has instead more gently moulded Harry's transcript into chapters and let the Master speak his mind.

And I, for once, will sit back and enjoy his reminiscences and his company.

MICHAEL BROADBENT
Christie's

I USA, April & May 1978

Westchester
April 9 1978

After the long drab winter and the seemingly endless grey skies over London, how stimulating it was to step out into the brilliant sunshine at John F. Kennedy airport. Waiting to meet me were Ron Fonte, the president of Les Amis du Vin, and my first host of this journey, Arnold Kowalsky, who with his wife Dorothy and their daughter – lives in Yonkers, Westchester County. By profession a teacher of music, Arnold Kowalsky founded the Westchester Chapter of Les Amis du Vin only a year ago and through his drive and enthusiasm has already made it one of the most active among the 209 Chapters now spread across the country.

A short rest after the long flight was necessary to enable me to enjoy the excellent dinner party arranged for me later that evening. My fellow guests were Mr. and Mrs. William Deutsch (Bill is a director of Somerset Wine Company) and Signor and Signora Gaetano Bertani, prominent vineyard proprietors from Verona in Italy. Signor Bertani produces Valpolicella and is particularly noted for his Amarone. Mr. and Mrs. Philip di Belardino, the U.S. agent for Bertani, were also present, as well as a freelance writer, Barbara Edsun.   In accordance with the pleasant custom they have in America of serving appetisers, really a first course before a meal, there appeared a fabulous spread of seafood – oysters, clams, mussels and crab – and, as though that were not enough, there was also a choice of pâtés. The opening wines were 1975 Crémant de Bourgogne tasteviné and Pommery N.V. from a magnum, the latter much the better of the two. The first course at table, a spicy *saucisson* (*boudin blanc*) was accompanied by three rather rare Vouvrays, all from the firm Mouzay-Mignot.

Wine	Characteristics
1953 Vouvray (*doux*)	Very pale in colour, a trace of sulphur on the nose which probably accounts for its having kept so well, medium sweet, but unusually fresh for its age.
1955 Vouvray (*doux*)	Darker colour, much fuller bouquet, a pleasant full flavour, with good fruity acidity, quite different in style, more rounded and frll-bodied with a hint of *botrytis* at the end.
1959 Vouvray (*moelleux*)	Pale colour, richer bouquet, a fuller but less refined flavour.

Of these three I preferred the older 1953. With roast beef came 1953 Château Lascombes, dark in colour with a delightful bouquet, typically

[9]

Margaux. Good fruit but drying off at the finish. At over 20 years old, it does not look as though this will improve any more.

With our cheese we tasted two vintages of Signor Bertani's Amarone, 1964 and 1958 and at 15° alcohol they were both rich and strong. Signor Bertani explained that the best Amarones are matured in wood for ten years before bottling and that they show at their best when served with game. Although our Italian friend did not agree, I found a suspicion of oxidation on both of the Amarones, particularly the 1964. Ten years in wood is a long time for any wine and the risk of oxidation must be great. However being an ignoramus on the subject of Italian wine, I am in no position to judge but imagine this is how Amarone has been drunk through the centuries and how the Italian connoisseur has grown to like it.

Then followed two Durkheimer Spielberg Riesling Ausleses (Johannes Kaunst & Sohne)

Wine	Characteristics
1976	Attractive nose, fruity and delightful, full but not so overwhelmingly so.
1975	A richer bouquet, not quite so sweet, but with greater depth of flavour and of finer quality.
	These provided a good contrast between the two fine vintages.
Sandeman Port 1950 Vintage	Good colour and bouquet, not a big wine but very good. For this light vintage the Sandeman had kept very well.

Dinner at Auberge Maxime
Monday 10 April

A day of rest at the Kowalsky's with a slow recovery from jet lag – just as well in view of the sumptuous dinner in store that evening at the nearby Auberge Maxime. Maxime Ribera has made a considerable reputation for himself at his restaurant Argenteuil, and so successful has he been that recently he has opened this smaller and more intimate place in North Salem. As the cost was 90 dollars per person, something rather special was expected and if the truth be known it was really more than I, at any rate, could manage. Here is the menu: Canape de Saumon froid, La Salade de Laitue et Homard, Le Pâté de Sole en Feuillette aux deux sauces, Sorbet au Calvados, Côte d'Agneau Maintenon, Caille Farci au Foie Gras, Fromage, Bombe Glacée aux Pralines.

Canard Côteaux Champenoise, still champagne, formed the aperitif, fresh and very dry, good of its kind, but like many of these Côteaux Champenois, it has a little too much acidity for my personal taste. The delectable baby lobster was accompanied by Meursault Perrières 1974 (Bichot) a little oxidised and in consequence disappointing. That was amply made up for by the Sole en Feuillette; indeed it was difficult to decide with which sauce it tasted better, the lobster or that made with champagne, a fine dish. The spring lamb cutlets also in a delicious sauce made a good foil for the 1970 Cos d'Estournel. The latter, dark of colour, a full bouquet, deep flavour and plenty of fruit, was in my opinion served before its time, i.e. there was still far too much tannin and quite a lot of acidity to lose. Anyway time will tell! Although each course had been purposely kept as small as possible, the next, the cold quail stuffed with real foie gras, was almost too much of a good thing.

Midway through this gargantuan feast I had been asked to enlarge upon the situation in France where I had been only the previous week. One question crops up regularly, namely why nowadays is it that red burgundy is so disappointing. Having just expounded (at least according to my own theory) that either the vines are exposed to excessive fertilisation (or is it a more prolific clone?), causing the pale colour, the quick maturity and the much shorter life than in pre-war days, immediately I was confounded by the Echézeaux Domaine Clos Frantin 1971 (Bichot) which had just been poured. To begin with, it had a good dark colour, almost as dark as the Cos 1970, a lovely bouquet and a remarkably rich flavour; in fact exceptional quality such as I have not encountered for a long time. So impressive was this wine shipped by Schenley that I had to get to my feet once more to confess I had to swallow some of my previous words! Here was a demonstration that at least a few growers are still making wine in the old manner. How sad, though, for all would-be burgundy lovers that there are not more of them!

There were still two wines to come, magnums of 1976 Guntrum's Niersteiner Oelberg Trockenbeerenauslese and Sandeman 1963 vintage port and lovely as each was they proved almost an *embarras de richesse*. Even so here are my notes: The Rhine wine, although full and sweet, fortunately was not too rich, its youthful freshness being most attractive; the Sandeman of the now famous 1963 vintage had been well chosen; although still really too young, it was perhaps more enjoyable to drink at this moment than one of the normally bigger wines made by, say, Taylor or Fonseca.

Among the pleasant surprises of that evening was to find among the guests my good friends Carlo and Sheila Russo from Ho Ho Kus, N.Y. The excellent Carlo is one of the leading wine merchants on the East Coast. Also present were Charles and Gloria Mandelstam who live nearby and who were to give me a bed for the night. A lawyer by profession, Charles is one of the principal owners of Domaine Gerin, one of the finest vineyards of Côte Rôtie in the Rhône Valley.

North Salem
Tuesday 11 April

A peaceful day with Charles Mandelstam in his comfortable house in North Salem. Originally an 18th-century farm, it overlooks fields, woods and a large lake. I noticed the vegetation was a long way behind even that in England where our spring was some two weeks behind. The late spring had also been evident the week before when I had been staying at Château Latour in the Médoc. While many of the trees were bursting into leaf, only the *merlot* vines were showing signs of budding. What a contrast from the year before when all the vines were in early leaf by the end of March. I well remember the growers' anxiety about frost. As it turned out how right they had been, for the April frosts reduced the 1977 crop by almost 50 per cent. Charles Mandelstam has what must surely be an ideal cellar underneath his old house and while down there he selected a bottle of his 1969 Côte Rôtie which we enjoyed with our lunch.

The meeting that evening took place at the Tarrytown Hilton Hotel in Tarrytown close to the Hudson River and once again Arnold Kowalsky excelled himself. The subject was port and my task as lecturer was made all the easier by the choice of wines he had made. As a result I was able to demonstrate fairly effectively the possibilities of this post-prandial nectar as yet so little understood by the American public. It is just as well perhaps because once the delight of vintage port becomes appreciated, inevitably there will be too little to go around.

This assembly provided a good opportunity for a gossip with various members of the wine trade whose firms represented Warre, Sandeman and Rebello Valente in the U.S. Also present were Shelly and Pauline Wasserman who have now written three books: on the wines of Italy, the Côtes du Rhône and white wines in general.

Following an aperitif of a chilled and rather good white port from Sandeman this is what we tasted.

Wine	Characteristics
Christian Brothers Tina Cream	Quite a nice tawny colour, bouquet fair, a different flavour from port as I know it, but definitely tawny in style. Not bad.
Paul Masson	(From a dreadful heart-shaped bottle. that alone was enough to put one off.) Colour fairly dark, the bouquet on the heavy side and the flavour altogether too sweet and plummy. The name port deserves better treatment than that!
Croft's Ruby	Medium colour, good fruit with pleasing finish.
Sandeman Partners	An attractive reddish tinge, a fairly full, but fine bouquet and quite full flavoured, good quality.
Warre's Nimrod	A lovely tawny colour, distinguished bouquet and a good example of a fine tawny of some age.
Warre's Warrior Vintage Character	Good dark colour, a full fruity bouquet, full-bodied and quite robust, good quality.
1969 Warre's Late Vintage (bottled 1971)	Good colour, a good full-bodied wine.

The wines before the break had mostly been what can be described as wood ports, i.e. matured in wood and bottled for ready sale. Wood port should be consumed reasonably quickly because unlike the vintage it does not continue to improve after bottling.

The second part comprised the vintage wines, i.e. those matured in bottle. To digress, a vintage for port is only declared when the climatic conditions have been exceptionally favourable. For example, only three vintages were declared in the fifties (although a few houses did ship a 1954, it was not general) 1950, 1955 and 1958. Likewise in the sixties there were also only three, 1960, 1963, 1966, plus two or three houses such as Cockburn's Sandeman and Martinez, all of whom shipped a 1967 instead of a 1966. During recent years there has been a radical change over vintage port. In the past it used to be matured in wood in Oporto for two years and then shipped to England where it was put into bottle by the old established wine merchants as well as some of the brewers. Now, according to Portuguese law, all vintage port since 1970 has to be bottled in Oporto.

The first wine after the break was a crusted port, the 1961 of Quinta do Noval. From its name it is obvious that it is handled more or less on the same lines as vintage port, the difference being that it is seldom produced from a famous vintage but usually from a off-year such as this 1961. Also at times it is bottled after perhaps three years in wood instead of two. In my early days in the wine trade, most of the leading British retail firms bottled and sold a crusted port under their own name. Two well-known ones are Croft's Roeda and Taylor's Vargellas. In fact at home in London I am enjoying very much at this moment the 1965 Taylor's Vargellas. Not quite so expensive as vintage port and without perhaps the renown, it is surprisingly good. Vargellas is of course the name of the vineyard from which that particular wine is made, in other words a single *quinta*.

Wine	Characteristics
1961 Quinta do Noval (crusted)	Colour beginning to turn a little mahogany, an attractive bouquet, a huge wine which provided a considerable contrast after the wood ports. Very good quality.
1971 Rebello Valento (Robertson)	Dark colour, rich rather plummy bouquet, immature but powerful, showing good underlying quality.
1970 Sandeman	Dark colour, distinguished bouquet, not a big wine but has a delicious taste. This should make a fine bottle in the years to come.
1966 Warre	Dark colour, distinctive bouquet, still very immature, nevertheless a full rich wine. Will also make an excellent bottle.
1963 Rebello Valente	Dark colour, superbly rich bouquet, full-bodied and of great quality. Not yet ready to drink.
1934 Rebello Valente	Colour almost tawny, an old but gracious bouquet; aged, yes, but remarkably good.

I considered myself fortunate to have such a fine range of wines to discuss. At the end of the proceedings I said farewell to my previous hosts, the Kowalskys and joined my new one, Michael Douglas, for quite a long drive to his home on Long Island. After that particular tasting I was glad not to have to drive myself! This was to be my second visit to the Syosset Chapter. On the previous occasion I remember we had compared some of the excellent Pomerols of 1970. One can only hope the local members took the opportunity to lay them aside at that time because they are now turning out remarkably well.

Fox Hollow Inn
Wednesday 12 April

Michael Douglas and his partner, Jim Galtieri, own a first-class wine business in Syosset called Post Liquors and between them they direct the Syosset Chapter of Les Amis du Vin. The meeting that evening took place at the Fox Hollow Inn, where I feel almost at home for the rooms are embellished with an interesting collection of nineteenth century hunting and racing prints.

Earlier on at dinner with the Douglases and the Galtieris, we drank two good vintages of Château Gruaud-Larose. The 1966, full of fruit, is still somewhat severe and in consequence it was overwhelmed by the delicious 1962.

About 120 people assembled for a blind comparison of California Cabernet Sauvignons with red Bordeaux. All the wines had been poured by the time we sat down but in view of the fact those from California were of more recent vintages, they were poured first and this seemed to work out well. While the Californians were younger, at least two of them were of the highly successful 1974 vintage. These are the wines and the result in accordance with my own personal notes.

[13]

Wine	Characteristics	My Placing	Group Placing	My Points
Château Giscours 1971, *Margeaux*	Retail price $7.99. Dark colour, pleasing bouquet, good fruit but on dry side, plenty of tannin and a slightly sharpish finish.	4th	8th	14/20
Robert Mondavi Cabernet Sauvignon 1974 (Regular)	Retail price $7.99. Dark colour, nice nose, good fruit, a lot of tannin but good quality.	5th	5th	13/20
Château Ducru-Beaucaillou 1971 *Saint-Julien*	Retail price $10.95. Good colour, attractive bouquet, good fruit and flavour.	2nd	4th	16/20
Burgess Cellars Cabernet Sauvignon 1974	Retail price $7.50. Somewhat heavy bouquet, too full and too massive for me, lacks finesse.	6th	2nd	12/20
Château Lafon-Rochet 1970 *Saint-Estèphe*	Retail price $7.99. Good colour, fruity bouquet, medium body, some tannin to lose, rather good.	3rd	7th	15/20
Les Forts de Latour 1971 *Pauillac*	Retail price $7.99. Colour medium, attractive bouquet, good fruit and body, well balanced with a distinctive flavour. By far the best wine in my opinion.	1st	6th	18/20
Spring Mountain Cabernet Sauvignon 1975	Retail price $9.75. Good colour, pretty bouquet, a big fruity wine but too much acidity for my liking.	8th	1st	10/20
Mayacamas Cabernet Sauvignon 1973	Retail price $12.75. Dark colour, heavy herby bouquet, a massive affair, lots of tannin, rather coarse with a sharpish finish.	7th	3rd	11/20

As may be imagined this was not at all an easy tasting All most of us knew was that there were four Cabernets from California and four from Bordeaux. The only wine I definitely knew to be present was Lafon-Rochet but have to admit that I did not actually recognise it. So far as I was concerned, the first step was to sort out the apples from the oranges, i.e. the red Bordeaux from the Californian. In this, in view of their more massive structure, it was not too difficult to pick out numbers 4, 7 and 8 as from California, but on account of its extra quality, at least in my opinion, the Robert Mondavi 1974 presented more of a problem, a good wine under any circumstances. Having decided (hopefully) which were the French wines, I had then to put them in order of preference and, had I seen the crib, I could not from my own point of view have been more pleased with the result. I was unaware Les Forts de Latour 1971 was present, but for me it was easily the best and, since I am such an admirer of all modern vintages of Ducru-Beaucaillou, it was equally satisfying to find I had placed that second.

Incidentally at a blind tasting of the 1970 vintage (excluding first growths) a month before I had placed the Ducru-Beaucaillou and Les Forts de Latour equal first and well ahead of all other growths.

It will be noticed that there was a considerable difference between the group's ratings of these wines and my own. Had the tasting taken place in California, with their natural in-built predelection for the taste and style of their own wine I would not have been surprised to find the Californias being preferred. However in the case of this group, the reason I think for their preference for numbers 4, 7 and 8 is because the tasters may have been confused by their more obvious style.

Knoxville, Tennessee
Thursday 13 April

Having boarded the plane at John F. Kennedy airport we sat there for two hours while repairs were made to one of the engines. Having consequently missed my connection from Washington D.C. to Knoxville in Tennessee, I was advised to remain on the plane until it reached Charleston and from there catch another plane to Knoxville. By the time we approached Charleston, I feared I would miss this second connection, but we arrived with literally a second to spare. Briefcase in hand I had to run like a hare to become the last boarder before the Knoxville plane set off. Despite the loss of my baggage, mercifully at Knoxville my luck began to change. Although we were already half an hour late my sympathetic hosts, Dick Reizenstein and the Killifers, were reassuring, telling me that the man in charge of the airport was a fan, who followed all my writings. The splendid man found my bags and delivered them himself to the Killifers house during the early hours of the morning.

We then went straight to the house of John and Betty Threadgill, the hosts for the tasting, and what a tasting it proved to be.

Some recent vintages of Château Pétrus and Château d'Yquem

Château Pétrus

Wine	Characteristics	Price	Points
1974	Quite a dark colour, fairly full bouquet, plenty of fruit, somewhat harsh, probably on account of its vintage. On the rough side too in relation to other vintages of Pétrus; some acidity at the finish did not add to its attraction. This 1974 probably needs some three to four years before it will be ready.	$15.00	11/20
1973	Quite a good colour for a 1973, pleasant bouquet, on light side but nice and easy to taste, almost ready now.	$16.95	13/20
1972	Medium colour, not a bad nose, good fruit and an unexpectedly pleasant flavour. A little acidity naturally, but should be ready before too long. It provided an agreeable surprise.	$13.95	14/20
1971	Good colour and an attractive almost perfumed bouquet, rich and round, lots of tannin of course but oh so good! Needs two or three years.	$27.50	18/20
1970	Good colour, fine rich bouquet, delightful flavour, heaps of fruit, still tannin to lose.	$20.00	17/20
1969	Good colour and bouquet, not such a big wine as the others naturally, but its very special flavour was unexpectedly nice, especially for a 1969.	$16.80	15/20

[15]

The author

| 1967 | Dark colour, splendid mature bouquet, full-bodied with a wonderful flavour, a lovely taste was left in the mouth. This confirms to me once again that the Pétrus is the best of all the 1967s. | $20.95 | 19/20 |
| 1966 | Dark colour, rich bouquet, heaps of fruit, still closed up and very backward. If you have any of this in your cellar, don't touch it for several years. | $32.25 | 17/20 |

The surprises among this *embarras de richesse* were the two off-vintages 1972 and 1969 and they underline the skill of Jean-Claude Berrouet who, as well as Pétrus, also makes all the other Pomerols of Jean-Pierre Moueix, La Fleur-Pétrus, Latour-Pomerol and so on.

It is unfortunate for us all that the vineyard of Pétrus is so small that the average annual production is no more than roughly 4,000 cases. The scarcity must no doubt add to its value but in view of the consistently high quality it is understandable that Pétrus is now fetching a higher price even than Lafite. My fatigue was kept at bay because there was more to come in the form of some vintages of Château d'Yquem.

Château d'Yquem

Wine	*Characteristics*
1971	Pale golden colour, fresh flowery, fragrant bouquet with a similar taste, fresh and fragrant, a delightful wine, more forward than the 1970, if not so serious.
1970	Pale golden colour, a fine deep aroma, wonderful depth of flavour, more concentrated than the 1971. Splendid quality.
1967	Golden colour, a truly fabulous bouquet, a heavenly rich wine. A masterpiece and about as good a Sauternes as one could ever wish to find.

The all-famous 1921 d'Yquem must have been a few years older, i.e. around 15 years old, when I first began to make its acquaintance before the war, an incredible wine while in its prime, better perhaps than now. Nevertheless the 1967 must be more or less in the same high class. After the remarkable 1921, the other really great pre-war vintages of Château d'Yquem were 1928, 1929 and 1937.

Friday 14 April   Fred and Raisa Killiffer, who gave me a bed for the night, live in a pleasant house directly overlooking the river. Knoxville, close to the Smokey Mountains, has a lovely setting and is among the four or five cities in the U.S. most noted for its dogwood trees. Mr. and Mrs. Patrick Beeker called to take me for a most enjoyable drive embellished by innumerable azaleas in full bloom. In front of many houses there were colourful banks of multi-coloured phlox.

We finally arrived at the Reizensteins house, where brunch was awaiting us and to accompany it a bottle of Louis M. Martini's delectable Moscato Amabile. A few weeks before Dick Reizenstein and his wife had been to California and with my imminent arrival in mind had tried but failed to find any Moscato Amabile in the shops. He had no alternative but to get in touch with Louis'daughter and persuade her to extract this bottle from her father's personal cellar! The one disadvantage of this fragrant, fresh nectar is that it has to be kept under refrigeration, so Dick Reizenstein had had quite a time keeping that bottle chilled in his hotel room before his departure home. The final enjoyment was well worth his care and trouble.

That however was by no means the end of my vinous experience in Knoxville. Dick Reizenstein, a marketing consultant by profession, as well as manager of a highly successful wine school, had also brought back from California some treasured bottles of Late Harvest Bunch Selected Rieslings. As I explained in my seventh Diary these *botrytis* dessert wines are a new development, now all the rage in California, and it was therefore a wonderful opportunity to taste some of them again. There were four altogether and I was thankful I had asked for them to be tasted anonymously, especially since as it turned out, there was a German Trockenbeerenauslese among them!

	Wine	Characteristics	My points
Late Harvest Bunch Selected Rieslings	1. Edelwein Gold Freemark Abbey 1976 (Residual sugar 16%)	Pale golden colour, a somewhat musty nose which, however, improved with airing, rich with a pleasant flavour and tasting better than the bouquet foretold. *Note* A year later this mustiness on the bouquet had disappeared.	12/20
	2. Wachenheimer Mandelgarten Scheurebe Trockenbeeren-auslese 1971 Burklin-Wolf	A wine which was awarded a gold prize at an exhibition in Germany in 1973. Golden colour, distinguished bouquet, a rich but delicious taste with a lovely finish. Superb quality.	19/20
	3. Joseph Phelps Late Harvest Select 1976 (Residual sugar 23.1%)	Slightly deeper golden colour, fine bouquet, rich and fuller than No. 2, very good. All the same super quality.	18/20
	4. Château St.-Jean Johannisberg Riesling 1976 Robert Young Vineyard (Residual sugar 25.4%)	A pale golden colour but as with No. 1 the nose a bit musty, a huge rich wine though with a hint, was it, of apricots? If one can criticise, there appears to be a lack of acidity to ensure longevity.	16/20

To sum up, there was more finesse on the bouquet of Nos. 2 and 3. The bouquet of 1 and 4 seemed similar in style but No. 4 was a much fuller wine. Until I knew the final result I was under the impression that 2 and 3 came from Germany and 1 and 4 from California.

Atlanta, Georgia
Saturday 15 April

A pleasant surprise lay in store in Atlanta where my hosts were Jim and Sue Hinsdale, whom I had met in London last year at the International Wine & Food Society Convention. The weather both at Knoxville and here at Atlanta has been superb and such an agreeable change after the winter at home.

At the dinner before the tasting Jim produced a real surprise, a bottle of 1968 Grange Hermitage, the finest red wine made in Australia. Full-bodied and powerful, it went well with the spring lamb.

The tasting took place at a local country club and after all the tension and fatigue of recent travelling, it was a relief to learn that the comparison between some red Bordeaux and wines from California was to be in the open, i.e. not a 'blind' affair. While a blind tasting is always a challenge too many of them on a tight schedule such as this can add to the general strain. After an aperitif of iced Lillet, these are the wines the regional director, Parkes Redwine, had chosen for us.

Wine	Characteristics	My points
Haut-Brion 1967	Dark colour, distinguished bouquet, good flavour and did not appear to have so much acidity as at my last tasting of this particular wine, fine quality.	17/20
Heitz Cabernet Sauvignon 1968 *Napa*	Dark colour, nice eucalyptus bouquet, but more plummy, more obvious, more full-flavoured than the Haut-Brion.	14/20
Lafon-Rochet 1970	Dark colour, good bouquet, medium body, some tannin and a trace of acidity, attractive all the same.	14/20
Giscours 1970	Very dark colour, good nose, a delightfully rounded quite rich wine. Well balanced and of excellent quality, still needs a year or so.	18/20
Robert Mondavi (unfined) 1970	Good colour, well-bred bouquet, good fruit, a little acidity at the finish.	15/20
Les Forts de Latour 1970	Very dark colour, deep bouquet, a fine full-bodied wine with a pleasant finish. Given time this should make an excellent bottle. Already it has made quite a name for itself in the U.S.	18/20

The Midnight Sun Restaurant

At dinner the previous evening my fellow guest was Mrs. Nancy Lester, the curator of Swan House, which, although only built in 1928, is a landmark of Atlanta and houses a fine collection of antique furniture originating mainly from England. The original owners, the Inman family, had collected all these treasures between 1900 and 1928 at prices which no doubt would be laughable today.

A dinner had been arranged at the Midnight Sun restaurant in Atlanta and was attended by about 20 people, a mutual affair, each couple bringing two bottles. There was thus a somewhat unpremeditated yet interesting selection of wine.

Before we sat down we enjoyed some remarkable Pinot Chardonnay but perhaps it is better to include that in my notes:

The white wines

Wine	Characteristics	My points
Heitz Pinot Chardonnay 1973	Nice nutty bouquet, full-bodied yes, but fresh with an excellent flavour. This had been brought along by my friend Ben Mazzara who manages the Grapevine wine store, Birmingham, Alabama.	17/20

Callaway Blanc Fumé 1974	Only a faint taste of the *sauvignon-blanc* grape and not very exciting.	12/20
Sterling Blanc de Sauvignon 1973 (from a magnum)	Pleasant bouquet, good flavour and a nice finish.	15/20
Château Grillet 1970	Fragrant bouquet, a full, rounded wine with just a hint of sugar at the finish. As fine as it is rare.	18/20

With a production of only around 4,000 bottles it is understandable why one comes across Château Grillet so seldom. Incidentally this vineyard, near Condrieu, in the Rhône Valley, is planted with *viognier* vines and has the distinction of being the smallest in France to bear its own *Appellation Controlée*.

The red wines

Wine	Characteristics	My points
Rioja Frederick Paternino Grand Reserva 1955	Good colour, an unusual bouquet, agreeable flavour, fairly full-bodied but could have more breeding. Perhaps the most notable thing about this is that it had come from the cellar of the late Ernest Hemingway!	13/20
Concannon Cabernet Sauvignon 1969, limited bottling	Dark colour, a rather roasted 'hot climate' bouquet, lots of fruit though and more sugar than usual. Massive, but lacks finesse.	11/20
Lynch-Bages 1970	Almost black in colour, a real Pauillac bouquet, with a hint of cedar. A huge wine packed with fruit. Although quite unready to drink now this has a splendid future.	18/20
Lascombes 1962	Dark colour, excellent nose, a really good Margaux flavour and beautifully modulated. Easily the finest of the evening.	19/20
Warre 1955, late bottled 1959	Incidentally when this bottle was decanted it was found it had thrown a huge deposit. While not so outstanding as the real 1955 Warre (bottled after two years), it provided a pleasant finish to the evening.	–

Sunday 16 April

The rest of my stay in Atlanta was in the home of Bill and Fran Graves. I had met Bill during my last visit to Atlanta when together with Russ McCall and Dr. King we had tasted some interesting California Chardonnays. Among the guests for dinner that evening was Morton Hodges, who brought with him the two Dr. Barolet burgundies, and Russ McCall, who was responsible for the 1961 La Mission-Haut-Brion.

Here are details of the wines we enjoyed during that meal, the Chardonnays being tasted anonymously.

Wine	Characteristics	My placing
1973 Sterling Chardonnay (magnum)	Very pale colour, fine nose, light but clean and fresh.	1st

1967 Meursault Genevrières *Hospices de Beaune*	A more golden colour, a fuller but tired bouquet, full-flavoured with a dry finish. Oxidised and past its best.	4th
1973 Chalone Chardonnay	Good colour, fruity bouquet, full-flavoured with trace of sweetness at the end.	3rd
1973 Spring Mountain Chardonnay	Good colour and bouquet, fairly full-bodied but rather nice.	2nd

In view of its age the poor Meursault Genevrières 1967 was at a disadvantage in this blind comparison. Even we humans have to age sometime! On the other hand, the Sterling, which most of us liked best, had the advantage of coming from a magnum.

Wine	Characteristics
1935 Bonnes-Mares *Dr. Barolet*	Medium colour, good bouquet, on dry side but still all there. Remarkable when one considers its age and the fact that the 1935 vintage was pretty poor anyway.
1929 Gevrey-Chambertin *Dr. Barolet*	Good dark colour, fine bouquet and a lovely, lovely taste. Oh for fine pre-war red burgundy!

Amazed as I was groping my way down those cellar steps of the late Dr. Barolet's cellar in Beaune, little did I imagine the astonishing repercussions which those excellent red burgundies would cause, particularly on the U.S. market. A comparison with the style of wine made then with much of what is produced on the Côte d'Or nowadays should give some of the growers cause for reflection.

Wine	Characteristics
1961 La Mission-Haut-Brion	Very dark colour, lovely deep bouquet, *un grand seigneur* combining both personality and distinction, splendid finish.
1945 Latour	Very dark colour, a huge wine, still plenty of tannin, exceptional quality.
1963 Quinta do Noval	Dark colour, nice nose, not one of the biggest of this unusually fine vintage, nevertheless lots of body and with a good future before it.

Mobile, Alabama
Monday 17 April

I had been told that I would like Mobile, Alabama, and certainly it is a pretty place, notable for its fine trees.

I was met by Spud (Howard) Schramm, the regional director of Les Amis du Vin and a nice reporter, Mrs. Charlotte Hall.

After a brief TV interview I was taken to lunch at the Bienville Club on the 34th floor of a building from which there is a spectacular view of the Mobile river and all the broad delta beyond. Present were a group of wine lovers, including Albert Reynolds and Harvey Jones.

Our aperitif, Concannon 1974 Rkatsitele, had been made from Russian vines planted in the Sonoma Valley, unusual perhaps but, although fresh, none the better for that. Mobile prides itself upon its seafood, so the other wines were also white:

Wine	Characteristics
1976 Château St.-Jean Chardonnay *Sonoma and Mendocino Valleys*	Clean, fresh and slightly *pétillant*.
1974 Château St.-Jean Chardonnay *Napa Valley*	Good flavour and I preferred this to the 1976.

The event that evening at the Constantine restaurant was built around a comparative tasting of red Bordeaux and California Cabernets.

Wine	Characteristics	My points
Cabernet Sauvignon 1974 *Louis M. Martini*	Good colour, pleasing bouquet, not a big wine but with an agreeable flavour. Absolutely ready and, while it may never make a great bottle, it was easy to drink. Reasonably inexpensive and ideal for the not too exacting lover of wine.	12/20
Cabernet Sauvignon 1973 *Inglenook Cask B4*	Darker colour, quite a nice nose, more body and certainly more tannin. Could have had more finesse.	13/20
Cabernet Sauvignon 1973 *B.V. Private Reserve*	Good colour, nice fruity bouquet, good fruit and flavour, well-balanced and of better quality. Not yet ready but should make a good bottle from 1980 onwards.	15/20
Château Fourcas-Hosten *Listrac 1973*	Good colour, attractive bouquet and tasting as it smells.	15/20
Château Palmer 1973 *Margaux*	Colour rather pale, well-bred bouquet but that was about all. It lacked body, in fact was almost skinny with some acidity thrown in for good measure! Not much future there. A telling example of how diluted some of the 1973s can be.	14/20
Château Latour 1973 *Pauillac*	A better colour than the others, greater depth of flavour and sitll plenty of tannin. If really necessary almost ready now, in fact very forward for Latour.	17/20

Dining later with a small group who attended the tasting, I ate some of the nicest fish I have come across for a long time. Scamp (not scampi) from the Gulf of Mexico is somewhat rare and is found here in Mobile as well as nearby Pansacola, but seldom if ever in New Orleans. This freshest of fish was served with sauce Amandine, which basically is made of butter and lemon juice, and sliced almonds, to which strangely enough is added some beef stock. The result was unforgettable.

Bad weather had been forecast and we certainly got it, a thunderstorm and torrential rain. In consequence my plane arrived two hours late, so another connection was missed and I had to proceed in a tiny plane on to Alexandria in Louisiana.

In view of the by now almost inevitable late arrival there was not a moment to spare and with this in mind my most thoughtful of hosts, Dr. James White, had brought in his car an ice bucket containing a bottle of Moët Jubilee 1971 champagne and two glasses! We had never met before but, believe it or not, there was so much to talk about that we forgot all about the champagne until we arrived at the hotel where the wine tasting was to take place. I had just 15 minutes before I was 'due on', but during that time managed to down a couple of glasses of that delectable and much needed 'reviver'.

Long before I had left England, James White had written to ask what I would like to talk about and, expecting to have many tastings of California versus French wine, I had asked for red Bordeaux. Having studied my books with considerable forethought, James had chosen some of my favourite *châteaux*.

Wine	Characteristics	My points
Gloria 1973	Quite a good colour for this vintage, pleasant bouquet, good fruit and flavour but some acidity. *Note.* The acidity often appears to be more in evidence here than in Bordeaux. Can this be on account of the journey over? I am beginning to wonder.	11/20
Gloria 1971	Dark colour, delightful bouquet, more body with plenty of charm.	15/20
Gloria 1970	Very dark colour, fine deep bouquet, lovely flavour.	17/20
Lanessan 1970	Very good colour, nice bouquet, plenty of fruit but some acidity.	13/20
Lanessan 1967	Good colour, nice bouquet and flavour, good for a 1967.	14/20
Lanessan 1966	Dark colour, lovely deep bouquet, good fruit and well made, still some tannin so should continue to improve.	15/20
Les Forts de Latour 1967	Dark colour, powerful bouquet, strong flavour, needs at least two more years.	17/20
Latour 1967	Very dark colour, typical Latour bouquet, full-bodied, heaps of fruit and flavour. Still rather immature.	19/20

As well as being interesting, this turned out to be an educational exercise. After it was over, James White said that perhaps in spite of its younger vintages the Gloria should have been tasted after the Lanessan. With this I agreed, for the overall quality of the Gloria was greater. The range of vintages was well spaced, 1973, 1971 and 1970, three 1967s and one 1966. Although still immature, what a good vintage 1966 is proving. At long last it is beginning to demonstrate its potential.

That was not the end of the proceedings though, because at the dinner which followed James had chosen no less than six red burgundies, all of the fine 1971 vintage!

Wine	Characteristics	My points
1971 Vosne-Romanée, Clos des Réas *Domaine Jean Gros*	Dark colour, full bouquet, full-bodied.	15/20
1971 Nuits St.-Georges, Les St.-Georges *Domaine Maurice Chevillon*	Dark colour, full bouquet, good fruit but rather thin with some acidity.	12/20
1971 Grands-Echézeaux *Domaine René Engel*	Medium colour, attractive bouquet, good fruit and flavour but still hard and closed up.	15/20
1971 Bonnes-Mares *Remoissenet*	Medium colour, distinguished bouquet, too much acidity though, disappointing for this fine vineyard.	14/20
1971 Clos-de-la-Roche, Cuvée Vieilles Vignes *Domaine Ponsot*	Dark colour, rich bouquet, delicious flavour, great quality.	18/20
1971 Chambertin-Clos-de-Bèze *Domaine Marion François Lebaron*	Dark colour, fine rich bouquet, a powerful rich wine, great quality.	18/20

Tired as I was, I could not fail to appreciate the quality of these wines. So seldom do I have an opportunity to taste red burgundy of this calibre.

Houston, Texas
Wednesday 19 April

Before catching my plane, James, or rather Jeems as he is known (an old negro slave version of his name), drove me to his home in order to inspect his unusually fine cellar wherein there is a huge quantity of well chosen wine. During my earlier visits to the U.S. I have been taken by many a proud owner to view his collection, but all too often the wines had been bought by the label regardless of quality. Nowadays I find people's cellars are being assembled with considerably more knowledge and discrimination. The swimming pool at the White's home must be unique because it is laid out in the guise of a huge Bordeaux bottle. The steps are situated in the neck and, in view of its extraordinary length, it looked more practical than usual for energetic swimmers. In my second book, *The Changing Face of Wine*, published in 1969, I wrote about the Grand Cru Club founded in the early sixties by a group of my friends in the Bay Area of San Francisco. After reading that book, 'Jeems' had formed a club on the same lines in Alexandria, which now meets bi-monthly. He was not alone in this, because many friends throughout the U.S. had the same reaction and in consequence there must now be many similar clubs in existence. Thus the Grand Cru Club, which began with the first growths of 1959, must be the forerunner of many a pleasant dining club throughout the United States.

After changing planes again at New Orleans, I arrived at Houston where in true Texan style I was met by Mike Voulgaris in a smart pale blue Rolls Royce. With him was my host, the regional director of Les Amis du Vin, Jules Silvers, a wine merchant and another Rolls Royce enthusiast, owning himself a splendid 1927 Phantom open tourer which had been made in the U.S.

The Houston Chapter, one of the early ones, had been allowed to lapse but has recently been revived and reinvigorated by Jules Silvers together with another Houston merchant, Joseph Ellison.

A dinner had been arranged that evening in a restaurant called The Depot, whose decoration was intended to give the impression of a railroad depot and led one to expect the worst – railways are seldom noted for their food! Naturally the organisers were disappointed by the poor quality, but selfishly I welcomed the lack of inducement to overeat. Anyway the wine was another matter. Château Millet 1975, one of the lesser growths from Bordeaux, formed the aperitif and we drank Château Latour 1971 with the meal. It was the first time I have actually drunk this 1971 and instead of the rather undeveloped wine I had expected, it seemed quite forward and agreeable to drink. The Dow 1963 was extremely successful and, as I had expected, a great number of the 100 members present had never tasted vintage port before. One has only to read the notes of this particular visit to the U.S. to realise how the interest in vintage port is growing.

As I had to get up at 5.45 next morning it was against my better judgment that I accepted an invitation from Jim de George to look in at his home to inspect his wine cellar, which turned out to be chock full of goodies. Requested to choose any bottle I liked, for education as much as anything else, I picked out a bottle of the already quite famous Fonseca 1963. It wasn't really ready to drink of course, but oh my, how good that was! At the tasting of the 1963 vintage described in my Volume Seven, this Fonseca had emerged as the best and it looks as though that assessment was pretty well on target.

Austin, Texas
Thursday 20 April

After a painfully early departure I was in Austin (Texas) by 8.40 a.m. Reuben Kogut took charge and, after a newspaper interview, led me to a shop where I was able to satisfy a request from my twins for cowboy hats. Reuben Kogut owns and, with his son, manages a large new wine store which, after only two years, is already proving too small. As with most cities in the U.S. there appears to be untapped prosperity for the good wine merchant.

An excellent meal before the tasting had been prepared at the Galleria restaurant near Austin. Besides his skill as a restaurateur, Bob Lowe is an active supporter of Les Amis du Vins as well as a lecturer on wine for the University of Texas. Among the others present were Mr. and Mrs. Don George (the president and the cellarmaster of the chapter), Bill Arnold and Dr. Warren Ross, all of whom were accompanied by their wives. Incidentally I have to thank Don George for a bottle of 1969 Haut-Brion which, when tasted, proved to be unusually good for this rather uninteresting vintage. The wines enjoyed at this meal were repeated at the tasting and a description follows.

Les Amis du Vin tasting 1978

White wines

Wine	Characteristics	My points
Fontana Candida	$2.99. This attractive fresh Italian wine came as a pleasant surprise. It restored my faith in the wines of Frascati which, from my admittedly small experience, have almost invariably been oxidised. Apparently it had been shipped over in a refrigerated container – the extra expense involved seems to have been well worth while. As will be seen, the wines were rather a mixed bag.	14/20

Husch Vineyards Pinot Chardonnay 1976	$9.49. Pale colour, slightly earthy nose, good varietal flavour.	14/20
Chassagne-Montrachet, Embrazées 1973 *Albert Morey*	$8.95. Delightful bouquet, delicious flavour, full of charm. By far the best of the white wines. Much better value than the preceding Pinot Chardonnay at $9.49.	17/20

Red wines

J. Heitz Cabernet Sauvignon 1973 *Napa*	$8.99. Good colour, good varietal bouquet, plenty of fruit and quite a striking flavour. There was nevertheless a certain degree of harshness.	15/20
Château Mouton-Rothschild 1967	$24.95. Colour quite good, attractive bouquet with lots of flavour but afflicted somewhat by the failing of its vintage, a sharpish finish.	16/20
Zeltinger Sonnenuhr Auslese 1976 *J. Ehses-Hansen*	$6.99. Pale colour, fragrant bouquet, flowery and delightful, a wine to buy.	17/20
Burgess Selected Late Harvest Johannisberg Riesling 1976	$9.99. This should have preceded the Zeltinger, for it was more clumsy and lacked the flowery bouquet. In its own context however it was agreeably fresh and pleasant.	15/20

In Dallas/Fort Worth
Friday 21 April

A short flight to Dallas where I was met by an old friend, Victor Wdowiak. I had met him in the early sixties in the wine department he created so successfully for Nieman Marcus.

After a lengthy interview for *Trend* magazine, we arrived late for lunch at the Balcony restaurant in Fort Worth. There patiently awaiting us were Marvin and Sue Overton at whose home I was to spend the next two days. It is a small world because, having heard I was to be in town, Robert de Goulaine arrived to say hello. In 1973, Prue and I had passed several unforgettable days with him and his wife, Gundred, meeting many of the growers in the Muscadet district, where of course Robert is a leading figure.

Not long ago, the Overtons moved into a large house with a classical frontage. On entering the capacious hall the first thing to strike one is the fascinating collection of cowboy paintings which deservedly have become so popular and hence unfortunately very hard to find. From my short acquaintance with Marvin, I have a sneaking feeling that apart from the other charms of this house, he must have been influenced by as good a cellar as I have ever seen. He personally has laid out his bins in a practical but spectacular manner. His stock of illustrious wine must be as large as, yet far superior to, that of a first-class wine merchant. The quality of the rarities displayed is breathtaking, and the contents are so important they will appear, necessarily abridged, later on.

To meet his friends, Tom and Lou Ann Lipscomb, a small dinner party had been arranged at The Old Swiss House, where the Swiss owner is a chef of great local repute. Having decided we would have a 1924 evening, following an excellent 1966 Montrachet, Jacques Prieur, these are the *châteaux* Marvin gave us to assess anonymously.

Wine	Characteristics
Cheval-Blanc 1924	Medium colour, naturally showing its age, but a nice nose and an attractive flavour, still some sugar even. This I liked best, remarkable for a Saint-Emilion at over 50 years of age.
Lafite 1924	Good colour for its age, the best bouquet of the three, plenty of fruit but with too much acidity at the finish. Nevertheless it improved somewhat as the evening wore on.
Margaux 1924	Dark colour, good depth of flavour, but a very frail old gentleman, in fact only just with us.
d'Yquem 1924	A lovely almost tawny colour, a rich but maderised bouquet, no longer very sweet, enjoyable all the same.

Saturday 22 April

At last two nights in one place and what a relief. While going through Marvin's cellar with him the previous afternoon I must have mentioned that the Latour and Mouton 1949 are considered about the best of that vintage. I had also been told the Mouton was slightly the better of the two, but had never had an opportunity to compare these two giants directly with one another. When we arrived at The Shady Hill Country Club for lunch I found my thoughtful host had decanted a bottle of each! The two other guests were Tom Lipscomb and Joe Ballard, so with onion soup followed by Southern 'chicken fried' steak we settled down to a blind comparison of the two wines.

Wine	Characteristics	My points
Latour 1949	The redder colour of the two, superb bouquet, drier but with heaps of fruit and a lovely finish. A wine of great distinction.	18/20
Mouton-Rothschild 1949	Browner colour, a richer bouquet, a wonderful rich wine, sweeter perhaps and with lots of flavour, although possibly a bit more obvious.	19/20

In spite of the lower rating I gave the Latour, I think on the whole it had more elegance and, dare I say it, breeding! My fellow guests placed them in the same order as myself, but from the very beginning Marvin Overton preferred the Latour.

Waugh and Warre

The focal point of the *grand diner* at the Overtons that evening was an extraordinary range of vintage port all from one shipper. When I arrived Marvin had explained that since, on a similar occasion in 1977 when Henri Martin and Michael Broadbent had been present, he had produced an astonishing number of vintages of Château Latour, he could not very well repeat that for me. He had therefore chosen my second favourite subject, vintage port, and who was I to complain? The whole evening was so outstanding that I scarcely know where to start.

Altogether 18 of us sat down, among them being several old friends, Ben Ichinose and John Parducci, both of whom had flown in from California, Henry Kucharzyk and Victor Wdowiak. While some of us ate fresh Gulf shrimps grilled on spits, the rest were photographed removing the necks of the bottles of the older vintages by means of red hot tongs. The reason for this

The Waugh and Warre
tasting at Fort Worth — Joe
Ballard, Harry Waugh,
Jack Holmes and Ben
Ichinose.

Tasting 15 vintages of
Warre with Marvin C.
Overton III, Fort Worth.

treatment is that the corks in bottles of very old vintage port tend to soften and consequently disintegrate when a corkscrew is used. Tongs remove the whole neck cleanly with the cork inside.

We all trooped below to the cellar, but to list all the gems in this Aladdin's Cave would be impossible. Except perhaps in a few private cellars of *châteaux* in Bordeaux I can never remember seeing such an assembly of large bottles. In fact, perhaps the last time I have seen a cellar of such importance was on that day when some ten years ago I brought to light the Dr. Barolet collection. This Fort Worth cellar houses fabulous vintages from both Burgundy and Bordeaux, all admirably binned and displayed. There is a worthy representation of the wines of the Côte d'Or, for instance all the good vintages of the Domaine-de-la-Romanée-Conti, including double and triple magnums of La Tâche, Richebourg etc. as well as other great *domaines*; in common however with the present day trend, the emphasis is on red Bordeaux.

To give but a brief idea of the pre-eminence of the latter:
Pétrus – practically every vintage back to 1945, including magnums and double magnums.
La Mission-Haut-Brion – similar.
Haut-Brion – back to 1907, also magnums, double magnums, as well as a jeroboam of 1924.
Latour – nearly all vintages back to 1920, magnums of 1949, jeroboams and one imperial (eight bottles) of 1961, double magnums of 1959, 1961 and 1966.
Mouton-Rothschild – similar, with jeroboams of 1953, 1957 and 1967 (I bet the 1953 is good).
Lafite – similar in all respects including bottles of 1874, 1878, 1893 and 1899!
One could go on and on, for other *châteaux* are also well represented.

The same story applies to Sauternes and Barsac; there are vintages of d'Yquem and Lafaurie-Peyraguey, all the way back to 1900! As for the port, most of the vintages at our tasting had come from this cellar and of course most of the good vintages of the other port shippers are lying there as well.

The California wines date back to the 1935 vintage of Simi, both Chardonnay and Zinfandel. I can vouch for the excellence of the 1935 Simi Zinfandel because I opened my one bottle in London a month ago, and words fail me in its praise. That bottle had been given to me some years ago by my friend Dr. Stanley Burton of San Francisco and it was opened on a fitting occasion at the first committee of the Zinfandel Club we have formed. Two of the founder members are well known to the vinous public of America, John Avery and Hugh Johnson.

The large menus were entitled 'Waugh and Warre. A very English event honouring Harry Waugh'. In spite of the fact there was a large watercolour portrait of myself on the cover the menu looked highly decorative. The details of the meal, in fine calligraphy, appeared on the middle page and those of the vintages on the last, but headed by two further drawings entitled *Les Enfants Bacchus père et fils*. Each had been based on photographs from my books, one of myself aged five, and the other of my son Jamie, at the age of two and a half. These delightful paintings had been done by the talented Lou Ann Lipscomb and to say they were a surprise would be an understatement.

Although many of the vintages were already lying in our host's cellar, he had taken immense trouble to find the others from elsewhere. Christie's and Sotheby's had been called in to help and in fact the bottle of 1927 had only arrived from Sotheby's, London, by air that very morning – it was a miracle it was in such good condition. As a reserve, from his own cellar in California, Ben Ichinose had brought a bottle of the 1924 vintage. The ramifications had been widespread, but nevertheless it was a close run thing. Marvin was lamenting he had failed to find any 1948, but that, like the 1927, has become extremely rare.

When one sees the vintages we tasted it must be agreed we had little to grumble about. To simplify the proceedings, the wines were tasted in four groups.

Group one

Eighteen vintages of Warre's port

Wine	Characteristics	My points
1970	Very dark colour, powerful but immature nose, full of fruit, but quite undeveloped. Clearly, however, this 1970 has a splendid future.	18/20
1966	Good colour, another young and powerful bouquet, a great mouthful of fruit, still immature but of excellent quality.	18/20
1963	Good colour, splendid bouquet, a full-bodied wine already good to drink, but with a great future before it. To reach its best, this needs another two to three years.	19/20
1962	(Late bottled 1966.) Paler of colour, a fruity but very different bouquet, quite a powerful flavour, good in its own way but lacking the charm and style of either the 1963 or 1960.	8/20
1960	Good colour, lovely bouquet, a splendid wine with a delicious tast. Probably at its best now.	18/20
1958	Paler colour, the spirit beginning to come through a little on the nose, a lighter wine, attractive all the same. 1958 was a light vintage which matured early and the best time to drink it was some years ago. It was never a vintage for long life.	14/20

Assessing this first group, by general consensus of opinion we preferred the 1960 to drink now, the 1963 vintage was considered best with regard to potential, following which came the more immature 1966. The late-bottled 1962 did not stand much of a chance against the regular vintages, but provided an instructive comparison.

Group two

Wine	Characteristics	My points
1955	Dark colour, delightful complex nose, a superb complete wine, a heavenly flavour and it finished well. A perfect example of a fine vintage.	19/20
1950	A paler colour and not quite bright, in fact still suffering from recent journey from New York. Bouquet fair, quite sweet but signs of the brandy coming through.	12/20

| 1947 | Medium colour and more perfumed bouquet, pleasant but on the light side, a little hollow now perhaps. | 13/20 |
| 1945 | Good colour, deep, deep bouquet, wonderful concentration of fruit and flavour, magnificent from an outstanding vintage. | 20/20 |

Of the above, the 1945 came first but fairly closely followed by the 1955, then, some way behind, the 1947. Up to that point the order for them all came 1945, 1955, 1960 (for present drinking), 1963 and 1966.

Group three

Wine	Characteristics	My points
1935	Good colour, pleasing bouquet, softer, sweeter and easier than the 1934, in fact more feminine, a very nice after taste.	15/20
1934	Paler than the 1935, good bouquet, more masculine and vigorous but a little spirit coming through.	16/20
1927	Good dark colour, very good bouquet, heaps of fruit and quite powerful, just a hint of the brandy there. 'Oh for the snows of yesteryear'. Alas the 1927s are now only a pale shadow of what they were as I remember them in the late forties and early fifties.	18/20
1924	Paler colour, a nice chocolatey nose, full-bodied and delicious, has kept wonderfully well.	19/20

I found I was in a minority with my preference for the 1934 over the 1935. Perhaps it was nostalgia for in the past I had always considered the 1934s better; it is a matter of opinion. The wines were assessed with the 1924 first, the 1935 second and the 1927 third.

Group four

Wine	Characteristics	My points
1922	Paler colour, full nose, good considering its age, still heaps of fruit and sugar. Clearly this has kept well and was much better than I ever anticipated. *Note*. I remember in the Hitler era before the war, business was so bad in England one could hardly give these good 1922s away even at the equivalent approximately of a dollar a bottle!	17/20
1920	Good colour, a rich almost perfumed nose, showing its age a little but still has charm.	16/20
1912	Pale colour, rather a spiritous bouquet, resembling more a tawny port, an old lady somewhat wrinkled and faded yes, but full of grace. Perhaps it was nostalgia again but I had expected more from this fine vintage; however, the 1908 more than made up for it.	12/20

"A thing of beauty is a joy forever;
Its loveliness increases; it will never
Pass into nothingness; but still will keep
A bower quiet for us, and a sleep
Full of sweet dreams, and health, and
        quiet breathing" Endymion 1818 ~Keats

MENU

Roasted Fresh Gulf Shrimp	Aperitif
Roast Suckling Pig	1900 Chateau Branaire·
Fresh Steamed Asparagus	Ducru en Marie-Jeanne
Wild Rice ~ Olives	
Cheese ~Nuts ~Fruits	1970 Bollanger Cuvee
	Ichinose en Magnum
Cigars ~ Café	1924 -1974 Remy Martin
	Grand Fine Champagne
	Cognac

GUESTS

Joe Ballard	Tom Lipscomb
Bruce Barker	Willis McIntosh
Karl Brandenberg	Marvin C. Overton, III
François Chandou	John Parducci
Jack T. Holmes	Ray Raney
Benjamin Ichinose	Bobby Smith
Rodney Johnson	Robert Travis
Stinson Jones	Harry Waugh
Henry Kucharzyk	Victor Wdowiak

April 22, 1978 ~ 5100 Crestline Road ~Fort Worth, Texas

The menu and guest list at Fort Worth

[32]

| 1908 | Paler colour, but good considering its age, wonderful bouquet for a septuagenarian, a staggering amount of fruit and body, almost miraculous. | 19/20 |

Following some discussion, this is the order in which the whole group placed the nine leading vintages, 1945, 1908, 1924, 1955, 1935, 1963, 1960, 1927 and 1947. From my personal point view the top eight were in this order: 1945, 1908, 1924, 1963 (higher of course for potential), 1955 , 1960 and 1966.

Besides being thoroughly enjoyable, this experience has been highly educational. With those 18 glasses before us what a unique opportunity we were afforded to be able to go back and forth among the younger and older vintages so as to appreciate fully the differences of maturity and to make comparisons. Indeed, how seldom does good fortune such as this come one's way.

The sucking or suckling pig, the finest I have ever tasted, was roasted on a spit by two young Mexicans from a local restaurant which specialises in this type of cooking. This proved an excellent foil for the *marie-jeanne* (three bottles) of Château Branaire 1900 – a brilliant ruby colour with plenty of fruit and flavour. There was some acidity at the finish but that may account for the wine having kept so well. Usually by that time of the evening I find champagne too sharp for my liking but somehow the Bollinger seemed just right. Incidentally it was from a special lot of some 500 cases reserved for Ben Ichinose around 1970 and bore his name on the labels, in itself unusual.

The conversation, mainly about wine of course, was stimulating and particularly interesting was the talk by John Parducci, who not only explained his problems as the proprietor of a well-known winery in California, but brought us up to date on the general situation there. Many of the hard liquor and cocktail enthusiasts of America have turned to the consumption of white wine as an aperitif and, in consequence there is currently a widespread shortage of this particular beverage. John told us he could not produce it fast enough and already had had to uproot many of his red vines for replacement with white ones, an operation not to be undertaken lightly since at least three years are lost before the new vines begin to bear fruit. So acute is the situation that some growers are trying to make white wine from the not-so-fashionable *pinot noir* grapes and there is even a white Zinfandel on the market.

The cognac from Remy Martin had been blended for their 200th anniversary.

Brunch with the Lipscombs

The final treat in Fort Worth was a Sunday brunch given by Tom and Lou Ann Lipscomb, at which were present their two sons aged 11 and 13. It was a pleasure to see how their father was gently introducing them to the study of wine. Speaking personally I shall never cease to be grateful for a similar education at more or less that age. But with my youthful palate it was the vintage port I preferred to the more austere red Bordeaux.

The venue was the Coffee House in Fort Worth, whose owner had been present at our dinner the evening before and whose two chefs had prepared the meal. Thus it was the Pickwickian-looking Mr. MacMcIntosh who personally supervised our delectable lunch. I am addicted to southern cooking, so happily for me fried quail had already been ordered together with the traditional cream sauce as well as some grits, and how good it all was!

c

[33]

Nevertherless Marvin and I were made to work because there were three red Bordeaux to be assessed and named and this proved to be anything but easy.

Blind tasting

Wine	Characteristics	My points
Jurade de St.-Emilion 1947	A big fruity bouquet and a pleasant taste, on the dry side but fairly ample.	16/20
Château Monbousquet 1947 *St.–Emilion*	Lovely nose, by far the best, much fuller, well rounded, excellent.	18/20
Château Lafite 1947 *Pauillac*	An elegant bouquet but that was the best part; sufficient fruit, but too much acidity for comfort.	14/20

With a blind tasting such as this comes the moment of truth but in fairness to the Lafite I do not think the Latour of that year would have fared any better. So charming while they were young, in general the Médocs of 1947 did not live up to their early promise and it was the wines from St.-Emilion and Pomerol which proved more successful.

The Jurade of Saint-Emilion is a glamorous public-relations body similar to the Bontemps-du-Médoc or if you like, Les Chevaliers-du-Tastevin. That particular wine had been blended under their supervision from some of the finer vineyards of Saint-Emilion.

After a much needed rest (only four hours sleep the night before) Tom and Lou Ann Lipscomb drove me to the Les Amis du Vin tasting in Dallas, and evening which had been splendidly organised by Victor Wdowiak, the regional director.

1973 claret

Wine	Characteristics	My points
Château Giscours *Margaux*	Good colour, a pretty nose, heaps of fruit and unusually full-bodied for its vintage, pleasing finish.	17/20
Château Troplong-Mondot *Saint-Emilion*	The colour was too pale, not much bouquet, or body for that matter, sharp and ungenerous.	10/20
Château Mouton-Rothschild *Pauillac*	Good colour, although the nose was fruity, a light wine for Mouton-Rothschild, an agreeable finish but it does not appear to have a long life ahead of it.	16/20
Château Haut-Brion	Good colour, elegant, typical Graves bouquet, plenty of fruit and in spite of some acidity at the finish easily the best. With time no doubt one hopes some of this sharpness will disappear.	18/20
Château Lafite *Pauillac*	Medium colour, distinguished if somewhat thin bouquet. Not a big wine but is has a good flavour, a little acidity at the finish.	17/20

A tasting such as this more or less confirms that these 1973s have only a short lifespan before them. This may of course be an incorrect assessment because one never knows with wine, but I personally would not buy them to keep for more than a few years. Nevertheless with their charm, the better of the 1973s should provide a useful stop-gap until, say, the 1971s are ready. Even so, as demonstrated so clearly by the Troplong-Mondot, this was not a successful vintage for the wines of Saint-Emilion and Pomerol. Prior to the harvest of 1973, excessive rain swelled the grapes so much that resultant wine was diluted, hence the anaemic colour of many of them. If one were to go by price, the Giscours represented the best value among this group.

Phoenix, Arizona
Monday 24 April

The two hours' flight to Phoenix, Arizona, led us over desert and jagged mountains. The town of Phoenix lies in a valley in which there are picturesque outcrops of rock called buttes and all around the skyline is formed by range upon range of mountains. Thes buttes together with the tall organ pipe cactus provide a scene which hitherto I have only witnessed at the cinema: the climate is hot (95° on my arrival) but very dry on account of the desert and thus more supportable than the heat and humidity of some of the cities I have been visiting around the Gulf of Mexico.

At a sandwich lunch, my host, Walter Kendall, introduced me to Jock Wulffson who to help down our picnic had brought with him an attractive bottle of 1976 Pinot Blanc from Château St.-Jean.

Before dinner, the Wulffsons arranged a vertical tasting of Beaulieu Vineyards and all the wines were from the Private Reserve which, generally speaking, is of superior quality to their regular Cabernet Sauvignon.

Beaulieu Vineyards
Cabernet Sauvignon
Private Reserve

Wine	Characteristics	Group placing	My points
1973	Good dark colour, plenty of bouquet, lot of fruit, needs time, has a good future.	5th	14/20
1972	Medium colour, indifferent bouquet, some fruit, but disappointing.	9th	6/20
1971	Medium colour, attractive nose, plenty of fruit, good flavour, some acidity and some edges to be rubbed off.	7th	15/20
1970	Very good colour, excellent bouquet, lovely big wine with a fine finish.	1st	18½/20
1969	Good colour, attractive bouquet, heaps of fruit and body but somewhat fierce.	3rd	16½/20
1968	Very dark colour, aromatic bouquet, full-bodied, good finish.	4th	17/20
1967	Medium colour, fruity bouquet, but not great, has fruit but on light side and seems to lack distinction.	6th	12/20
1966	Beautiful colour, full bouquet (cedar or eucalyptus) well balanced. A beauty.	2nd	19½/20
1965	Colour browning, query a roasted bouquet, lacks middle, tannic with some acidity.	8th	14/20

1964	Beautiful colour, rather dull bouquet, plenty of fruit but badly oxidised.	10th	6/20
1963	Pale colour, but since this bottle had died many people did not vote on it.	–	–

According to the group it seems that my assessment of the 1965 vintage was over generous. While discussing the final result afterwards our host opened a treasured bottle of Moscato Amabile from Louis M. Martini. It was the first time most of those present (about 16 all told) had come across this rare wine and it was a pleasure to watch the surprise and delight on their faces as they tasted it. (See my previous comment.)

Not wishing to subject me to more so-called French cuisine, my hosts had decided to give me a proper cowboy dinner, good simple food in an unusual setting. The entrance to the Pinnacle Peak Patio, some 20 miles from Phoenix, is a copy of the old ranch gates made of wooden poles etc. After passing through, you come across a simulated grave of a man executed in 1907 for 'claim jumping', all sham of course. The effect is also enhanced by bits of old covered wagons and other bric-a-brac of the early settlers dotted around in the foreground. The waitresses are becomingly attired as cowgirls, all of course wearing cowboy hats, likewise the barmen who, so I was informed, still carry revolvers in their belts. The food is simple but good, just salad, a steak and beans, cooked cowboy style.

Jock Wulffson an *afficionado* of Zinfandel had brought along three examples for comparison, but I fear I disappointed him with my lack of enthusiasm.

Zinfandel

Wine	Characteristics
Ridge Montebello 1974	Good colour and a nice bouquet, far too sharp for my European palate, although there was clearly a good underlying flavour.
Clos du Val 1973	Dark colour, a more refined bouquet, plenty of fruit but again this strike of acidity.
Chateau Montelena 1973	Dark colour, not much bouquet, not so full-bodied as the others but on the same lines.

No doubt these three may turn out well once the acidity has worn off but at the moment it was too intense for my personal taste.

Tuesday 25 April

After a light lunch Walt Kendall introduced me to the famous desert, but on account of recent heavy rain, it did not look nearly so arid as I had expected, being greener apparently than for many years. As the road wound up into the hills more and more cacti appeared; indeed they became so numerous that they began almost to resemble a forest.

The dinner preceding the tasting took place at Vita Scampi, justifiably noted for its Italian cooking. Since the restaurant has only an average wine list, happily for us Jock Wulffson had brought one or two bottles with him and as a result we were able to enjoy far better quality than the restaurant could have provided.

How things have changed since around 1969 when I began seriously to study these domestic wines. Apart from numerous enthusiasts actually within the State of California, hardly anyone elsewhere in the U.S. took much interest and indeed knew very little, about their own domestic wine. In those days there were remarkably few knowledgeable merchants, indeed very few of them ever tasted the wine they had in stock but sold by the label. As for the rest of the country, there were vast areas where the wine bug had not bitten at all. Witness the scores of newly formed chapters of 'Les Amis' I have visited during the past few years, a tribute to the excellent pioneer work that has been done. Now thanks to the astonishing increase in quality and better distribution I meet enthusiastic *afficionados* all over the country, people who live far from the West Coast but who have made a special point of studying their own domestic product. While it was fashionable to prefer imported wines it is becoming increasingly evident how through high prices the French are losing their former pre-eminent position in the market to the Italians and, to a lesser extent, the Spanish.

These are the unusually good wines Jock Wulffson had brought along for us to enjoy during that well-cooked meal.

Wine	Characteristics	My points
1975 Chateau St.-Jean Chardonnay *Robert Young Vineyard*	Quite a striking bouquet, typical as someone said, of the Sonoma Valley. Fine flavour though with first rate fruit acidity.	17/20
1975 Burgess Cellars Chardonnay	Lovely, fresh bouquet, excellent flavour, in my opinion the better of two really good Chardonnays.	18/20
1968 Mountain Barbera Private Reserve *Louis M. Martini*	Unusually dark colour, rich bouquet, immensely rich and powerful. Great quality.	17/20
1968 Cabernet Sauvignon Special Selection *Louis M. Martini*	Very dark colour, a good *cabernet* bouquet, lovely flavour and an attractive finish.	19/20

Until I tasted this Cabernet Sauvignon I had thought the quality of the Barbera outstanding, but the 1968 Cabernet had so much more style and breeding that I had to reduce my original elevated marking down to 17 out of 20. A 1976 Caymus Chardonnay (the grapes had been heavily infected by *botrytis cinerea*, 31 per cent residual sugar by weight) had a delightful rich yet fresh bouquet, an equally lovely taste. The outstanding features were the lightness and the freshness as well as an excellent finish.

I seem to remember that some years ago Joe Heitz had made a very good *botrytis* wine from *chardonnay* grapes, which he named Alicia, after his wife. In the normal course of events the dessert wines of California are made from the *riesling* grape so this one from *chardonnay* was a pleasant experience.

After an aperitif of Firestone Chardonnay the tasting for the Phoenix Chapter of Les Amis du Vin represented what had become for me an almost automatic blind comparison of Cabernet Sauvignons with wine from Bordeaux.

Wine	Characteristics	My points
Clos du Val 1974	$9.50. Dark colour, pleasant California bouquet, plenty of fruit but a bit fierce.	9/20
Beychevelle 1971	$15.00. Slightly browner colour but much better fruit and well balanced.	16/20
Robert Mondavi 1973 Reserve	$15.00. Dark colour, a dry rather unsympathetic bouquet, medium body but quite a good finish, more tannin.	12/20
Latour 1971	$31.00. Dark colour, richer bouquet, richer flavour, considerably more body and quality than No. 3.	16/20
Heitz 1973	$7.75. Dark colour, fine bouquet, good fruit, well balanced, has quality.	17/20
Burgess 1974 Vintage Selection	$13.00. A rich nose, a massive rich full-bodied wine, good quality.	15/20

I learnt a lesson that evening; owing to a shortage of glasses, the above had to be tasted in pairs. When an anonymous comparison between California cabernet and that from Bordeaux is to take place, since one is likely to forget from pair to pair, it is essential that all wines, six in this case, should be poured out at once for direct comparison. On this particular occasion the shortage of glasses caused confusion.

The evening ended with two vintage ports:

Wine	Characteristics
1975 Quady made from *zinfandel* grapes	A rather odd bouquet, sweet and rich yes, but it lacked something and fell away at the finish; it bore a resemblance to port but that was all.
1963 Croft	Dark colour, infinitely more distinction on the bouquet and a heavenly flavour.

The Quady, labelled as 'vintage port', was quite a travesty of the genuine article. In my humble opinion the sooner domestic port and domestic so-called champagne appear under other labels, the better. Good as they may be in their own right, these two misnamed styles of wine are detrimental to the good reputation California has acquired.

San Francisco
Wednesday 26 April

San Francisco and how lovely to be back. My good friends Barney and Belle Rhodes, to whom I owe all I know about the wine of California, are providing a much needed rest from the treadmill, nice as it has been. As on previous similar occasions, the first meal Belle provided was the delicious Dungeness crab now in season and for which San Francisco is noted, and I can think of nothing better with this than the two vintages of Harbor Chardonnay we compared.

Since quite understandably on this journey I have met many people who had not heard of Harbor Winery, a few words of explanation may not come amiss. Here in California there has always been a number of enthusiastic amateur wine makers, some of them so efficient that they have at times produced results unequalled by the professionals. Those readers who have followed my books will often come across the name of one of these, Charles Myers, a professor of English at Sacramento City College. Apart from other successful varietals, his speciality has always been *chardonnay*, with which in my humble opinion he obtains a finesse infrequently encountered elsewhere. So great has been my respect for his *chardonnay* that I must digress a little.

When I was asked to make the wine list at the Ritz Hotel in London, if possible the finest in Europe, I discovered that California wine had never been included on it. In order to rectify this lapse I decided to list at least one red and one white, each of the best possible quality. Thanks to the assistance of Barney and Belle Rhodes I was able to obtain a few cases each of Harbor Chardonnay 1974 and Caymus Cabernet Sauvignon 1974, both wines recognised by authorities to be of outstanding merit. There is some irony to this story, however, because thanks to the unawareness in Britain of the immense increase in quality of California wine, these two have remained virtually untouched during their first year on the wine list, so it is profoundly hoped that one of these days visitors to the Ritz will appreciate the treasures available in the cellar, treasures which in California are regarded like gold dust.

Wine	Characteristics
Harbor Winery Chardonnay 1975	A nice pale colour, fresh bouquet and a lovely clean taste, excellent quality.
Harbor Winery Chardonnay 1974	Pale colour, beautiful bouquet, a delightful complex wine, great style.

These two are of first rate quality.

The Napa Valley
Thursday 27 April

At eight o'clock on a sunny morning Barney and I set out for the Napa Valley. Our first stop was at the spectacular Rutherford Hill Winery which from its hillside enjoys such a splendid view across the valley. Originally known as Souverain, this property has changed hands three times within a short period – evidence of the recent economic stresses. Now under new ownership, several of the directors are the same as the good team at Freemark Abbey. With Phil Baxter as the wine maker, this efficient winery has every chance of success.

Some old friends had gathered to meet us, Bill Jaeger, Chuck Carpy, Brad Webb and Phil Baxter. Here are details of the wines we tasted.

Wine	Characteristics
1977 Pinot Noir Blanc	In spite of its name actually a rather pretty *rosé* colour (0.15% sugar by residual weight) clean, fresh bouquet, clean and very dry with a fresh finish.

Since, perhaps deservedly, the *pinot noir* grape has lost popularity, in accordance with the current trend to assuage the demand for white wine as an aperitif, attempts are being made at Rutherford Hill and elsewhere to make white and *rosé* wines from this varietal. It would appear that unlike the *pinot noir* of Champagne which produces a white wine, the juice from the Californian varietal is pinker.

Wine	Characteristics
1977 Gewurztraminer (0.85% residual sugar)	Delightful bouquet, clean and dry with a delicious flavour, this should prove a success.
1977 Johannisberg Riesling	Bouquet still undeveloped, a trifle sweeter but nicely balanced, good fruit acidity at the finish.

Four Chardonnays followed, all from the Curtis Ranch and of the same vintage. They provided an insight into the endless experiments being made all the time.

Wine	Characteristics
Matured in stainless steel	Pleasant bouquet, with perhaps less elegance than the others, a good flavour, if a little more obvious.
Matured in large American oak cask	A finer bouquet than No. 1, full flavoured but pleasantly dry, also had a good finish.
Aged in new Limousin oak barrel	More finesse on bouquet, in fact the best nose. Similar taste to No. 2.
Composite of all, 1–3	Very nice bouquet, good fruit and flavour, nice fresh finish. Very good.

Pinot Noir blends, all of 1976 vintage (all three from Curtis Ranch)

Not barrel aged	Medium colour, fresh but was it a slightly metallic nose? Light and fruity, finished well.
Blend of barrel aged wines	Dark for Pinot Noir, a fuller, rounder bouquet, good fruit but a slightly tart finish.
Blend of 1 and 2	Good colour, a round and pleasantly sweet bouquet, less body than No. 2 but a fresh finish.

Three Zinfandels all with a good dark colour and all from the Mead Ranch on Atlas Peak.

Wine	Characteristics	My placing
1975	Matured 70% American oak barrels, 30% French. A huge fruity bouquet, good depth of flavour with agreeable after taste.	2nd
1976	Very dark colour, a big but drier bouquet, full flavoured, attractive taste.	1st
1977	Very dark colour, youthful but good nose, very young and immature, really too young to judge.	3rd

Thanks no doubt to the drought, the crop of 1976 was, generally speaking, relatively small. While there was no irrigation during the winter of 1975/6, with the experience behind them, the growers used some during the following winter, so while the 1977 crop still suffered from the continuing drought, the effect on quantity was not so serious as in the year before. There was also some rain late in May, in consequence of which more wine was made. If one is forced to take this step, it would appear that the best time to irrigate is during the winter months, otherwise the effect is negligible. Whether it provides any proof or not, the quantity of wine made in 1976 was 35,000 tons and in 1977 53,000 tons. Here are the results of further tests, this time with *cabernet sauvignon* and *merlot* grapes.

Wine	Characteristics
1975 Cabernet Sauvignon (with 22% *merlot* added)	Very dark colour, fine well bred bouquet, a nice complex wine.
1975 Merlot (with 20% *cabernet sauvignon* added)	An enormous bouquet, full fruity flavour, lots of charm.
1977 Merlot (100%)	Very dark colour, good varietal and rather rich nose, good fruit with some acidity but this should diminish with time.
1977 Cabernet Sauvignon (100%)	Very dark colour, a powerful very immature bouquet, full flavoured, good depth with pleasant after taste. Very good.

Spring Valley

A pleasant surprise awaited me in Spring Valley, for no sooner had we arrived than there at the door appeared Miles Maskell. Miles' father, Max Maskell, had been a good friend in pre-war days when he was a director of Percy Fox, the London importers among whose products were Lanson Champagne, Langenbach German wines and Warre's Port. (I remember we used to buy a lot of these from him at that time when I was working for that fine old firm, Block, Grey & Block). Just before the war Max met his South African wife, Fay, and from then until some time after the war he was the owner and wine maker at the noted Constantia Vineyard near Cape Town.

After he left University, I got Miles his first job with Harveys of Bristol, which I hope proved a useful training, for now he is part owner of the well-known firm of Green's in the City of London. His present visit to California had been sponsored by the Bank of America for the promotion of California wine in England.

The weather was so beautiful that Joe Heitz moved a table out into the sunshine so that we could enjoy tasting his wines in the open. Our friend, Martha May, was also present. She and Tom are the owners of Martha's Vineyard, and I think it was as instructive for her as the rest of us to see how her latest vintages were turning out. She sells her grapes to Joe who then makes what has possibly become California's leading Cabernet Sauvignon.

A 1974 Martha's Vineyard Cabernet Sauvignon was purple rather than dark, with the typical minty bouquet, and a lovely full flavour. This should make a great bottle.

As Joe pointed out, Martha's Vineyard is not by any means the only fine Cabernet sold under the Heitz label, so we then proceeded to taste some of his other Cabernets. For instance, he also buys grapes from a neighbour called Fay and recently he has begun to buy from the Bella Oaks Vineyard. The vines of the latter are still young but clearly full of promise. Incidentally the Bella Oaks Vineyard belongs to my friends Barney and Belle Rhodes, who originally planted out what is now known as Martha's Vineyard. How exciting it will be if with Bella Oaks they can pull off a double!

Tasting with Joseph Heitz

Wine	Characteristics
1975 Martha's Vineyard	Very dark colour and a nice rich bouquet, the richer of the two, some youthful exuberance to lose but a fine flavour.
1975 Fay Vineyard	Very dark colour, lot of breeding on the bouquet, also on the palate, should be ready earlier.
1976 Martha's Vineyard	Unusually dark colour, a deep fruity, minty bouquet, still powerful but a delicious flavour.
1976 Fay Vineyard	Very dark colour, rich bouquet, powerful with plenty of fruit.
1976 Bella Oaks Vineyard	Very dark colour, not a big wine but well balanced.
1977 Martha's Vineyard	Very dark colour, super minty bouquet, a lovely mouthful of flavour, should make a fine bottle. Tremendous character.
1977 Fay Vineyard	Very dark colour, well-bred nose, a full, delightful flavour. Should also make a good bottle.
1977 Bella Oaks Vineyard	Very dark colour, nice bouquet, on light side, good fruit and flavour though considering Bella Oaks was only planted in 1972, this vineyard appears to be doing nicely.

Pinot Chardonnay

1975	Pale colour, pleasant nose, good fruit and flavour. Liked this best.
1974	A paler colour, good nose and taste.

During an alfresco lunch in the garden we enjoyed the 1973 Chardonnay and an older range of vintages, all Martha's Vineyard.

Wine	Characteristics
1973 (bottled June 1977)	Delightful bouquet, full-flavoured and very good. Ready now.
1972	Dark colour, pleasant bouquet, good taste but needs more time.
1970	Delightful typical nose, plenty of body, very good indeed.
1969	More aromatic bouquet than most, more mint! Full of character and style. An astonishing wine which Joe now prefers to his already famous 1968.

After this plethora of goodies, neither Barney nor I were in the best of form for our next but important stop just down the road, namely at the winery of

Joseph Phelps. Joseph was there himself together with his skilful wine maker, Walter Schug. The latter received his vinous education at Geisenheim in Germany, the result of which is clearly to be found in the quality of his white wine.

Joseph Phelps tasting

Wine	Characteristics
1977 Johannisberg Riesling (early harvest)	Clean bouquet, dry fragrant taste, very good.
1977 Johannisberg Riesling (*Späestlese* style but not so labelled)	Fuller bouquet and flavour, preferred the first one.
1977 Johannisberg Riesling (Late Harvest 7% residual sugar)	Altogether good, lovely fruit acidity at the finish.
1975 Cabernet Sauvignon (94% *cabernet sauvignon*, 6% *merlot*)	Dark colour, pronounced *cabernet* bouquet, good fruit, will make a nice bottle.
1975 Insignia (86% *merlot*, 14% *cabernet sauvignon*)	(Insignia is Joseph Phelps' designation for his outstanding claret blend of a given vintage). Very dark colour, pronounced varietal bouquet, attractive flavour.

The above two 1975s made a good comparison between the *cabernet sauvignon* and the *merlot* taste.

Wine	Characteristics
1975 Single Vineyard Cabernet Sauvignon (Eisele)	Dark colour, fine rich bouquet, full-bodied, very fruity, excellent.
1976 Cabernet Franc	Colour almost purple, the bouquet different from yet similar to that of the Cabernet Sauvignon, an attractive flavour.
1976 Syrah (not to be confused with Petite Sirah)	Dark colour, totally different bouquet from preceding wines, good flavour and remarkable considering this was made from three-year-old vines.
1977 Gewürztraminer (*beerenauslese* style)	Rich, rich bouquet, sweet, but light and elegant.
1976 Selected Late Harvest Johannisberg Riesling	(The same as I had tasted in Knoxville, Tennessee.) Golden colour, glorious taste and a splendid finish, 1.2 fruit acidity.

The remarkable thing about Walter Schug is that not only does he make outstanding wines of this description but he succeeds equally well with his reds.

Warren Winiarski, is now among the most noted of the growers in the Napa Valley but regrettably by the time we reached his premises we were two very tired people. Since my last visit two years ago he has built a fine new annexe to his winery. Exhausted as we were, we tried two of his wines and very good they were; at least as best as we could judge!

With Warren Winiarski	*Wine*	*Characteristics*
	1976 Stag's Leap Wine Cellars Chardonnay	Delightful bouquet and a most attractive flavour, well balanced with noticeable elegance.
	1975 Stag's Leap Wine Cellars Cabernet Sauvignon	Good colour, pleasing bouquet, heaps of fruit and a nice finish.

More elegant than many wines of this varietal, clearly Warren is steering in the right direction, at least, that is, from my European point of view. Without direct comparison this appears to be as good as his 1974. As he was about to cross the Atlantic on the QE2, he would have a chance on board to drink not only his 1974 Cabernet Sauvignon but also his 1976 Chardonnay.

Friday 28 April The day of the 'Grand Cru' dinner and what an evening this proved to be. Thanks to the kindness of the members over the years, this must make the fourth or fifth meeting I have been privileged to attend. The members present besides my host, Barney Rhodes, were Bob Adamson, Bill Dickerson, Harry Drescher, Jack Tupper, George Linton and Robert Knudson. My fellow guests were Phil Baxter of Rutherford Hill and Mario Aguirre.

The 1961 Pommery Avize served before the meal had tremendous elegance and showed no sign of age. It was reputed to come from a single vineyard and is only made occasionally.

The wines to accompany the meal following the tasting were:

Wine	*Characteristics*
1961 Chevalier Montrachet *Henri Clerc*	Pale golden colour, attractive rich bouquet, showing a few signs of age but a delightful flavour, a fine bottle.
1961 Le Corton *Bonneau de Martray* (magnum)	Good colour, distinguished bouquet, fairly dry but a rich wine. Has kept extremely well.
1949 Wachenheimer Gerumpel Riesling (*trockenbeerenauslese* Fass No. 2 Burklin-Wolf)	A deep golden colour, the bouquet aged but still rich; rich and wonderful on the palate too, an unforgettable bottle.
Croft 1912 Vintage Port	Colour rather pale, fine bouquet, still a very good taste but the brandy had come through. Barney told us his remaining bottles of Croft 1912 have begun to vary from one to the other. It was very good all the same.

The 'Grand Cru Club', *Subject:* The *Grands Vins* of 1970 – blind tasting

Wine	*Characteristics*	*My placing*	*Group placing*	*Points against*
Mouton-Rothschild	Good colour, attractive bouquet, good fruit, medium body, dry finish.	7th	3rd	40
Pétrus	Good colour, distinguished bouquet, Saint-Emilion or Pomerol, richer flavour, very nice.	1st	2nd	35

Latour	Very dark colour, fine very full bouquet, full-bodied still very powerful, heaps of tannin.	= 2nd	1st	29
Ausone	Pale colour, Saint-Emilion nose, mellow and easy to taste.	4th	8th	60
Margaux	Dark colour, attractive bouquet, good fruit but lacks charm, sharp finish.	8th	4th	45
Cheval-Blanc	Medium colour, pronounced bouquet, different somehow from the others, plenty of body but an off taste, a bad bottle perhaps.	5th	7th	57
Lafite	Good colour, dry bouquet, full-bodied, some acidity.	6th	5th	46
Haut-Brion	Medium colour, different bouquet, a fine full-bodied wine, great flavour but some acidity.	= 2nd	6th	47

The last time the club studied this vintage was two years ago with the result as follows: 1st, Latour; 2nd, Pétrus; 3rd, Mouton-Rothschild; 4th, Cheval-Blanc; 5th, Lafite; 6th, Haut-Brion; 7th, Margaux, and 8th, Ausone.

The general impression was that these great 1970s have rounded off and matured considerably since then. They appear to be turning out every bit as well as expected. The only one still very backward is the Latour. It is interesting to note that the order for the first three was the same as before.

Back to the Napa Valley
Saturday 29 April

To the Napa Valley again and on another glorious day. The vines, with their vegetation about three weeks in advance, run the seasonal risk of frost. So far few of the vineyards have been cultivated because, on account of the recent rain, either tractors cannot get on to the soft ground or, if they do, there is the risk of caking the soil underneath. Before our first rendezvous we passed by the Rhodes' own vineyard, Bella Oaks, where I noticed the vines are trained rather high, this of course to avoid the frost low on the ground.

Our first call was at Grgich Hills, one of the many new wineries which have come into existence since my last visit only a year ago. The two partners are Mike Grgich and Austin Hills. Situated in an excellent part of the valley alongside the vines of Beaulieu Vineyard, a compact little winery has been built on some 20 acres of land suitable for eventual planting of vines. Formerly a partner and the wine maker at Chateau Montelena, Mike's 1973 Chardonnay achieved fame at the much publicised blind tasting in Paris, when California wines caused such a sensation by receiving higher points than many of the best Médocs and white burgundies from France. Indeed, his Chateau Montelena 1973 Chardonnay was one of those which emerged with flying colours and thus it was particularly gratifying to be told that before that tasting I had been the only person who had recognised its special quality. The proof was, as he said, the favourable comment on it in my seventh Diary written and published, of course, before the event took place.

So new is this winery of Grgich Hills that the first wines were only released in March 1978. These are the ones he showed us.

Wine	Characteristics
1977 Chardonnay (from the barrel)	A pleasant perfumed bouquet, lots of fruit, good dry finish. To be bottled June 1978.
1977 Johannisberg Riesling	Already on the market. Delightful varietal bouquet, fragrant flavour with breeding.
1977 Johannisberg Riesling (late harvest)	Bouquet still undeveloped, much richer of course, one can really taste the fruit in this.

My goodness how these Johannisberg Rieslings have improved during the past two or three years! I used to consider the Chardonnay California's best wine and perhaps it still is, but the Rieslings which formerly I used to find almost too perfumed and certainly too clumsy are beginning to improve enormously, especially from wineries such as this.

Late harvest wines are all the rage now but as Mike explained the vines from which this particular wine was made had had what could only be described as a galloping attack of *botrytis* at the critical moment and he had thus no alternative but to produce a late harvest wine from them.

Wine	Characteristics
1977 Zinfandel	Still in stainless steel tank, will be put into barrel in June and kept there for another year. This wine had a very dark colour, pronounced fruity bouquet, quite full-bodied, very nice.

My readers will know that for years I have wondered why such a plethora of varietals have been produced at the wineries; if nothing else, even the administration of them alone must cause a problem. It would appear that Mike is one of the forerunners to concentrate on just one or two varietals, at present *chardonnay* and *riesling*. He said however that the soil being suitable, he would like to reduce his varietals to one only, a *chardonnay*, and specialise in that. Incidently the attractive labels for this new winery were designed by Sebastian Titus, whose ability I have commented upon on previous occasions.

Our next stop was at another new establishment which has also blossomed since my last visit. For years Roy Raymond has managed the vineyards and winery at Beringer and left them only when the estate was bought by Nestlé. Now, together with his two sons, he has launched this new winery called Raymond where, from some 90 acres, the family hopes to produce about 20,000 cases a year. Their first releases last year, received instant acclaim.

Wine	Characteristics
1977 Chardonnay	Pale golden colour, a full very fruity bouquet, a very nice clean wine with good fruit acidity at the finish.
1976 Cabernet Sauvignon (with 10% *merlot*)	Good colour and distinct varietal nose, heaps of character and better still not massive. This is to be bottled later this month (May 1978).

1977 Zinfandel	Unusually dark colour, good nose, lots of fruit. Has tannin and acid but not too accentuated. Zinfandel unfortunately comes in many styles but this was cumbersome.
1977 Merlot	A pretty ruby colour, strong varietal bouquet, not a big wine but it has considerable charm.

Walter Raymond informed us that this will be used a little for blending but mainly for selling as a varietal on its own. Finally we tasted his 1977 Late Harvest and how delicious it was with its honeyed bouquet. In a few years' time this should make an excellent dessert wine.

How thoughtful it has been of Barney and Belle Rhodes to bring me to see new wineries such as these, both of them first class and each in its own way representative of the snowballing quality of these exciting wines of California.

Spring Mountain – what a magnificient property this is! Set in the most beautiful surroundings, altitude about 500 feet on the west side of the Napa Valley, whence in every direction there is a lovely view. When Mike Robbins bought this estate some years ago the nineteenth-century house had looked decrepit, gloomy and depressing. Having restored it to its original Victorian style, Mike and Shirley Robbins can be justly proud of their superhuman effort.

When I was here two years ago the building of the actual winery had scarcely begun; now besides being possibly the most up-to-date in design and equipment in the Valley, it is a joy to behold. A perfectionist if ever there were one, Mike, at least in my eyes, has the added attraction of admiring Château Latour above all wines of Bordeaux; indeed he has many different vintages of Latour in his personal cellar. In return it is nice to record that his 1975 Chardonnay from Spring Mountain is the most popular of all California wine on board the QE2.

As a summer lunch Shirley gave us *prosciutto* followed by delicious fresh salmon. The first wine, 1974 Sauvignon Blanc, was one of the best I have tasted here on the West Coast, resembling more than usual the Blanc Fumé or Sancerre from the Loire. The second, the 1975 Chardonnay, had a fine flavour and a really good bouquet. Distinguished and very dry.

Wine	Characteristics
1975 Cabernet Sauvignon (with 6% *merlot*)	Very dark colour, full bouquet, plenty of fruit, still a bit too strong on account of its youth and there was some acidity to lose.

Dinner at the Caravanserai

The Rhodes gave a little dinner party at a San Francisco restaurant, the Caravanserai, for John and Diane Carpenter and myself. John, who has recently launched The Wine House in San Francisco, is the merchant responsible for the local chapter of Les Amis du Vin. With that meal we had an attractive 1975 Zinfandel from Joseph Phelps.

The tasting for the San Francisco Chapter took place conveniently in the same building, and there I met my old friend, Jay Jacobs, and the Haskell Normans. It was the Normans who helped to make the 'Call of the Vintage' cruise so enjoyable for us last September on board the MTS Daphne, organised by Alexis Lichine. The subject of the tasting was the 1975 vintage of Bordeaux, just beginning to arrive from France. Actually I felt those particular 1975s were not showing nearly so well as in Bordeaux, no doubt because only three weeks after arrival, they had not recovered from the journey.

The 1975 vintage from Bordeaux

Wine	Characteristics	My points
La Tour de By *cru bourgeois*	Very good colour, a rich bouquet if a little rougher perhaps than that of some of the more classic Médocs, nevertheless though still firm and tannic it had heaps of fruit and flavour. Definitely a wine to buy with an eye to the future.	14/20
L'Eglise-Clinet *Pomerol*	Good colour, if a trifle browner, attractive bouquet, rich flavour still very immature but this also appears to have a good future.	16/20
Pavie *Saint-Emilion*	Good colour, tinged brown, some fruit, but too thin. May be suffering from the journey.	13/20
Brane-Cantenac *Margaux*	Good colour, very marked Margaux bouquet, light and gracious, real Margaux style. *Note.* Some members did not approve of this very different taste and smell.	17/20
Léoville-Poyferré *Saint-Julien*	Dark colour, full fruity nose, heaps of fruit and flavour, well balanced.	16/20
Lynch-Bages *Pauillac*	Dark colour, powerful, yet different bouquet, quite a big wine; is it oxidised? Perhaps the journey is the cause of disappointment? *Note.* Yes, it was the journey for tasted a year later it is showing splendidly, likewise the Pavie.	13/20
Montrose *Saint-Estèphe*	Dark colour, lovely nose with heaps of fruit in it. A fine big wine but very backward, indeed this may not be enjoyable for seven or eight years.	17 plus/20
Mouton-Rothschild *Pauillac*	Superb colour, full powerful bouquet, a big wine with plenty of fruit.	18/20

We shall have to wait many a year before this vintage is ready. At first glance I had been disturbed by the paler colour of these 1975s, especially in view of the fact that one of their assets in Bordeaux is their dark hue. What may also have happened to me during these past two days in the Napa Valley is that I have become accustomed to the almost black colour of these red wines of California and they have made the 1975s from Bordeaux appear much paler by comparison.

Russian Easter party
Sunday 29 April

Stanley and Ruth Burton invited me to join them at the annual Russian Easter party given by André and Dorothy Tchelistcheff. I was originally introduced to André, the father figure, as it were, of California wine, in April 1969 when the Rhodes took me to Beaulieu Vineyard in the Napa Valley, where he was the wine maker. I recorded that meeting in my third Diary, *The Pick of the*

Bunch, and it is memorable to me not only for the pleasure of getting to know this delightful man but also because it was there for the first time that I tasted the 1968 vintage. I wrote: 'It is obvious that 1968 is an exceptional vintage for California and as good for cabernet sauvignons as say 1961 was for Bordeaux . . .'

Time has proved this statement pretty well correct. I also added: 'If I had the good fortune to live in this pleasant land, like a gun dog after game I would soon be sniffing around to flush some of these fine 1968s from covert . . .'

After retiring from Beaulieu Vineyards, André became a wine consultant and is now regarded as among the greatest in the world. The wineries he assists with his sage advice are myriad, covering the whole of the state of California as well as Oregon and elsewhere. That lunch also provided an opportunity to meet prominent members of the wine world, among them the Heitz, the Stanley Hoffmans, Dick Graf of Chalone and Theo Rosenbrand, the new winemaker at Beaulieu Vineyard.

When, after our return to Oakland, Barney Rhodes asked if there was anything further I would like to try before my imminent departure, I leapt at the opportunity to compare a few more Cabernet Sauvignons of 1974, easily the finest vintage since 1968. All five were tasted anonymously.

Some Cabernet Sauvignons of the excellent 1974 vintage

Wine	Characteristics	My points
Stag's Leap Wine Cellars (Cask 23, 100% cs)	An attractive bouquet faintly reminiscent of chocolate, heaps of lovely fruit. This will make a splendid bottle.	17/20
Raymond (6% *merlot*)	Immature bouquet which improved with airing, a lot of flavour, some tannin to lose.	16/20
Caymus (100% cs)	A charming bouquet, a superb wine beautifully balanced.	19/20
Trefethen	Distinguished bouquet, delightful flavour, plenty of fruit and has complexity, of quite a different style from no. 3 but equally good.	19/20
Burgess (regular)	Pleasing bouquet, reminiscent of fine tobacco, good fruit but too much acidity for my liking. *Note.* This did not seem to compare with the much bigger 1974 Burgess tasted in Phoenix, Arizona.	14/20

Exactly how does one assess this vintage for California Cabernet Sauvignon: with regard to quality, possibly it is in the same category as the best from Bordeaux, i.e. 1970 or 1975. As for California itself, 1974 is the best for many years, transcending maybe even the noted 1968s. Inevitably the 1974s are already expensive, some costing more than 12 dollars a bottle, with the Heitz Martha's Vineyard, usually the most expensive, yet to appear. The 1974 Caymus is the same wine as on the list of the Ritz Hotel, London (as well as the 1974 Harbor Chardonnay already mentioned in these notes); however,

I repeat sadly that so far nobody has asked for either of them!

Even though this visit has been so brief, as always I have noticed improvements in quality as well as some subtle changes. It is difficult not to be unfair to Bordeaux since I go there so often (at least nine times in 1977) but although there is always a new vintage to assess, where signs of improvement might be beneficial at many a *château*, they are not everywhere in evidence. Undoubtly there is vast experience behind the Bordelais growers, and progress continues to be made but apart naturally from certain instances, somehow one misses the bubbling over of enthusiasm one encounters here in the new world of wine.

Although not in all cases, the fashion in the recent past in California has been to produce massive Cabernets, the bigger the better, but among some of the growers a striving is evident to attain more finesse. Indeed, the result is already discernible, so eventually this may tend to narrow the gap between the Cabernets of Bordeaux and those from California. While it has become a popular pastime to do so, the Cabernets of California and Bordeaux should not really be compared directly; they both stem from the same noble family, and should be regarded more as cousins than as brothers. The difference stems no doubt from the soil, that priceless swath of infertile pebbly soil along the left bank of the Gironde, and the generally cooler, if unreliable, climate, two reasons surely for greater elegance in the wine.

Up to date the most successful wines from California, at least in my humble opinion, have been the Chardonnays. During blind tastings I have found them considerably more difficult to separate from those of the Côte de Beaune than is the case with the Cabernets. There used to be only one or two vineyards which produced exceptional Chardonnays but now their number is increasing all the time.

The real surprise this time has been the Johannisberg Rieslings. During the last two visits in 1977 and 1976 excitement has been concentrated around the late harvest wines. These have now become the 'in thing' and instead of just one or two enlightened growers specialising in them, one seems to encounter a late harvest wine in most of the places one visits.

It is not, however, the late harvest Rieslings which have been so startling this time, but the improvement so evident among some of the straightforward ones. On previous occasions, the regular Johannisberg Rieslings have been either too oaky, too perfumed, too sweet and certainly too clumsy for my particular taste. What has impressed me so much on this journey has been how, at several of the wineries, much of the clumsiness has been ironed out with more elegance taking its place. Should this continue, the Germans too may have to look to their laurels.

The two varietals which have not crossed my path on this visit have been *chenin blanc* and *pinot noir*, but there is no sense of loss for so far neither has appealed to me. *Prenez garde* however; one can never be too dogmatic about the wines of California. If such astonishing results can be obtained in so short a space of time, as with the Cabernets, the Chardonnays and now the Johannisberg Rieslings, anything can happen!

Supper with the Robertsons
Monday 1 May

Boise, Idaho – 'famous potatoes' as one reads on the registration plates of all the cars. An exciting surprise was in store, for there at the airport to meet me with Brooks Tish, the regional director of Les Amis du Vin, were my chums from Salt Lake City, Dr. Owen Reese and Stanley Katz, who with their wives had flown up in the latter's plane. Later on Colonel Jack Daniels also arrived; his journey by car from Salt Lake City had taken him seven hours, so there's enthusiasm for you!

Brooks and Dorothy Tish drove us to the home of Steve and Lesley Robertson, where spread before us lay the most appetising buffet supper one could imagine – what is more it all tasted as nice as it looked. Steve Robertson owns a fish restaurant as well as a retail wine store, hence the wide variety of seafood – Dungeness crab, lobster, Oregon cocktail shrimps on coleslaw, smoked salmon, baby asparagus and so on and so forth. That part of the meal had been prepared by Mrs. Ed. Robertson. Lesley Robertson, Steve's wife, had made no less than three kinds of cheesecake as well as chocolate, orange and almond fudge, but by the time we had reached that stage I could only manage the almond fudge.

So far on this journey no Chenin Blanc had come my way but the four to be described fully made up for that lapse. As mentioned earlier the Chenin Blanc from California so far has not captured my enthusiasm but at least two of these wines were to prove an agreeable surprise.

The Chenin Blanc 1977 from San Michele in the State of Oregon was a little too sweet and too bland for my personal taste, but nevertheless it indicated the progress made in this comparatively new wine region. The 1976 Bell Canyon, although pleasant, was not out of the ordinary in so far as style and quality are concerned. However, the two Chenin Blancs from the Hoffman Mountain Ranch were undoubtedly a revelation. I had met Dr. Stanley Hoffman and his wife, Jane, on the Alexis Lichine cruise in September 1977. It is actually his two sons who manage the vineyard and make the wine, but he had told me then that their consultant is André Tchelistcheff. During this present journey I have encountered the HMR wines on several occasions and their quality has been worthy of André's skill. These are my notes on the nicest Chenin Blanc I have so far tasted, both of them from the Hoffman Mountain Ranch.

Wine	Characteristics
1977 Chenin Blanc Sec H.M.R.	Pronounced perfumed bouquet, good fruit acidity and fairly dry.
1977 Chenin Blanc H.M.R.	Good bouquet, a fuller wine, richer but certainly not too sweet and rather good.

Then followed two 1974 Cabernet Sauvignons, the Caymus 1974 from a magnum and the Burgess Vintage Selection (i.e. the best Cabernet from that winery). I was permitted to taste these blind, and to begin with was put off by the musty bouquet of the wine which turned out to be the Caymus, totally different from the bottle of the same I had tried only the day before with Barney and Belle Rhodes. This may or may not have been on account of the magnum, because later on some of that mustiness wore off.

Wine	Characteristics
1974 Cabernet Sauvignon, Caymus	Very dark colour, slightly musty nose, all the same the good fruit and delightful after taste were discernible. This could, of course, have been a faulty bottle.

1974 Burgess Vintage Selection	Very dark colour, attractive bouquet, not a big wine but well balanced and good all through.

In view of the disappointing bottle of Caymus, I preferred the Burgess Vintage Selection, in any case a very good wine.

Two notable dessert wines were served with the cheesecake, 1973 Freemark Abbey Edelwein and 1976 Joseph Phelps Late Harvest.

Lunch at Morgan's Exchange
Tuesday 2 May

About 20 people gathered for lunch at a club called Morgan's Exchange, where most of us chose the seafood platter, shrimp, Dungeness crab, onion rings and melon. This formed a good background for the Johannisberg Rieslings from the local winery of Ste. Chapelle.

Our hosts, the owners of Ste. Chapelle, were Bill and Penny Brioch and their young Canadian wine maker, Bruce White. The latter had received his training at Fresno. I personally thought the white wines were better than the red. It appears there have been vineyards here for a long time but unfortunately the old ones were discontinued and all the vines pulled up long ago.

Ste. Chapelle

Wine	Characteristics
1976 Johannisberg Riesling (14% alcohol)	Pale colour, bouquet quite pleasant, fresh and clean with fruit acidity at the finish. Reasonably dry.
1977 Johannisberg Riesling (11.9% alcohol)	Fresh varietal bouquet, fuller, fruitier and sweeter, in fact too sweet for me.
1977 Johannisberg Late Harvest	Flowery bouquet, richer flavour but with attractive fruit acidity.

Before tasting these wines of Idaho I was afraid I might have to make polite noises, so it was all the more pleasant to find that at least the whites if not the reds appear to have promise. There was also a rather nice Rosé de Cabernet Sauvignon, but it was on the sweet side. Vinously, this is an unsophisticated area, so I was told they have to make all their wines rather sweet otherwise there would be no sale for them; this is also the case in many other parts of the U.S. Once the local people have become more accustomed to this relatively new hobby, then perhaps this winery can consider producing a drier style.

Another facet of this situation was pointed out by Steve Robertson, who told me that of all the customers who come to his shop (where wine only and no spirits are sold) only about two are above 40 years of age!

The tasting took place just out of town at a catering establishment called Chapon and on arrival I noticed the bar was crammed with people having a high old time, so much so that I remarked that the place appeared to be doing unusually good business; it turned out to be an Irish wake! For many years it seems the deceased had worked at the Chapon as a barman and in his will had left a generous sum of money for his friends to have a final fling, this time at his expense.

From the cheerfulness of the Amis du Vin members assembling, it was possible from the outset to sense that our part of the evening was also about to go well; indeed the meeting of about 100 people had been heavily oversubscribed.

The aperitif, the Ste. Chapelle 1977 Johannisberg Riesling, tasted well and the selection of wines Brooks Tish had made gave plenty of cause for discussion.

<table>
<tr><td>Tasting with the
Amis du Vin</td><td>Wine</td><td>Characteristics</td><td>My points</td></tr>
<tr><td></td><td>1974 Clos du Val Cabernet Sauvignon</td><td>Dark colour, a fruity but somewhat coarse bouquet, plenty of fruit, agreeable to drink but lacks elegance.</td><td>12/20</td></tr>
<tr><td></td><td>1975 Spring Mountain Cabernet Sauvignon</td><td>Dark colour, attractive bouquet, delightful flavour, perhaps just a little too much acidity.</td><td>14/20</td></tr>
<tr><td></td><td>1974 Stag's Leap Wine Cellars Cabernet Sauvignon (cask 23)</td><td>Dark colour, a rich complex bouquet, well balanced, delicious flavour and an excellent after taste; a real winner.</td><td>16/20</td></tr>
<tr><td></td><td>1974 Haut-Brion</td><td>Good colour, distinguished bouquet and good fruit, but the tannin coupled with some sharpness detracted from its attraction. This needed at least two years.</td><td>16/20</td></tr>
</table>

Being rounder and richer, the Stag's Leap appeared the more attractive of the four; on reflection, however, it lacked the breeding and finesse of the Haut-Brion. It is perhaps natural that most people preferred the former, so much easier to taste.

Wine	Characteristics	My points
1970 Ducru-Beaucaillou	Dark colour, elegant bouquet, lovely flavour, has great style.	18/20
1967 Latour	Dark colour, deep bouquet, heaps of fine flavour, plenty of tannin; in spite of a trace of the inevitable 1967 acidity, it was for me nevertheless the best wine of the evening.	19/20

On account of its indifferent vintage, this comparison with the Stag's Leap of a great year was a somewhat unfair test for the Haut-Brion. All the same, if immediately after tasting the Haut-Brion one went back to the Stag's Leap, the latter, although with much more, as it were, in the shop window, had a thicker and perhaps more plummy taste. There, maybe, lies the essential difference between the great wines of California and those of Bordeaux, a lack of ultimate elegance. This, however, is by no means the end of the story for I am sure the Californian growers will not allow matters to rest there!

The evening was rounded off with a glass of delicious 1971 Château d'Yquem.

Denver, Colorado
Wednesday 3 May

The plane to Denver crossed the desert and stopped en route at Salt Lake City. It was interesting once again to see the Salt Lake and admire the snowclad Rocky Mountains. From then on there were mountains all the way, seemingly of immense height especially as we descended into Denver.

I never managed to see the city of Denver, because Paul McEnroe drove me direct to his restaurant and liquor store at El Rancho, 8,000 feet up in the mountains. In spite of some much-needed rain the mountain air was wonderful.

While it appears possible to obtain the run-of-the-mill California wines from distributors, the retailers around here clearly have a problem with anything out of the ordinary. For instance our evening had been planned around the wines of St.-Estèphe but in spite of long notice they had not turned up. Instead we had to go 'slumming it' with two first growths from Pauillac – one could fare worse I suppose!!!

In fact, we came up against a setback fairly common in this country and especially so in cities far from the coast: wine which had suffered either through transport or bad handling. I had heard of this many times but never before had experienced it quite so blatantly. Although the distributor had assured my hosts that all the cases of wine had come straight from Bordeaux within the past year, it was not only a question of some cases being faulty but also individual bottles as well. For instance, knowing how good the Mouton 1970 can be, I could not believe what I had in my glass and when I checked the contents on other tables and from different bottles their wine was much better. Since that was by no means the only instance of variation of bottles from the same case it is doubtful whether these notes will be of much value.

Wine	Characteristics
Mouton-Rothschild 1970	Good dark colour, a full bouquet, not yet properly developed, a bigger wine than the Lafite, good flavour.
Lafite 1970	A pretty, if less dark colour, distinguished bouquet, good fruit and flavour, not a big wine, has a pleasant finish and seems more forward than the 1970 Mouton.
Mouton-Rothschild 1967	Medium colour, a full fruity bouquet, plenty of flavour, some acidity.
Lafite 1967	Colour rather weak, elegant bouquet, not so big a wine but the flavour overwhelmed by the acidity. *Note.* At another table this acidity was less pronounced.
Mouton-Rothschild 1964	Colour poor, even cloudy, pleasant bouquet, flavour only fairly good.
Lafite 1964	Brilliant ruby colour, not much bouquet, but excessive acidity. Here again other bottles tasted were better.

To Indianapolis
Thursday 4 May

So far on this journey I had been favoured with fine weather but my luck was now to change for it was raining hard by the time I arrived in Indianapolis. Charles and Jill Thomas live in a lovely house some miles outside the city, where I was to pass two pleasant days.

A dinner had been arranged that evening at the Chanteclair restaurant in Indianapolis. They must have a good chef at that establishment because the standard of the meal was far above average. It seems that writing books has a built-in advantage for by now future hosts of Les Amis du Vin have a pretty

George Lokey makes Harry Waugh an Honorary Citizen of Amarillo.

Indianapolis: Maggie and Bill Dick, HW, Charlie and Jill Thomas.

good idea of most of my favourite vineyards in Bordeaux, hence a dinner such as this based on the wines of Château La Mission-Haut-Brion.

By far the best white Graves I have had on this visit, the Laville-Haut-Brion 1974, went very well with the lobster Provencale; three of the red wines were served alongside so that they could be compared. All had a good dark colour.

Tasting of La Mission-Haut-Brion

Wine	Characteristics	My points
La Mission-Haut-Brion 1967	A good Graves bouquet, plenty of fruit and flavour; happily there was only mild evidence of the weakness of the 1967 vintage, acidity; in fact, it is really 'greenness' as the late Henri Woltner used to describe it. Henri, the genius who for nearly half a century made so many outstanding vintages for La Mission, often told me that many of the *cabernet* grapes of 1967 were not entirely ripe at the time of that harvest. He had therefore taken the precaution to eliminate all the unripe bunches he could before the grapes went into the press. Hence the success of this particular 1967.	14/20
La Mission-Haut-Brion 1964 (From a magnum)	Possibly this would have been better from a bottle because from such a large container it was still very backward. Heaps and heaps of fruit and a success in a vintage when a number of well-known *châteaux* did not distinguish themselves.	16/20
La Mission-Haut-Brion 1957	A beautiful bouquet of considerable depth, a supple, delectable flavour and surely at its best now.	17/20
	As a general rule most 1957s were unbending, unattractive wines in which both acidity and tannin predominated. So far as I am concerned, among the few successful were this La Mission and Lynch-Bages. Although a bit out of chronological order Charles Thomas had wisely reserved the two biggest wines for the cheese:	
La Mission-Haut-Brion 1966	Very dark colour, splendid bouquet, a huge wine full of concentrated flavour, needs a few more years to reach its summit.	18/20
La Mission-Haut-Brion 1961	Very dark colour, splendid bouquet, with a glorious rich flavour, also needs some years to reach its best. This must surely be among the greatest pearls of this fabulous vintage.	19/20

What a tribute these wines are to the genius of Henri Woltner; a dear friend was lost when he died in 1974. Happily, Monsieur Lagardère, his manager who worked alongside him for 20 years, is still there, together with his son, Michel, to ensure the future. Since both the Woltner brothers Henri and Fernand are now dead, the vineyard is now in the able hands of Francis and Françoise Dewavrin, the daughter of the late Fernand.

One of the vintage ports, the Croft 1963, has already been commented upon in these notes, but the 1896 Brooks Empress was something way out of the ordinary. In dumpy golden bottles, it would appear this particular wine had been bottled in Oporto to celebrate the Golden Jubilee of Queen Victoria.

As pale as a tawny port it was not only highly enjoyable but remarkably well preserved. Although on the label it stated vintage 1896, I have a sneaking feeling this was not a vintage port as such but a fine tawny which provided a fitting end to an extraordinarily good dinner.

Friday 5 May

Dr. and Mrs. Thomas gave a dinner party before the tasting during which we drank two vintages of Château Gruaud-Larose, the 1959 and the 1949. Opinions differed but I personally preferred the younger of the two.

Wine	Characteristics
Gruaud-Larose 1959	Good dark colour, attractive bouquet, a lovely wine full of fruit and flavour and a very pleasant finish.
Gruaud-Larose 1949	Good colour, fine old bouquet, still has sufficient fruit and flavour, now drying off a bit at the finish. All the same it was extraordinarily well preserved for a 30-year-old.

The turnout was impressive, over 170 people, the largest apparently they have ever had and three times as many as usual. Charles Thomas had shown considerable imagination over his selection of wines, which were served anonymously in four pairs. We were allowed to know the names of the pairs but not the order in which they were to be presented.

An anonymous tasting of Saint-Juliens and Margaux at the Latour restaurant in Indianapolis

Wine	Characteristics	My points
Malescot 1967	Medium colour, attractive bouquet, on the thin side, much too sharp and singularly lacking in charm.	10/20
Léoville-Barton 1967	Plenty of bouquet, much more fruit and altogether a better finish.	15/20
	The voting on these was slightly in favour of the Malescot, Margaux. The points out of 20 are my own.	
Gruaud-Larose 1970	Very good colour, fine bouquet, good fruit, some acidity to lose. Needs two to three years yet	13/20
Giscours 1970	Nice dark colour, lovely full bouquet, a huge wine, excellent. Needs four or five years.	18/20
	Voting was almost unanimously in favour of the Giscours. The Gruaud-Larose could have been suffering from poor handling.	
Brane-Cantenac 1966	Medium colour, a rather special yet attractive bouquet, good fruit, finished only fairly well. Ready now.	14/20
Léoville-Las-Cases 1966	Good colour, a sweeter, very good bouquet, medium body but good flavour, some tannin still to lose, ready soon.	16/20

[57]

Voting overwhelmingly in favour of the Léoville-Las Cases.

Beychevelle 1967	Good colour, pleasant bouquet, good fruit, just a little acidity at the finish.	16/20
Palmer 1967	Good colour, quite a powerful bouquet and a big impressive wine, needs some years yet. First rate quality and the best of the evening.	18/20
	The voting was overwhelmingly in favour of the Château Palmer. This must be among the top flight of the 1967 vintage, an example of how well Château Palmer is made; somehow the almost universal acidity of the 1967 vintage has been excluded.	

Percy Simmons, English by upbringing and a first-class timber merchant, has for many years been the backbone in Indiana of the propagation of the wines of France. For the good work he has done in this field and also as French Consul he has been awarded the Order of Merit. On behalf of Les Amis du Vin of Indianapolis I deemed it an honour to be asked to present him also with an award from Les Amis du Vin.

Dinner with the Chentniks
Saturday 6 May

The drive of some 90 miles from Indianapolis to Logansport took us through the village of Waugh. Richard Chentnik had done some research since my visit in 1976, and had discovered that it had been named after a trapper who had settled there with his family from the lowlands of Scotland around 1840. Since my own forebears had for centuries been yeoman farmers near Jedburgh, that early settler could well have been of the same family.

A dinner party was given that evening by Richard and Annette Chentnik at the Ambers restaurant in Logansport, one of the earliest townships to be settled in Indiana. Correctly surmising that many of my previous tastings would be based around either red Bordeaux and the Cabernet Sauvignons of California, Richard had chosen bottles from the Domaine-de-la-Romanée-Conti, which were tasted with really good lamb chops.

Wine	*Characteristics*
La Tâche 1967	Good colour, but oh dear, there was a touch of volatile acidity on the nose, a fuller wine than the Richebourg but its soundness was questionable.
Richebourg 1967	Colour rather weak and nose distinctly frail. Well bred yes, but thin and disappointing. Richard said he was certain that both cases had been delivered to his house within a month of arrival in the U.S. and had been in his cellar ever since, so that the question of bad storage did not arise.
La Tâche 1969	Good colour, attractive bouquet, more body than the 1967s and of course tremendous breeding but if this is the best that some of the best-known post-war red burgundy can do, well it makes one wonder!
Grands-Echézeaux 1937 (Dr. Barolet collection)	Medium colour, fine bouquet, good complex flavour and a fine finish. This bottle put the Domaine-de-la-Romanée-Conti wines into the shade.

Dr. Richard Chentnik, who buys many of the wines for the local chapter of Les Chevaliers du Tastevin, stated that he has to scour the country to find wine of sufficient quality for his meetings and all too often after all the trouble taken the result is disappointing. Many Burgundians are fully aware of the dismay of their vinous followers, yet so little is done about it. One of these days perhaps they may find it is too late!

An outstanding 1875 Malvasia, Henriques Y. Henriques, bottled in 1967, was enjoyed with a chocolate mousse. So lovely was this Madeira, it must be one of the highlights of the entire visit.

Sunday 7 May

Percy Simmons, the special guest of honour, arrived from Indianapolis around 5.0 p.m., as well as Mr. and Mrs. Carl Banholzer. Some years ago Mr. Banholzer planted a vineyard at La Porte in Indiana, a courageous operation in view of the northern climate, but before doing so he had taken the trouble to ascertain that there was an unusually good micro-climate in that particular area. Mr. Banholzer produced two wines that evening. The 1975 Cabernet Sauvignon, although on the light side, had a pleasant varietal bouquet and flavour. His white La Fleur, however, was much more serious, indeed an attractive aperitif wine, dry with just a trace of sugar and a slight prickle. Indiana is not exactly a state where one expects wine to be made, so the result he had achieved was indeed praiseworthy. This La Fleur is made from 55 per cent white *riesling* and the rest mainly from a French hybrid called *vignoles* (Ravat 51).

In order to change the theme Richard had chosen some Zinfandels for the evening event. Following a glass of Schramsberg Cuvée de Gamay 1973, these are the wines we discussed:

Zinfandels

Wine	Characteristics	My points
Burgess 1974 *Napa and Sonoma*	Big fruity nose, lot of oak though, plenty of fruit, seems rather coarse.	14/20
Mirassou 1974 *Monterey, Santa Clara*	Musty bouquet, very obvious flavour, some acidity, all in the shop window.	10/20
Simi 1973 *Sonoma*	Not much bouquet, good fruit and quite well made.	16/20
Mayacamas Late Harvest 1974	Dark colour, bouquet hard to find, the fruit overlaid by considerable acidity. Query what it will be like if and when the acidity has disappeared?	

At the end of the proceedings it was my pleasant task to make Dr. Chentnik a Chevalier of Les Amis du Vin. Apparently only three similar awards are being presented this year, to individuals who have done particularly well for the cause. Cause it is, because during my travels around the U.S. it is impossible not to be impressed by the good being achieved by 'Les Amis'. I have been engaged upon these lecture tours for a number of years now, and every time the whole project seems to get better and better. Apart from the pleasure of going to new places and making new friends, my more recent journeys have been concentrated on areas where the chapters have either been newly formed or revived. The spread of new chapters is highly encouraging and through them it is possible to gauge the depth of interest in table wine throughout this huge country. There are now well over 200 and I can see no limit to further increase. The fundamental question all beginners ask is: 'Apart from reading books on the subject, how can I actually learn about it?' In the U.S. at any rate the answer is simple and is being proved again and again all over the country: 'Join Les Amis du Vin'.

Monday 8 May	Since my last visit to Logansport, my host Richard Chentnik has planted out about an acre of vines alongside the Eel river and has a further 40 acres already cleared ready for planting. In view of the severe winters, I had always imagined the area unsuitable for the planting of anything but hybrids. It appears, however, that all along the valley of the Wabash river, of which the Eel is a tributary, there is a much milder micro-climate and thus the planting of *vinifera* grapes becomes a feasible proposition.

How times are changing. While in the past the main wine producing areas were the Finger Lakes and California now, thanks to general enthusiasm, enterprising people are planting vines all over the country. To mention but a few states: Arkansas, Texas, Idaho and even northern Arizona if my information is correct. Doubtless not all wineries will succeed, but how exhilarating it is to watch the enthusiasm.

If one can judge by the way the American public is taking to the drinking of table wine, these additional vineyard areas will serve a useful purpose. Only a year or so ago California was considered to be overplanting vines and a glut of grapes was feared. As it has turned out there has been no glut at all, any possible surplus having been absorbed by the masses of people who have been giving up hard liquor and taking instead to the juice of the grape. What certainly was not envisaged was the present popularity of white wine.

Travelling as I do in aeroplanes, I do not see as much of the country as I would like, and consequently the drives from Indianapolis to Logansport and on to Fort Wayne, each about 70 miles, have been an agreeable change.

Thanks to a change of timetable poor Richard Hadad had to go to Detroit airport twice, my plane having been re-routed from Fort Wayne back to Indianapolis! The weather was bad ever since I left Idaho and it was even worse when I arrived in Detroit with even a tornado warning in the offing.

At the Dearborn Inn where the tasting was held, it was a pleasure to meet many friends, including Bob Simburger, and Dick and Sally Scheer. The Scheers, who own the Village Corner at Ann Arbor, have possibly as good a wine list as any in the Mid-West, and they had brought along their entire staff to the tasting. To give a rough idea of this remarkable firm, there are over 360 red Bordeaux on its list including all the very finest!

To make a change for me the local director had arranged a tasting of red Burgundy and had scoured the country to find wines out of the ordinary.

	Wine	Characteristics	My points
Red Burgundy, the 1973 vintage	Gevrey-Chambertin *Domaine Armand Rousseau*	Rather a feeble colour, well-bred bouquet, on light side and a little sharp.	10/20

Wine	Characteristics	
Vosne-Romanée *Louis Latour*	Slightly darker colour, more depth of bouquet, more body, less sharp than the Gevrey-Chambertin, but still too thin.	12/20
Corton-Grancey *Louis Latour*	Medium colour, fuller bouquet, more fruit to it. A much better wine, rounder and well made.	16/20
Echézeaux *Domaine Dujac*	Medium colour, my immediate reaction to the bouquet was 'Ah, now we are getting somewhere'. It had that delightfully perfumed bouquet one sometimes comes across in fine red Burgundy. Not a big wine, perhaps even a bit meagre, but with a flavour similar to the bouquet, a burgundy with style.	15/20
Morey St.-Denis, Clos de la Roche *Domaine Dujac*	Not dark, but a much better colour, the same beautiful bouquet as the other Dujac wine, lovely flavour and well balanced.	18/20
Gevrey- Chambertin Clos St.-Jacques *Armand Rousseau*	A paler colour, good bouquet, again on the light side, but well made.	15/20

As with Bordeaux, 1973 was a copious vintage for red Burgundy. There are masses of pale coloured, rather light wines, few of which appear to have a long life before them. Although the Echézeaux had more style, contrary to many of the group I personally preferred the Corton-Grancey on account of its better balance. The Corton was ready to drink but I think the two wines from Domaine Dujac may improve over the next two years; neither, however, is to be considered for the long term.

Detroit
Tuesday 9 May

The Hadads have a delightful house on Grosse-Ile, bordering on Lake Erie with Canada only a few hundred yards away across the water. I had been looking forward to some repose by the lakeside but in pouring rain and gales of wind the lake resembled a rough sea.

My fellow guests for dinner that evening were Norman and Rita Simpson. Norman, like Richard Hadad, is also a member of our London Chapter of Les Compagnons du Beaujolais. Another guest was Dwayne Kremko, a wine merchant. The meal Shirley prepared was simple but outstanding, *vichyssoise*, rolled ribs of beef and cheesecake. The beef, cooked impeccably, had as fine a flavour as any I have ever eaten. There were two Chablis: a 1974 Vaillons (Schoonmaker), correct but rather severe, no doubt due to the vintage, and a 1975 Chablis Le Clos de L'Hospice, and how good that was. Two red Bordeaux accompanied the meat:

Wine	Characteristics
Pichon-Lalande 1967	Good colour and bouquet, full-bodied for a 1967 better than most perhaps, even so, some of the acidity of the vintage was in evidence.
Margaux 1962 (magnum)	Good colour and bouquet, plenty of fruit and flavour but could perhaps have had more charm. Even in magnums it seems as though the 1962 Margaux needs drinking.

The Graham 1960 vintage port, surely now at its peak, provided a splendid finish to the meal.

Fleeing from the grey skies of Detroit to the warm sunshine of Louisville, Kentucky, presented an agreeable change, added to which was the personality of my hostess, Judi Haas, who had come to meet me.

As well as being the regional director of Les Amis du Vin, Judi Haas is a film director. On arrival I was swept off to a formal garden on the university campus where a short documentary was made. This took at least three hours but the time passed rapidly in that sunswept garden. Although Louisville is a new chapter it is remarkable what Mrs. Haas has accomplished in so short a time, especially since she has to work under all the disadvantages of a controlled state, i.e. difficult licensing laws. Happily for this chapter, Louisville is situated on the border of Indiana where things are more civilised and it is thus possible to buy fine wine from a merchant whose premises are just over the state line. In fact all the wine for our tasting came from his store.

A host and hostess are appointed in rotation for each meeting and on this particular occasion they were a young couple called Joseph. Not only were the arrangements admirable but Mrs. Joseph had prepared no less than three large quiches for the 80 odd people who attended, cheese, spinach and quiche Lorraine.

This chapter in Louisville is an example of what a useful purpose Les Amis du Vin can perform. On account of the fact that Kentucky is a controlled state it is only natural that with all the goodwill in the world, the local inhabitants know very little about wine. Consequently I was asked to keep my talk on the wines of Bordeaux as simple as possible. All the same it was encouraging to be asked a considerable number of knowledgeable questions. Judi Haas had carefully chosen the wines to show as far as possible some of the basic differences in style of the various districts.

Wine	Characteristics	My points
Bouscaut 1971 *Graves*	Pretty colour, typical taste and flavour of its district but too thin for general approval.	12/20
Brane-Cantenac 1971 *Margaux*	Good colour, distinguished bouquet, not a massive wine but very attractive, finishes well. Needs several years before it will be ready, certainly worth waiting for.	16/20
Clerc-Milon 1970 *Pauillac*	Dark colour, full bouquet, plenty of fruit, but rather sharp at the finish. *Note.* Tasted a 1971 Clerc-Milon five days later in London and it had the same sharp finish.	13/20
Cos-d'Estournel 1970 *Saint-Estèphe*	Dark colour, heaps of fruit and tannin and at the moment excessive acidity. Ready by, say, 1982/3.	15/20
Cheval-Blanc 1970 *Saint-Emilion*	Dark colour, fine bouquet, rich rounded flavour and a good finish. Fine quality, needs three or four years.	18/20
Latour 1964 *Pauillac*	Served as a kind of *bonne bouche*. Dark colour, lovely Latour bouquet, a fine well-made wine. Not yet at its best but will surely make a good bottle. One of the successes of this somewhat irregular vintage for the wines of the Médoc.	18/20

There was an exciting conclusion to the meeting for me when Dick Haas, Judi's husband, presented me with a certificate to the effect that I had been commisioned a Kentucky Colonel. The framed certificate is now hung with pride at my home in London, since it is an honour not freely awarded and therefore one to be cherished.

Washington, D.C.
Thursday 11 May

Washington D.C. was looking at its best in the lovely spring sunshine. There was a reception at the British Embassy to celebrate the 300th anniversary of the Oporto firm of Croft & Co. Apart from their cream sherry and a fine ten-year-old tawny port there were three vintages also to taste, the 1935, 1945 and 1904. Although showing some age the 1904 was most enjoyable. The 1935 has kept well and the 1945 was outstanding.

Lunch at the Jean-Pierre restaurant
Friday 12 May

Harold Baron, whom I had met in Westchester, at the beginning of this visit, had flown down to give a magnificent lunch party for me at the Jean-Pierre restaurant, one of the finest in the city. Those present were Kathy O'Reilly, Barry Breen, Larry Clatt and Larry Bartleman. They all work for the firm of Schenley, of which our host is a vice-president. Incidentally, it is Dreyfus Ashby, a subsidiary of Schenley, which over the past ten years have done such a good job getting Château Latour into the right restaurants in the U.S. Also present were Ron Fonte, Marvin Stirman (of Wines Ltd.) and David Purseglove, who writes for the *Washington Star* as well as a syndicate for 800 newspapers across the country.

Here are the details of this outstanding meal:

Hure de Saumon
An unbelievably good *remoulade* in slices with jelly herbs and ale.

Grilled Shad Roe Beurre d'Anchois
It is now the season for shad. The roe was served *en croûtons* with a strong anchovy sauce. The Americans have every right to make such a fuss about this dish.

Gratin d'Ecrevisses
Tiny tender *écrevisses* with sliced mushroom and I think some lettuce in a lovely cheesy sauce and, of course, some truffles.

A sorbet not on the menu then appeared with red and white grapes on top and a pronounced taste of *marc de bourgogne*, somewhat out of place!

Filet de Boeuf en croûte, sauce Perigeux
By this time I could eat no more but all I tasted was excellent.

This was by no means the end though because cheese and a delicious coffee soufflé followed.

Three white Burgundies served in succession were to accompany the two fish courses:

Wine	Characteristics
Chablis Les Beugnons 1974 *Domaine Albert Long Depaquit*	Lots of lovely flavour, fine quality.

[63]

Chablis le Clos 1975 *Moutonne*	Even finer than Les Beugnons and as fine as Chablis can be.
Montrachet 1974 *Marquis de Laguiche*	Not a very big wine, at its best though with a delightful long after taste.
Beaulieu Vineyard 1964 (private reserve)	Very dark colour, full Cabernet nose, but a very plummy grapy taste and a 'strike' of was it severity towards the finish. It was unfortunate to have it served alongside the Mouton and Lafite for it did not stand a chance.
Mouton-Rothschild 1959 (magnum)	Fine dark colour, a huge wine full of fruit, the true Mouton flavour. Not in fact quite ready yet in a magnum but of great quality.
Lafite 1955	Distinguished bouquet, nothing like so full-bodied as the Mouton but it had a very nice flavour and of course was full of race and breeding.
La Romanée 1970 *Château de Vosne-Romanée*	Good colour for a 1970, fine bouquet, lovely flavour, had heaps of style.
La Romanée 1971 *Château de Vosne-Romanée*	Dark colour, more concentrated nose and flavour, solid and well made, excellent quality, will improve.

These two fine Burgundies were in fact the purpose of the lunch because when I had so admired the 1971 Echézeaux Domaine Clos-Frantin in Westchester, Harold had promised to let me taste some more wines from the same stable. Since these two La Romanées as well as the two Chablis had come from the house of Bichot, clearly the latter have some aces in their pack!

As though that were not enough, to round off the proceedings a magnum of 1976 Niersteiner Oelberg Riesling Trockenbeerenauslese appeared. Fresh, not too heavy, and delightful (but this has already been described earlier in these notes). When Harold Baron first came across it, he liked it so much that he ordered a quantity of magnums, and a magnum of fine German wine is a rare bird.

Naturally there was no question of any meal before the tasting that evening and after all those good things I wondered how I was going to manage! The subject was the 1975 vintage from Bordeaux and since the wines were served anonymously, it provided a most interesting evening.

Some 1975 Clarets

Wine	Characteristics	My placing
Garaud *Saint-Emilion*	Good dark colour, quite a decided bouquet, not a big wine, in fact a bit thin by comparison with the others and a sharpish finish, disappointing. Since all these 1975s had only been landed five weeks before, I got the impression they had not fully recovered from the journey across the Atlantic.	5th
Brane-Cantenac *Margaux*	Slightly pale colour, a sweet attractive bouquet, not a big wine but has good quality.	3rd
Ducru-Beaucaillou *Saint-Julien*	Good dark colour, a fine intense bouquet, quite powerful. Clearly of fine quality but still backward – as indeed it should be.	4th

La Lagune *Ludon*	Very dark colour, something odd about the bouquet, fairly full-bodied, lots of tannin but there was a query about it. Another instance perhaps of bottle sickness after the Atlantic crossing.	6th
Montrose *Saint-Estèphe*	Good colour, well-bred bouquet, good flavour, well balanced, backward of course but most attractive.	1st
Lynch-Bages *Pauillac*	Good colour, very fruity bouquet, full-bodied with heaps of tannin. Excellent.	2nd

This tasting confirmed the impression I had formed in San Francisco when we had tasted a range of 1975s. Although these particular wines had been landed some two to three weeks longer than those in San Francisco, they had still not recovered from the journey, and I feel sure they are tasting better in Bordeaux. For instance, while the Lynch-Bages had been 'all over the place' in San Francisco, here in Washington D.C. it was among the best. Similarly, the Ducru-Beaucaillou, which had shown so well in San Francisco, while good, was not nearly so outstanding in Washington.

At Heathrow airport, London, adding to the delight of being reunited with my family, to welcome me home were Prue, wearing the splendid cowboy hat presented to me when I was made an honorary citizen of Amarillo, Texas, and the twins, each wearing the cowboy hats I had sent them from Houston. They were causing quite a sensation.

II   That pre-phylloxera claret – was it really better?

Well, if it was better, how in fact did it differ from the red Bordeaux of today? Of course the only way to solve this problem properly is to compare like with like, but after a lapse of roughly a century, that clearly is impossible.

When in 1934 I joined the fine old firm of Block, Grey & Block in South Audley Street, London, there were still some bottles of the great vintages of the 1860s and 1870s in the cellar, in fact I clearly remember the excitement when we bought a good-sized bin of 1868 Gruaud-Larose from one of the Cambridge colleges.

If for nothing else that inter-war period was a splendid era for the retail wine merchants of London, a group of unusually erudite authorities. To mention but a few of them there were those two great personalities Walter and Charles Berry of Berry Brothers, Nick Block of Block, Grey & Block, Dick Richards of Chalié Richards (long since a subsidiary of Justerini & Brooks), Annie Irish of Christopher's, Jack Rutherford, of Rutherford, Osborne & Perkins – all heads of businesses established in the 18th century or even the 17th. In addition, among the importers there were other exceptional characters such as the delightful Ian Campbell as well as André Simon, who at that time had but recently founded the Wine & Food Society. Not to be forgotten also are the distinguished amateurs of that day, H. Warner Allen, Vyvyan Holland, Curtis Moffat, Maurice Healy and C. M. Wells. Happily for us, many of those authorities wrote the books which portray that interesting time, as well as the period covering the 'Golden Age' of Bordeaux, 1858 to 1880, together with the after-effects of the devastation of the vineyards by phylloxera, the latter an unkind blow inflicted upon the old world by the new.

The seniors among those men must have been in their twenties or thirties at the turn of the century and at a time when the great pre-phylloxera vintages, the 1864s, and 1868s and the 1875s had reached, or must have been reaching their peak of perfection. The resistent 1870s, some of the finest of all, did not mature until many years later. Not only was there a spate of exceptional vintages between 1858 and 1880, but in addition by that time the method (or art if you prefer) of vinification had recently taken a decided step forward, and consequently the wine was finer than it had ever been before.

It is really only since the last two decades or so of the present century that the Bordelais growers have mastered the art of handling relatively successfully a really bad vintage – but only just you may say! At least the produce of a bad year is drinkable now, *vide* 1968, but this was certainly not the case 50 years ago. Nevertheless, those men of the second half of the 19th century certainly knew how to produce a great wine when the conditions were favourable.

Although I was treated with immense kindness in those ominous days prior to the last war, I was in too junior a position to be invited regularly by the chairman, Gerard Robinson, when he entertained his best customers and cronies in the trade and regaled them with great wines. On account of my inexperience, they would probably have been wasted on me anyway, but I do remember the excellence of that 1868 Gruaud-Larose, then some 70 years old. Merely for the sake of comparison, where are the 1928s and 1929s now? There may be exceptions, but most of them 'turned up their toes' a good time ago! For me personally the 1929s were at their delightful best in the years just after the war, but the longer-lived 1928s continued in fine fettle for some ten or more years.

In the post-war period I did from time to time have the opportunity to share a number of pre-phylloxera wines and luckily I have kept my notes on them. But it must be remembered that by that time even the 1878s, the last of those spectacular vintages, must have been about 70 years old, a considerable age for any red Bordeaux. Forty odd years have slipped away since I had the good fortune to meet Ian Campbell and the other leading personalities of those days, but the impression I gathered from them was that the pre-phylloxera wines were definitely superior to their successors.

I have never been among those who pour adulation on a wine merely because it is old; there is no need merely on account of its age to bow and scrape over a decrepit bottle, but all too often I have seen that done. A pretty woman aged around 30 is surely more attractive physically than a once-famous beauty of over seventy! The fetish of ancient bottles is naturally remunerative for the auction houses and of course an attraction for the wine snobs, the number of whom fortunately is not great.

This is by no means to say that I have not been spellbound by many a pre-phylloxera wine. Mmy old tasting notes bear witness to that. Without wishing to be boring, I will quote only a minimum of fairly recent instances of masterpieces consumed. My last bottle of 1870 Lafite, bottled incidentally by Harveys, was drunk when it was 96 years old; and as the guest of Michael Broadbent I was privileged to share a splendid magnum of the same wine at 101 years old. Finally there is the bin of 1865 Latour in the cellar below the *château* which although not of an absolutely tip-top vintage, at 110 years old was still quite remarkable. When any very old bottle is opened, usually the wine stays at its peak for about ten to 15 minutes and then fades away, but I have known this 1865 to continue at its best for over an hour.

The point I have tried to make is that while not obsequious to a famous wine because of its antiquity, I freely admit that, tasted in their old age, those pre-phylloxeras certainly displayed quality and longevity to a remarkable degree.

While on this subject, I have found the perusal of the *History of Château Latour*, particularly the second volume, highly rewarding. It would seem that the mildew of the 1880s, really the more desperate foe of the two, destroyed entire crops, while the phylloxera was not a universal killer of vines. So for two or three decades leading *château* proprietors, especially the first growths, continued to replant original French plants until they were confident the produce from the grafted American stocks was truly acceptable. Indeed, in a contract signed during the first decade of this century between a Bordelais *négociant* and Latour, the former insisted that no more grafted vines should be planted during the period of the contract. It was not therefore the owners of the famous vineyards alone who were apprehensive about the 'new' vines, but the Bordelais *négociants* as well.

What then about the post-phylloxera wines, those made from vines grafted onto American roots and especially of vintages made after the vineyards had had time to recover from their afflictions? 1928 was a tough, tannic vintage, if ever there were one, but there cannot be many 1928s around now and it seems unlikely that few of those which remain will live to celebrate their centenary. The other comparatively recent vintage blessed with longevity is 1945, but it is doubtful whether many of the 1945s, not even the great Latour 1945, will become venerable centenarians similar to their predecessors of the last century.

Another factor to be taken into account of course is that thanks to the improvement in the art of vinification, the produce of stubborn vintages can now be harnessed. For instance the 1945s were not quite so hard and unbending as were the 1928s and the 1961s are less tannic than the 1945s. Compare for example these three very fine vintages with that of 1870. According to the pundits the 1870s did not become drinkable until they were about 40 and more years old, but then think of the age to which they have lived! It is improbable in this modern age that we shall ever see the like of a vintage like that of 1870 again.

The prime reason for raising this subject was the fascinating result of some tastings arranged for me by John Movius in Los Angeles in May 1978. These concerned the produce of ungrafted vines of California and although the wines had been made from young vines, the possibilities, if we had not been led astray by wishful thinking, were exciting to say the least. At John's request, I have made a little research among the books published by leading authorities just prior to and after the war, to see what they had had to say concerning the comparative merits of pre- and post-phylloxera wines.

Possibly the greatest collection of books on the subject of wine lies in the library of the Guildhall in the City of London and there is also a useful comprehensive library at the headquarters of the International Wine & Food Society in Pall Mall. Unfortunately, in so far as red Bordeaux was concerned, I could find very little – perhaps those writers did not like to commit themselves so definitely in print. It may also be that my search was not sufficiently thorough, and as a result the following is all I was able to find.

In *The Wayward Tendrils of the Vine* by Ian Campbell, published in 1947, the author discusses vines grafted on to American stocks: 'The vines had done their best and with age will it is sincerely hoped, regain a large part of their virtue.' He continues 'I doubt whether the vineyards have yet entirely recovered from the phylloxera infection'.

While discoursing on guessing the name and vintage of a wine, he wrote 'but it seems to me that in the old days, we would almost always make sure of spotting an 1858, an 1864 or a 1875 and other wines of the pre-phylloxera period. The phylloxera indeed may itself have robbed the vines of the power to impart a strong touch of personality to their product.'

H. Warner Allen in his *History of Wine* is perhaps more emphatic when writing about vintage port. 'In Portugal, it seemed at first that the Port Wine Trade was faced with extinction and that vintage port would soon become just a legend . . . In 1884 the grafted vines began to turn the tide. Human agency plays a more important part in the making of port than in that of natural wines and it is easier to correct shortcomings due to the thousand natural shocks the vine is heir to. There was a change in the character of the wines pressed from the grapes of the grafted vines. They were lighter and less full-bodied, maturing more quickly, not so solemnly and seriously worthy of Meredith's Dr Middelton's orotund commendations.'

An up-to-date and useful source of information has been through Louis Vialard, the owner of Château Cissac in the Médoc. He writes as follows: 'During my childhood and teenage years, I had the opportunity to taste many pre-phylloxera vintages made by my grandfather, the manager of Château Lafite until 1868 and a wine grower on his own estates at Château Anseillan, Clerc Milon and Cissac. I have found the pre-phylloxera wines were lighter in colour and in alcohol and more delicate than the post-phylloxera.

'There were certainly bigger differences between vintages before the phylloxera than very recently. In my opinion this is not because the grafted vines produce a more consistent quality, quite the contrary. I have at Cissac three hectares, roughly seven acres of vines of original ungrafted stock. The wines produced by these vine plants are more consistent in quality than those produced by grafted vines. They are lighter in alcohol and colour, but with a more delicate bouquet and taste.

'If there is less difference now than before in the quality of poor and good vintages, it is because the technology of vine growing and oenology allows the wine grower to transform healthier grapes into very good wine, even when climatic conditions have not been ideal. Nevertheless I intend trying to increase the acreage of my vineyard with ungrafted stock, even at the risk of another attack of phylloxera.'

The above remarks tie in with some of my own research and it is interesting to note what Louis says concerning the smaller variances in quality between modern poor and good vintages.

I would also like to mention the opinion of a friend of many years, Guy Schÿler, who for long has been associated with Château Lafite. Since the pre-phylloxera vines lived longer than do their successors with grafted root-stocks, obviously a larger proportion of grapes were available from old vines and it is a well-known fact that the grapes from old vines, say of 50 years or more, form the quintessence of the quality of a great wine.

What conclusion can be drawn from all this? It would appear that the grafting has reduced the longevity of present day claret, that it is a little heavier in alcohol and may perhaps lack some of the finesse of its predecessor? If so, the blame could perhaps be laid at the door of the American roots. But who are we to complain and where would we be without that grafting – our gratitude is everlasting.

III Bordeaux, October 1978

Château Latour

Many are the times we have taken the ferry across the Gironde from Blaye to Lamarque in the Médoc, but on this occasion we thought we would try the *bac* from Royan to the Pointe de Graves, at the very northern tip of the Médoc peninsula. It proved a pleasant experience and since our destination was Pauillac, we felt we had saved quite a lot of mileage.

Our hosts at Château Latour were the new president of the estate, the Hon. Clive Gibson and Anne, his attractive French wife, and with them we passed two most agreeable days. Among those who came to dine were Peter and Diana Sichel (Palmer and Angludet), Ronald and Phyl Barton (Léoville and Langoa-Barton) and Jean-Paul Gardère and his wife.

During the various conversations it was surprising to discover a shift of opinion regarding the much publicised 1975 vintage. While it is agreed on all sides that the 1975s have become far too expensive, almost dangerously so in fact, in some quarters there are now queries whether they are quite so good as they were claimed to be originally. Indeed, some people doubt whether they are any better really than the good 1970s. Since I was blessed with another ten days in Bordeaux, it would be instructive to find what further enquiries would bring to light.

For those people who may have vintages of Château Latour in their cellars, the following notes on one or two of them, made then, may be useful:

Wine	Characteristics
Latour 1960	Good dark colour, delightful bouquet, round, complete and charming. The quality is remarkable when one realises that most other 1960s are already dead and gone. Of course recent vintages of Latour such as 1966 and 1961 will be greater eventually, but for the past few years for pure enjoyment I have considered the 1960, now at its apogee, the most delightful of all from the private cellar. It is even better from a magnum!
Latour 1925	Dark colour, good bouquet, full, rounded and astonishing for such an indifferent vintage. Peter Sichel came wonderfully close when he assessed it as either 1920 or 1924. Apart from the very end of the taste one would never have guessed it was not of a good year. Faced with Latour 1925 on a restaurant wine list, I would have dismissed it out of hand, demonstrating how wrong one can be!

Château Latour: Jean-Paul Gardère, Clive Gibson and the author.

Latour 1962	Dark colour, lovely bouquet, not yet at its best, extremely good nevertheless. I agreed with Clive Gibson that the 1960 of the previous evening had been more attractive.
Latour 1958	Good dark colour, fine bouquet, not so big as usual for Latour, but complete, well balanced together with a good finish. From an off-vintage and with most other 1958s more or less memories of the past, this 1958 Latour still has plenty of life left.
Léoville-Barton 1961	Good colour, delightful bouquet and a fine flavour, probably at its best.
Latour 1947	Dark colour, nice bouquet, plenty of fruit with tannin very much in evidence, but it tailed off unattractively.

Unlike the Pomerols and Saint-Emilions of 1947, the Médocs were not generally successful. Immensely attractive when they were young, thanks to the over-hot summer that year, there was a definite lack of acidity. Even the long-lived Latour has not stood up to the test of time.

Before leaving, Clive Gibson took us up into a loft over one of the *chais* where there was laid out a mass of old equipment formerly used in the vineyard. Old ploughs and so on, but also several syringes used unsuccessfully in the last century to inject chemicals into the earth in order to counteract the phylloxera.

Château La Mission-Haut-Brion

We drove to Château La Mission-Haut-Brion in the Graves district to spend the weekend with Francis and Françoise Dewavrin. Françoise is the daughter of the late Fernand Woltner and she and her husband are now in charge of the *château*. We arrived to find general delight over the continuing good weather, particularly since some white wine (Laville Haut-Brion) is made at La Mission, and the last loads of grapes were being brought in under ideal circumstances. Whatever happens it looks as though 1978 will be a successful vintage for dry white Graves.

As for the rest of the vineyard, the *merlots* were ripe and every day of sunshine was adding to the maturity of the *cabernet-sauvignons*. One of the reasons for our visit was to see our friend Hélène Woltner. The widow of Henri Woltner whose genius as a wine maker brought La Mission-Haut-Brion to the forefront among the great wines of Bordeaux. We arrived in time for what the Dewavrins called a simple lunch; even so we had three wines.

Wine	Characteristics
1974 La Tour-Haut-Brion	Dark colour, full bouquet, full-bodied, well balanced with an unusually good flavour. Francis, who is delighted with this wine, considers that at the moment it is showing better than La Mission of the same year.
1960 La Mission-Haut-Brion	Good colour, beginning to turn a little brown at the edges, a fine well matured bouquet, remarkably well preserved for its vintage, must be among the best of the 1960s.
1955 La Mission-Haut-Brion	Very dark colour, delightful bouquet, fruity, full-bodied and quite excellent. Surely at its best now.

La Mission-Haut-Brion:
Francis Dewavrin, H. W.
Françoise Dewavrin and
Prue Waugh.

Harry Waugh with Eric
and Philippe de
Rothschild.

Discussing the property, Francis explained, the gravel on the estate averages in depth from between eight to ten metres. This means the vines have to force their roots pretty deep in order to find moisture.

It appears that in the past only a very little white wine was made and that was for the personal use of the proprietor; what is now known as Laville Haut-Brion began with one barrel in 1928 and three in 1929! Francis showed me the early labels, the first of which was identical to that for the red wine, except that the lettering was printed in gold instead of black. The second which must surely have been somewhat controversial, says 'Château Laville 1931' with printed underneath 'Terroir de Haut-Brion'. The final label as it is today appeared for the first time on bottles of the 1935 vintage. Over the past 30 years the average production of white wine has been around 1,800 cases while that of red has been 6,200 cases.

Those pre-war days were difficult for the two Woltner brothers; indeed it was a time of crisis for the wine trade everywhere. Wine was a luxury article and the world had not recovered from the economic crisis of 1929. After the two great vintages of 1928 and 1929 there had been three bad ones in succession, 1930, 1931 and 1932, all of which produced poor wine that no one wanted to buy. Not even the first growths were in demand because, according to the records at Château Latour, the cases accumulated in the cellars and were not finally disposed of until the early days of the 1939 war.

Meanwhile way ahead of his time Henri Woltner had blazed a trail with his *cuves vitrifiés*, steel vats with a glass lining. Likewise, he had been the first on the scene to use a tractor instead of the traditional oxen. By means of refrigeration he was able to control the temperature during the fermentation, i.e. if the fermenting must became too hot, he was able to reduce it to around 28° centigrade. He began with two trial vats and when they proved successful, all the rest of the wooden ones were replaced.

The vineyard of La Mission can be divided into roughly three parts, the vines which produce the *grand vin* La Mission Haut-Brion, those which make their second wine La Tour Haut-Brion, a similar wine to La Mission but with more tannin and lacking perhaps some of the finesse of the *grand vin*, and thirdly the *sémillons* and *sauvignon blancs* (growing on the lower ground) which make the white wine, Laville Haut-Brion.

Originally Frederic Woltner had come to France from Poland and by the turn of the century was working for the Bordeaux *négociants*, Schroder and de Constans. At that time the estate of La Mission Haut-Brion belonged to Monsieur de Constans who shortly afterwards sold it to a Monsieur Cousteau who happened to be a good friend of Frederic Woltner. Frederic told his son Henri that it had always been his ambition one day to become the owner of La Mission and that he had begged Monsieur Cousteau to let him know if ever he considered selling it. When, in due course, the latter decided to retire from active business, he remembered Frederic's request and handed over the estate saying Frederic was the one man who deserved to become the new owner.

This happened just after the end of the First World War when the vineyard, like many another at that time, was in a deplorable condition. Later on the widow of Monsieur de Cousteau bequeathed to Frederic that part of the present vineyard now known as Latour Haut-Brion.

All great vineyards also have their poorer portions and the lower ground of what is now Laville Haut-Brion is a case in point, but at that time it was planted with *cabernet-sauvignon* and *merlot* vines. Realising no good red wine would ever be made from that soil, Frederic pulled up all the vines and replanted with *sémillon* and *sauvignon blanc*, saying that by doing so his sons would never be tempted to make red wine from that part again. It seems that grapes for producing a white wine thrive better in soil where the *cabernet-sauvignon* does not fare so well.

To return to the present, throughout the vineyard at this important period just prior to the vintage, the grapes although smaller than usual, looked extremely healthy and being in such good condition would not suffer unduly if it were to rain during the harvest, a consoling thought at least! Those grapes had been smaller still only a week earlier, but heavy rain over the weekend of 29 September had done them a world of good.

On the Saturday evening, Charles Dobson came to dinner, a young Englishman who is responsible for the family's *négociant* business which has just been re-opened in Bordeaux. The wines we tasted were quite a revelation.

Wine	Characteristics
Laville Haut-Brion 1974	Powerful bouquet, full flavoured, but still too young and aggressive.
Laville Haut-Brion 1973	More finesse on the nose, a lighter wine but with ample charm.
Laville Haut-Brion 1972	Elegant bouquet, lovely taste, ready now.
Laville Haut-Brion 1959	Pale golden colour, splendid bouquet, delicious flavour, remarkable for a 19 year old.
Laville Haut-Brion 1948 (half bottle)	Golden colour, a nice nutty nose, full-bodied and packed with flavour, extraordinarily good for a half bottle of that age.
La Tour-Haut-Brion 1964	Very dark colour, a rather rich bouquet, just a little 'pruney' perhaps, but a big full-bodied rich wine which finished well.
La Mission-Haut-Brion 1964	Very dark colour, delightful bouquet, full of breeding, still backward, but well made with clearly a good future.
La Mission-Haut-Brion 1937	Dark colour, the bouquet well matured, quite a big wine with a fine flavour, but still a little hard, even after 40 years.
La Mission-Haut-Brion 1934	Dark colour, lovely mature bouquet, a huge wine with a splendid flavour. A success in a year when most of the great Médocs proved to be disappointing.

Saturday 7 October While writing to Francis earlier on, I had asked if it would be possible to taste some recent vintages from other *châteaux* in the Graves district and as will be seen, he responded most nobly to my request by inviting for lunch Monsieur and Madame Ricard, the owners of another notable Graves vineyard, Domaine de Chevalier.

In order that his wines would present themselves well, Monsieur Ricard had already sent over a selection of bottles. Some of these we tasted blind in the cellar before lunch and the remainder during the meal.

Blind tasting in the cellar
White Wine

Wine	Characteristics
Domaine de Chevalier 1976	A clean distinguished bouquet, the flavour fresh and very dry, some acidity still to lose.
Laville Haut-Brion 1976	Scented bouquet, a suggestion of honey and it tasted like a flower garden, a characteristic of this vineyard. There was also some acidity still to lose.
Laville Haut-Brion 1975	Elegant scented nose, lovely flavour, dry of course but plenty of it.
Domaine de Chevalier 1975	Fuller bouquet than the 1976 from the same vineyard, but fine and fresh. A very dry wine with magnificent breeding.

The difference in style between the wines from the two *communes* of Talence (or Pessac, if you like) and Léognan was marked. While the Talence wines were a little fuller and more honeyed in character, those from the Domaine de Chevalier were remarkable for their extreme elegance and finesse. All four wines were exceptional and ultimately it was a question of personal choice, the fuller, more flowery wine or the lighter and possibly more elegant one.

Red Wine

Wine	Characteristics
La Mission-Haut-Brion 1976	Medium colour, very pretty true Graves nose, medium body and with heaps of flavour, should make a good bottle.
Domaine de Chevalier 1976	Good dark colour, distinctive Graves bouquet, but more severe than No. 1. Strong and powerful, fine quality.
Domaine de Chevalier 1975	Good colour, very pretty bouquet, lots of breeding but still undeveloped. Has a strong flavour and a fine future.
La Mission-Haut-Brion 1975	Very dark colour, a powerful but closed up bouquet, a huge full-bodied wine which may take years to mature.

There had been little difficulty in putting a name and vintage to the white wines in the first section, but in the second I only succeeded with the unmistakable 1975 of La Mission. One cannot help being prejudiced by labels; indeed I am a fervent believer in blind tastings. I have little respect for those who prefer to taste with the labels showing.

Wines tasted during lunch
White Wine

Wine	Characteristics
Domaine de Chevalier 1970	Great finesse of bouquet, very dry, a wine of considerable distinction.
Laville Haut-Brion 1967	A richer more perfumed bouquet, with a fuller, more earthy flavour. Very good.

| Domaine de Chevalier 1962 | Pale colour for its age, heavenly bouquet, very dry, a wine of tremendous class. |
| Laville Haut-Brion 1955 | Slightly darker colour, rich bouquet, lovely full flavour. 1955 is one of the most successful vintages of Laville Haut-Brion. |

Red Wine

| La Mission-Haut-Brion 1974 | Very dark colour, a full fragrant bouquet, a full-bodied wine with a pleasant lingering after taste. Still needs three to four years. |

The 1974s, while not great, can be very attractive and clearly they were successful here. With less breeding perhaps, the La Tour Haut-Brion should develop earlier. I marked it down as one I shall try to buy for my own cellar. It is not easy to compare the 1974s with the 1973s because at one *château* the 1973 is better and at another the 1974. Generally speaking the good 1974s are bigger wines but more backward.

Wine	*Characteristics*
Domaine de Chevalier 1970	Dark colour, distinguished bouquet, not a big wine but well bred, needs three to four more years.
Domaine de Chevalier 1964	Dark colour, delightful bouquet, again not a big wine but of great distinction. This also needs more time to mature.
La Mission-Haut-Brion 1947	(Decanted at the table.) Very dark colour but turning brownish at the edges. Such a rich bouquet, a rich, rich wine, packed with flavour. Indeed a tribute to the late Henri Woltner. What a man to produce such a masterpiece!

The generosity of our host and hostess was unbounded for that evening they had invited for dinner the Baron de Luze and his wife, Chantal, and there was another magnificent display of gems from the private cellar.

Wine	*Characteristics*
Laville Haut-Brion 1970	Pale colour, a lovely bouquet and flavour, but it needs more time to develop. As Monsieur Ricard had said at lunch time, in order to develop their true potential the great white wines of Bordeaux need longer than is generally appreciated.
Laville Haut-Brion 1961	Heavenly bouquet, a superb wine and a perfect example of what is said above. At 16 years old this must be at its very best.
La Mission-Haut-Brion 1950	Good colour, attractive Graves bouquet, lighter in style but well balanced and has a delightful flavour.
La Mission-Haut-Brion 1949	A classic wine from this vineyard, fine colour, a rich, rich bouquet, delicious flavour, a great bottle. I can only think of two other 1949s in this class, Mouton-Rothschild and Latour.

La Mission-Haut-Brion 1948	Lovely colour, a full, very fruity bouquet, a lovely taste, full of fruit. Although most of the 1948s have gone downhill by now, this one is still at the top of its form.
La Mission-Haut-Brion 1945	Dark colour, good bouquet, but to our surprise disappointing for this great vintage, somehow it lacked charm and was also still chock-full of tannin.

By Sunday 8 October the wind had changed to the south, usually a bad omen at vintage time, for a south wind can bring rain. Surprisingly though the weather remained fine, if much more humid, a further bonus to assist any unripe grapes.

At Château de Fieuzal
Monday 9 October

On a hot rather sticky morning we made our way to keep an appointment with Gérard Gribelin, of Château de Fieuzal in Léognan. In fact this property belongs to his wife, whose family bought it in 1973 from an extraordinary local character, the late Monsieur Bocke about whom I have written in a previous book.

The vineyard, which has no actual *château*, is well situated on gravelly soil and on rising ground. The annual production is relatively small, about 6,000 cases of red wine and about 500 of white. There is thus no problem over distribution. Nevertheless, Gérard has two ambitions, to see his wine distributed in the right places and if possible to improve the quality. Being a young man, he has plenty of time to achieve both aims.

The percentage of vines on the property is roughly 50% *cabernet-sauvignon*, 30% *cabernet-franc* with the rest made up with *malbec* and *petit-verdot*, but no *merlot!*

In normal years proprietors do not necessarily begin to pick their grapes on precisely the same day, but this year, in view of the special circumstances, it has been generally accepted the vintage would commence on 9 October. Even so we found Gérard Gribelin somewhat doubtful about the ripeness of some of his grapes. Admittedly his own staff were picking the *malbec* but he was awaiting the result of this first picking before putting a full team on to the rest of the vineyard. On account of the proximity of the huge University of Bordeaux, the proprietors in the Graves district have few labour problems at vintage time. Students are always available, but since this year there is quite severe unemployment in France, Gérard intended to use some of the unemployed instead.

While driving through his vineyard it was possible to detect how this chancy year of 1978 differed in comparison with others. For instance, in places there were few if any bunches on a vine, yet in others there was comparative abundance. As at La Mission, most of the *cabernet-sauvignons* were very small (a day or two more of rain might have helped them) while the *cabernet-francs*, the *malbecs* etc. were much larger. All of them however looked extremely healthy with a nice bloom on them.

Here are some notes on the present state of recent vintages from Château de Fieuzal:

Wine	Characteristics
1977	Medium colour, fruity bouquet, medium body, perhaps a little short.

1976	(Just bottled.) Quite a good colour, medium body, good fruit but again a rather short finish. All the same, this will probably make a pleasant bottle in due course.
1975	Dark colour, full bouquet, much more depth and fruit, but, like most 1975s, on the dry side. Needs time.
1974	Good colour, attractive bouquet and attractive flavour. Still some tannin to lose, should make a nice bottle by, say, 1980.
1973	Good colour for a 1973. Nice bouquet, on light side as is to be expected, but has plenty of charm.
1972	Medium colour, a drier but fruity bouquet. Not much body but quite a nice taste. Still some of the acidity of its year but not aggressively so. Ready to drink now.
1971	Dark colour, attractive bouquet, well made, well balanced and very good. This must be among the most successful of the 1971s.
1970	Dark colour, very good bouquet, full-bodied with lots of flavour, tasting much better than a few years ago. A wine with plenty of character and a good future.
1969	Good colour, but beginning to turn brown at the rim. Lighter in style, in fact typical 1969, pleasant all the same. Probably at its best now.
1967	Dark colour, elegant bouquet. Attractive flavour and ready to drink now, nicer than many of the 1967s.

Martin Delahay arrived that evening in order to participate in all our tastings. Martin and I work closely together, for he is the official wine buyer for the Ritz Hotel and the Cunard Line.

To Ronald Barton
Tuesday 10 October

In spite of the south wind, the miraculous weather continues. With every succeeding day greater grows the chance of even better quality. Now only about two more weeks of sunshine are needed to see the vintage in safely – is this too much to hope for? Everyone connected with the vineyards is holding his thumbs and praying.

For a number of years my old friend Ronald Barton (I can so describe him for we have known each other since before the war) has arranged for me a classic tasting of the great wines of Saint-Julien. Beginning with the 1966 vintage, this has continued with the successful years ever since. The actual organisation has lain in the hands of another friend of long standing, Daniel Lawton, a noted wine broker whose family have been brokers since their firm was founded in 1740. Needless to say, he collects the bottles and arranges them so that no one has any idea which is which.

Generally speaking, those participating have been the proprietors of the *châteaux* whose wines were to be tasted, but on this particular occasion it must have been a record, because all 12 of them were present. Gruaud Larose and Talbot were represented by Jean Cordier and Madame Cordier respectively, Léoville-Lascases by Monsieur Delon and so on. Perhaps it is unnecessary to add that, apart from first growths, the *commune* of Saint-Julien is generally accepted to contain the greatest proportion of fine vineyards of the Médoc.

For me this is always the most testing tasting of the year; it is not so difficult normally to differentiate between a Médoc and a Pomerol, or even a Pauillac and a Margaux, but these were all Saint-Juliens, all of the same style. It is no wonder that the *château* proprietors themselves experience difficulty in detecting their own wine.

It would be hard to think of a more appropriate point of assembly than the courtyard outside Ronald's *cuverie* at Château Langoa where the first loads of grapes of the 1978 vintage were being brought in for crushing. It should be added that here too the grapes were looking unusually healthy with a really attractive bloom on them. There is excitement everywhere this year, because the grapes were registering from 12° to 12.5°.

The 1975 vintage; anonymous tasting of the wines of Saint-Julien

Wine	Characteristics	My points	Group total	Group place
Talbot	Pleasant bouquet, not a big wine but will make a good bottle.	3/10	86	11th
Gruaud-Larose	Good bouquet, full-bodied, plenty of fruit. Difficult to taste on account of considerable tannin. This nevertheless will make a fine bottle one day.	4/10	92	10th
Saint-Pierre	Quite a good bouquet, good fruit.	5/10	98.50	7th
Beychevelle	Powerful bouquet, a lovely creamy flavour, very good.	10/10	101	6th
Léoville-Poyferré	Full bouquet, a big wine, perhaps a little rougher than some of the others, also a lot of tannin.	7/10	101.50	5th
Gloria	Elegant bouquet, a distinctive flavour, plenty of tannin, but very good.	9/10	111	2nd
Langoa-Barton	Fine bouquet, medium body, rather hard.	5/10	91	9th
Ducru-Beaucaillou	Very good bouquet, well made, appeared rather on dry side and has a lot of tannin, a good wine though.	6/10	94	8th
Lagrange	Full bouquet, very hard and difficult to taste.	2/10	83.50	12th
Léoville-Las-Cases	Good bouquet, good fruit, well made, but still very backward.	4/10	109.50	3rd
Branaire-Ducru	Rather an obvious nose, a lot of fruit though with a very good, very definite flavour.	9/10	109	4th
Léoville-Barton	Big bouquet, good fruit, excellent flavour.	8/10	111.50	1st

There was no point in making special notes regarding the colour; all 12 of these wines were remarkable in this respect. In a tasting such as this, someone has to come last, so there is no disgrace entailed there. One has to remember 1975 was an exceptional vintage with regard to quality and the general standard was correspondingly high.

It is a vintage with much more tannin than usual so it is natural that after only a year in bottle many of these wines seemed rough, or dry or hard. In fact, a better time to taste them would be in five or even ten years when much of the tannin will have diminished. For instance, I am sure that the

Gruaud-Larose, the Talbot and Léoville-Poyferré will appear much more agreeable with more time in bottle.

Our duty done, we walked through the garden to the west terrace of this lovely 18th-century *château* and there as a reward for our labours we were offered a welcome glass of Perrier-Jouet. Later on some 25 of us sat down to a delightful alfresco lunch admirably organised as always by Ronald's wife, Phyl.

Wednesday 11 October A busy day commencing with a tasting of some classified growths of the 1976 vintage. In accordance with their usual generosity, Patrick Danglade and Jean-François Moueix had arranged a series of three tastings of this good vintage.

1976 vintage, blind tasting

Wine	Characteristics	My points	Total	Group place
Beychevelle *Saint-Julien*	Dark colour, nice bouquet, good fruit and flavour, some acidity still to lose.	4/10	97	=4th
Pichon-Lalande *Pauillac*	Medium colour, nice nose, good fruit, attractive and well balanced.	8/10	107	1st
Cos d'Estournel *Saint-Estéphe*	Dark colour, full bouquet, good fruit and flavour.	7/10	88	8th
Léoville-Barton *Saint-Julien*	Nice nose, fairly full-bodied, finishes nicely.	5/10	84	10th
Montrose *Saint-Estéphe*	Fine fruity bouquet, a big full-bodied wine, well made, good quality.	8/10	99	3rd
Ducru-Beaucaillou *Saint-Julien*	Distinguished bouquet, good fruit but some acidity at the finish.	5/10	97	=4th
Brane-Cantenac *Margaux*	Distinctive nose, individual style, lots of flavour, very good.	10/10	103	2nd
Léoville-Las-Cases *Saint-Julien*	Pleasant bouquet, good fruit, some acidity.	4/10	94	7th
Lynch-Bages *Pauillac*	Good bouquet, good fruit, but some acidity.	6/10	82	11th
La Lagune *Ludon*	The least agreeable of them all. It may have been a bad bottle.	4/10	87	9th
Calon-Segur *Saint-Estéphe*	Pleasant bouquet, not a big wine, but well balanced.	9/10	96	6th

All of the above had a good colour and, with the exception of the three which I felt had too much acidity, they were every bit as good as expected.

Later on at Borie-Manoux we were received by Emile Castéja, his son Philippe and Regis Argod, their general manager.

Before leaving for the Médoc we tasted one or two 1977s, but must confess so far I have not been able to raise much enthusiasm over that vintage. At the moment, they appear to be singularly lacking in charm. A consolation if any is that they are considered to be better than the 1968s and the 1972s, but that is

F

not saying much. **All the same they are relatively inexpensive and therefore have commercial value.**

Before sitting down to lunch at Château Batailley in Pauillac, Emile opened for us a range of recent vintages from the *château*.

Château Batailley

Wine	Characteristics
1977	Good colour and bouquet, has fruit but not much depth.
1976	Good colour, attractive bouquet, delightful flavour.
1975	Good colour, fine bouquet, greater depth of flavour than the 1976, but more severe; one day nevertheless this will make a fine bottle.
1974	Medium colour, more mature bouquet, good fruit and body, some acidity to lose.
1973	Medium colour, pretty bouquet, good fruit, pleasant and well forward.
1972	Paler colour, a well bred but drier bouquet, good flavour, still some acidity to lose.
1971	Medium colour, attractive bouquet, very nice flavour. Almost ready to drink now and will continue to improve.
1970	Good colour, fuller bouquet than the 1971, a good solid wine with a great future, needs some four to five years.

At lunch we enjoyed the Château Baret 1974, white Graves, and the excellent 1961 of Batailley, surely at its apogee now. As a relatively inexpensive white Graves, the 1974 Baret is proving popular on board the QE2.

That evening Jean and Anne Delmas gave a splendid dinner party for us. Their house at Haut-Brion was designed by Anne's brother and is one of the most attractive I have seen. Not too large, it is planned around a small open courtyard, almost in the Roman style. Anne herself, equally gifted, achieved a great success when some years ago she arranged the interior decoration at Château Bouscaut, also in the Graves district. There she manages both the vineyards and the making of the wine.

Needless to say, we had some excellent wine at dinner, 1971 Haut-Brion Blanc with grilled bass. In its way the white Haut-Brion is as unique as Château Grillet of the Rhône Valley. The unusually honeyed bouquet and individual flavour is quite exceptional. Unfortunately not a lot of it is made, so when you come across a bottle, treasure it.

With delicious wild duck and the cheese which followed we drank the 1967, 1962 and 1959 vintages of Haut-Brion, the 1959 showing exceptionally well.

Thursday 12 October   Another important morning at Duclot where once again we assembled, this time to taste the first growths of the same fine vintage, namely 1976. On this occasion it was a little easier with only eight wines instead of 12.

The Great Wines of 1976

Wine	Characteristics	My points	Total	Group place
Haut-Brion	Very nice bouquet, not a big wine but very well balanced, fine quality	8/10	121	1st

[82]

Pétrus	Not much bouquet, rounded and well made, considerable tannin.	9/10	106	7th
Mouton-Rothschild	Pleasant bouquet, good flavour, but at present too much acidity for my liking.	4/10	110	5th
Margaux	Bouquet fair, lean, austere, could have more charm.	3/10	97	8th
Ausone	Quite a full bouquet, a big rounded wine, perhaps a little flat.	7½/10	107	6th
Lafite	Good bouquet, a fine well made wine.	6/10	111	4th
Latour	Nice bouquet, excellent quality, full-bodied, fruity and well made.	8/10	113	3rd
Cheval-Blanc	Strong bouquet, excellent quality, well made, a lovely wine.	8/10	107	2nd

As usual, Margaux trailed behind the others. There is comfort to know there is a change of ownership at this distinguished vineyard. Conversely, how nice it is to see Ausone climbing up the scale. I was surprised to find Pétrus lacking general approval; usually on these occasions it comes out on top. Patrick Danglade also placed it first, but it seems we were in a minority. The extra tannin should have given me a clue to Latour, but at any rate I had given it a good report.

Clearly these 1976s are of very good quality and we shall be hearing more of them. Tearing himself away from his wine-making, it must have been satisfactory for Jean Delmas to see his Haut-Brion come out on top, and deservedly so.

The rest of the day was spent with Daniel Vergely, of the Maison Cordier, a great empire here in Bordeaux. At their office in the Quai Paludate we began with a tasting of a few of the lesser 1977s but it seemed unfair to taste these after the great 1976s, the difference in style and quality between the two vintages being far too great.

Daniel Vergely drove us to what is really the only good restaurant in the Médoc, La Mare aux Grenouilles. Somewhat rudely I turned up my nose when the 1968 Gruaud-Larose was suggested, but it turned out to be better than expected. On our way back we called at Châteaux Talbot and then Gruaud-Larose, both properties superbly kept.

Wine	Characteristics
1977 Meyney *Saint-Estèphe*	A good dark colour, fruity bouquet, some acidity of course.
1976 Meyney *Saint-Estèphe*	(Not yet in bottle.) Good colour, plenty of flavour, well balanced, but with some acidity to lose.
1977 Talbot *Saint-Julien*	Good colour, very good nose, not a big wine, quite a pleasant flavour though.
1976 Talbot *Saint-Julien*	Good colour, bouquet and flavour.
1977 Gruaud-Larose *Saint-Julien*	Good colour and bouquet, the best 1977 so far tasted.
1976 Gruaud-Larose *Saint-Julien*	Good colour, attractive bouquet, good fruit but also some acidity to lose.

This was the third morning at Duclot in order to cover the 1976 vintage. 'Cover' in fact is hardly the right word, because there are some 3,000 *châteaux* in the Bordeaux area! Nevertheless, with exceptions of course, a representative proportion of the most important vineyards had been included.

Patrick Danglade had led me to believe that on this third day we were to tackle some of the *crus bourgeois*. For that alone I would have been grateful, but on arrival we discovered the quality level was to be much superior, namely some of the better wines, mainly from Saint-Emilion and Pomerol.

Graves, Saint-Emilions and Pomerols of 1976

Wine	Characteristics	My points	Total	Group place
La Mission-Haut-Brion *Graves*	Very definite bouquet, heaps of fruit and flavour, a powerful wine, but very backward.	5/10	82	6th
La Fleur-Pétrus *Pomerol*	Attractive nose, lots of fruit, delightful flavour, well balanced.	9/10	91	4th
Figeac *Saint-Emilion*	Good bouquet, special flavour, medium body, but a most attractive wine.	6/10	79	=7th
L'Evangile *Pomerol*	Delightful bouquet, a full-bodied rounded wine, packed with charm.	10/10	93	1st
Haut-Bailly *Graves*	Nice bouquet, a different flavour from those preceding and lacking their charm.	4/10	70	10th
La Gaffelière *Saint-Emilion*	Very good bouquet, well made, with an attractive rich flavour.	8/10	92	=2nd
Trotanoy *Pomerol*	Pleasant bouquet, full-bodied with plenty of fruit, rather good.	7/10	88	5th
La Conseillante *Pomerol*	Fruity bouquet, fairly full-bodied, but harder and less attractive than many of the others.	4/10	79	=7th
La Grave Trigant de Boisset *Pomerol*	Very good bouquet, more acidity than the others which made it less attractive.	3/10	76	9th
Magdelaine *Saint-Emilion*	Good bouquet, full-bodied, rounded and very well made.	7/10	92	=2nd

It was amusing to perceive a look almost of beatitude on the faces of the participants as they began to discover the charm of some of these wines; truly they were an agreeable surprise.

Obviously this somewhat mixed bag was considerably more attractive to taste than the second and other classified growths of the Médoc had been on the first day. There is a lesson here somewhere, but nevertheless while the fine wines of the Médoc may have a more classic if more austere background, some of these Saint-Emilions and Pomerols of 1976 definitely have a greater attraction at the moment, and those merchants who have invested in them will have many satisfied customers.

Delor & Co. have now finally moved into their headquarters at Parempuyre in the Médoc, but somehow I missed the way among all the unmarked roads of the industrial estates that have sprung up on the outskirts of Bordeaux. Consequently we arrived rather late for the next tasting.

Among a range of inexpensive 1976s, those I liked best were Château La Croix-Millorit from Bourg and Château Graves de Portets. As a *bonne bouche* we were able to taste recent vintages of Château La Dominique, Saint-Emilion, for which Delor now hold the exclusivity.

Château La Dominique, *Saint-Emilion*

Wine	*Characteristics*
1975	Dark colour, good bouquet, fairly full-bodied, rather good, still has considerable tannin.
1974	Somewhat disappointing; there are some very nice 1974s around but this is not one of them.
1973	Medium colour, pleasant bouquet, not a big wine, attractive to drink now.
1972	Medium colour, nice bouquet, an unexpectedly nice flavour. By far the nicest 1972 I have so far come across. Not destined for long life but should be pleasant for the next year or so.
1971	Dark colour, fine bouquet, very good flavour, full of charm, a wine to buy.
1970	Dark colour, good bouquet, bigger and firmer than the 1971, but on account of its tannin etc. less immediately attractive. Needs three or four years to show at its best.

Monday 16 October

A final tasting at Duclot – Patrick Danglade, who passed the weekend getting in the vintage at his Château Rouet in the Fronsadais, had brought back with him some 1976s from that region.

1976 Fronsadais

Wine	*Characteristics*
Canon de Brem *Côtes Canon-Fronsac*	Good colour, still closed up, but has plenty of stuffing. Should make a nice bottle in due course.
Château du Gaby *Côtes de Fronsac*	Medium colour, has fruit but too much acidity for my liking.
Château Toumalin *Côtes Canon-Fronsac*	Medium colour, nice bouquet, good fruit and flavour, finishes well.
Château La Dauphine *Côtes de Fronsac*	Medium colour, deeper bouquet, plenty of fruit and flavour, some acidity.
Château Tessendey *Côtes de Fronsac*	Dark colour, good fruit and a definite flavour.
Château Rouet *Côtes de Fronsac*	Medium colour, quite a pretty bouquet, on light side, but elegant with some acidity to lose.

None of the above was really showing at its best; doubtless they had not yet recovered from recent bottling. Not only should they pick up colour and bouquet, but as time goes on, lose most of their present acidity.

During lunch at the Automobile Club de Bordeaux, we had the opportunity to compare two of the great Saint-Estèphes of 1970:

Wine	Characteristics
Château Montrose 1970	Extremely dark colour, full bouquet, a huge great wine, even the excess of tannin and acidity were not able to suppress the hint of richness which presages a great future for this wine. It could take a good five years for it to begin to show at its best, if then.
Château Cos-d'Estournel 1970	An equally dark colour, a fine deep bouquet, equally full-bodied with heaps of fruit and quality. There is nevertheless still a powerful strike of acidity which may retard development and it may take even longer to come round than the Montrose.

Château Rieussec
Wednesday 18 October

When a year or so ago Gérard Gribelin had been in London, he had brought to lunch with us his friend, Albert Vuillier, the proprietor of Château Rieussec (Sauternes), but it was only on this journey that at last we had an opportunity to take advantage of the latter's invitation to visit his vineyard. In fact I am ashamed to admit it was the first time I had ever been there.

Situated close to the illustrious Château d'Yquem, the vines of Château Rieussec grow on the highest ground in the district; in consequence from the château on top of the hill there is a splendid view looking westwards across the river Garonne.

Château Rieussec, classed as a *premier grand cru de Sauternes* at the time of the 1855 Exhibition has, like many another famous Bordelais vineyard, suffered from too many owners. The property of the church until the French Revolution, it passed from hand to hand until during the last war it belonged to the Vicomte du Bouzet.

The vines of Château Rieussec (75% *sémillon*, 20% *sauvignon*, 5% *muscadel*) cover some 112 acres where the flinty soil has an ideal mixture of limestone and gravel, all of which endow the wine with its special qualities of finesse and strength combined with a smooth richness. In accordance with the aim of all proprietors of the famous *châteaux* in the Sauternes district, i.e., only to produce the finest quality wine, the average production at Rieussec is no more than 9,600 cases.

During recent years there has been a tendency among some growers to make a dry white wine as well as their traditional one, but until now I have not been over enthusiastic over any of them. Somehow, however, the Château 'R' made by Albert Vuillier is different and I was impressed by the style of his first essay made from the 1977 vintage. Made from 75% *sémillon* and 25% *sauvignon* grapes, my notes read 'clean attractive bouquet, dry but full flavoured and very fresh and delightful'. The grapes for the 1978 crop of this dry wine were being picked as we arrived.

The vintage for the dessert wine was not due to commence for several weeks, late here as everywhere else. The prospects were favourable except that on account of the exceptionally fine weather much of the usual humidity, misty mornings etc. which prevail at this time of the year, had been missing. In consequence there was a certain lack of the necessary *botrytis*.

Albert had prepared a tasting for us in his *chai* and there we were joined by Peter Crameri, an Englishman who now lives in Bordeaux. On Albert's advice, allowing for the overwhelming richness of the 1976 and 1975 vintages which would have overshadowed the 1972 and 1973, we did not taste the wines in their usual sequence, i.e. youngest first.

Wine	Characteristics
1972	Pale colour, a nice Sauternes bouquet, we were informed in early days this had the typical acidity of its year and no great concentration. Apparently it has improved considerably since then and now is really quite attractive with plenty of finesse. This should improve even more as time goes by.
1973	A little more colour than the preceding wine and somehow a different bouquet. Much richer also but it did not appear so well balanced. We all preferred the 1972 which unexpectedly perhaps won on account of its finesse.
1974	The conditions were so bad that Albert sold his entire crop without his label.
1975	A pretty golden colour, delightful well bred bouquet, a wine of great breeding and superbly balanced. Will make a great bottle.
1976	(Not yet in bottle.) Deep golden colour, much deeper than I would have expected. A full, full bouquet, immensely rich and of wonderful quality, yet it has good acidity and therefore is well balanced. Albert told us the colour had been induced by the extraordinary concentration, some bunches had been so concentrated he had not been able to put them through the press. It is rare to encounter concentration of such depth and this 1976 could turn out similar to 1929, almost a freak vintage. We could understand now why he had made us taste the 1972 and 1973 vintages first!
1971	A pale golden colour, a lovely concentrated bouquet and flavour. Well balanced, this lovely rich wine was the first vintage made by Albert who told us it had caused him great anxiety at the time.
1970	A shade darker than the 1971. Bouquet less attractive at the moment. A more massive wine but in my opinion not so good.
1969	Golden colour, pleasant bouquet, but with less depth. Fairly rich but a lack of acidity, hence no doubt its tendency to flatness. Very sweet of course but a tiny trace of bitterness was discernible at the very end. Clearly less well balanced than some of the other vintages.
1967	(From a magnum) A lovely deep golden colour and a much older bouquet, the smell of young fruit was no longer there. A fine more mature wine and of excellent balance. Without undue flattery, it occurred to us all that while very good, the style of the wine made by Albert's

	predecessor was somehow flatter and had Albert made, say the 1970 and 1967 vintages, both famous years of course, they might well have been greater wines.
1964	Golden colour, some bouquet but nothing great, although fairly rich for its year, there was a trace of bitterness at the finish. Quite good all the same for this very ordinary vintage.
1957	Deep colour, very rich bouquet, reminiscent of good toffee, a mouthful of fruit and flowers. A wonderful beautifully balanced wine.

In view of this tasting it would seem that while this particular Sauternes has always been very good, under the direction of Albert Vuillier it looks as though it is going to be finer still, and Château Rieussec will certainly be a vineyard to watch.

In a letter written to me dated 17 November 1978, Albert wrote that he had finished his vintage two days before and while there had not been so much *pourriture noble* as in 1976 and 1973, he had never seen a crop looking so healthy. With less *rôti* (i.e. over-ripe grapes) than either the 1975 or 1976, his young 1978 appeared to have elegance, fruitiness, finesse and an exceptional flavour. This could well be something to look forward to.

In conclusion, a few words about Peter Crameri may be of interest to readers, because he represents what can only be described as a 'new look' on the Bordeaux scene. Many a *château* proprietor has suffered from poor representation abroad by big importers who have masses of bread-and-butter wine and many lines upon which to concentrate their sales effort. Thus his own *château*, however illustrious, has tended to appear as a small fish in a very big pond.

Briefly what a château proprietor is looking for is a closer relationship with the customer abroad and to pursue this a few of them have gathered together, namely Rieussec, de Fieuzal, Graves, La Tour de By – an excellent *cru bourgeois* in the Médoc – and Beauséjour in Saint-Emilion, to use Peter Crameri as their broker, and in consequence have found a much more satisfactory solution to their problem.

IV   Bordeaux, March 1979

In place of the intense cold experienced in England, the winter in Bordeaux has been one of the wettest for many years; fortunately this has done little or no harm to the vines. Certainly they appear to be more backward than at the same period in 1978 but that in view of possible spring frosts could be an advantage.

On the Tuesday evening we had a most enjoyable dinner party at Latour in the company of old friends, Guy and Nicole Tesseron (Pontet-Canet and Lafon-Rochet), Guy Schÿler, who for years has handled the public relations of Château Lafite, Arlette Kressman, the widow of Yves Kressman, and Evelyn Samazeuilh, whose husband François, the new head of Cruse, was in bed with bronchitis.

With whiting we drank 1962 Meursault Les Perrières Albert Morey, excellent and remarkably fresh. Then with lamb, Lafite 1961 in honour of Guy Schÿler. With lots of bouquet and flavour, it was showing very well. I had sold all my stock of the final wine, Latour 1952, long ago thinking it would never come round. In fact it has now lost its preponderance of tannin and at long last is fulfilling its promise.

Jean-Paul Gardère had promised to arrange a tasting of the 1978 vintage for me, but in view of its reputation – 'the miraculous vintage' – it seems samples were hard to come by. Such is the demand for the 1978s at this particular moment, the *château* proprietors are hard pressed to handle the distribution of samples. Anyway, these are the wines we tasted anonymously.

1978 Bordeaux	Wine	Characteristics	Placing
	Haut-Batailley *Pauillac*	Dark colour, pleasant bouquet, plenty of fruit and flavour but some acidity to lose.	7/20
	Branaire-Ducru *Saint-Julien*	Very dark colour, good bouquet, fruity, full-bodied with a good finish. Should make a nice bottle.	11/20
	Rauzan-Gassies *Margaux*	Very dark colour, good bouquet, a little lighter than the Branaire-Ducru, but well made.	9/20
	Pichon-Lalande *Pauillac*	Very dark colour, full deep bouquet, lots of fruit, excellent quality.	16/20
	Pichon-Baron *Pauillac*	Very dark colour, distinguished bouquet, lighter than the Lalande and lacks its charm.	10/20
	Pavie *Saint-Emilion*	Very dark colour, attractive bouquet, good fruit, medium body, well made.	12/20
	Lynch-Bages *Pauillac*	Very dark colour, good fruit, medium body and a good finish.	14/20

Beychevelle *Saint Julien*	Very dark colour, good bouquet, good body, plenty of tannin.	16/20
Ducru-Beaucaillou *Saint-Julien*	Very dark colour, attractive bouquet, lots of breeding and quality as well as plenty of tannin.	15/20

The dark colour of these 1978s was noticeable. While it may not be one of the great vintages of all time, the quality is definitely good. A minor criticism perhaps is a slight lack of acidity. It is far too early to say much, but so far people are saying the 1978s are certainly better than the 1967s and perhaps as good as the 1976s. We shall see.

After the amplitude of the 1978s it was not so easy to turn to the 1977s, a vintage of which the quality could perhaps be placed at least for Latour between 1963 and 1968. During the 1880s, thanks to mildew and the phylloxera, the vintages were known as *les maigres vaches*, so perhaps can 1977 be described. As always with any wine from the Latour *domaine* one has to wait for years before any sound judgment can be made. However so far as one can judge the 1977 Latour is not so disappointing as one might have feared, for there is some depth of flavour.

Ronald Barton dined with us that evening and we compared his delightful 1962 Léoville-Barton with Latour of the same year. The latter was almost too powerful and appeared to need a year or so yet to be at its best.

Almost exactly two years ago Patrick Danglade and Jean-Francois Moueix had arranged for me a magnificent comparison of the top wines of 1970 with those of 1971. Learning of my imminent arrival in Bordeaux, these two good friends prepared for me a repeat performance with the identical wines, inviting more or less the same authorities to participate.

Among the wine brokers were Messieurs Brun, Le Sauvage, Delbeck, Blanchy, de Lestapis, Lawton and Moses. The *châteaux* represented by proprietors or managers were Messieurs Cazes (Lynch-Bages), Berrouet (Pétrus), Delmas (Haut-Brion), Tesseron (Pontet-Canet and Lafon-Rochet), Prats (Cos), Eugéne and Xavier Borie (Ducru-Beaucaillou), Bassie (Ausone), Delon (Léoville-Lascases), Delor (Delor et Cie). There was also the famous oenologist Monsieur Ribereau-Gayon.

I think it would be no overstatement to describe the above as a pretty competent team of wine tasters. It was not at all easy and their skill was tested to the maximum. Here are the results:

	Wine	Characteristics	My points	Group average
Blind tasting comparing the eight great growths of 1970 and 1971	Mouton-Rothschild 1971	Not much bouquet, has distinction but seemed to lack body.	1/5	69.5
	Latour 1970	Good nose, a big wine with plenty of fruit, very well bred and very closed up, thus could have more charm, considerable tannin to lose.	2/5	81
	Haut-Brion 1971	Fine bouquet, good flavour, has breeding and more charm than Latour 1970.	4/5	79
	Margaux 1970	Rather severe bouquet, elegant, well made but very backward and not much charm.	1/5	71.5
	Ausone 1971	Charming bouquet, rounded and attractive, delightful after taste.	4/5	85

Lafite 1970	Well made, some tannin but lacks charm. (Note. This may have been a doubtful bottle because the bouquet was somewhat suspect.)	1/5	77
Pétrus 1971	Magnificent colour, full attractive bouquet, a huge 'plummy' wine, a proper mouthful of flavour, splendid quality, plenty of tannin.	4/5	95
Cheval-Blanc 1970	Very dark colour, still backward, *un vin solide*, full of charm, excellent.	5/5	87
Mouton-Rothschild 1970	Colour medium, pleasant nose and flavour, seems fairly forward.	1/5	75
Latour 1971	Dark colour, deep bouquet, full-bodied and full flavoured. Masses of tannin, very good all the same.	2/5	81.5
Haut-Brion 1970	Distinguished nose, full flavoured and attractive, very good quality.	3/5	77
Margaux 1971	This must have been a bad bottle and it was not fair for judgment.	0/5	55.5
Ausone 1970	Full, attractive bouquet, well made with a delightful flavour.	4/5	82
Lafite 1971	Very nice bouquet, strong and powerful, still plenty of tannin.	4/5	73
Pétrus 1970	Full very fruity bouquet, well balanced very good flavour, some tannin.	5/5	88
Cheval-Blanc 1971	Huge bouquet, a huge rich wine, almost too much of a good thing.	4/5	81.5

The final result then was as follows:

1st	Pétrus 1971	95 points
2nd	Pétrus 1970	88
3rd	Cheval-Blanc 1970	87
4th	Ausone 1971	85
5th	Ausone 1970	82
6th	= Latour 1971	81.5
	= Cheval Blanc 1971	
8th	Latour 1970	81
9th	Haut-Brion 1971	79
10th	= Haut-Brion 1970	77
	= Lafite 1970	
12th	Mouton-Rothschild 1970	75
13th	Lafite 1971	73
14th	Margaux 1970	71.5
15th	Mouton-Rothschild 1971	69.5
(16th	Margaux 1971	55.5)

When comparing the result of an identical tasting in 1977, this makes quite a fascinating study.

Average result of a blind tasting of the eight first growths 1970 vintage versus 1971, on 16 February 1977		
1st	Pétrus 1970	59.5 points
2nd	Cheval-Blanc 1970	53.5
3rd	Pétrus 1971	53
4th	Cheval-Blanc 1971	52.5
5th	Latour 1971	50.5
6th	= Ausone 1970 = Haut-Brion 1970	50
8th	= Latour 1970 = Mouton-Rothschild 1970	49
10th	= Mouton-Rothschild 1971 = Lafite 1970	47.5
12th	Haut-Brion 1971	47
13th	Margaux 1970	46.5
14th	= Margaux 1971 = Lafite 1971	46
16th	Ausone 1971	43.5

In each case the Pomerols and Saint-Emilions came out on top, but that can be explained by the fact that they always appear more attractive in youth. The more austere and aristocratic Médocs take a longer time to develop their full plumage.

It is therefore no surprise to find Pétrus and Cheval-Blanc stealing the limelight, but what about Ausone, which appears to be making a more than welcome comeback? One of the surprises of the 1979 tasting was to see the Ausone 1971 (at the bottom of the list in 1977) emerging in 4th place in 1979!

Closer home, the Latour 1971 preceded the 1970 on each occasion. This again is understandable because 1971 is an easier vintage to taste than the tougher 1970.

One other facet may be of interest, if one counts up the placings, 1st, 2nd, 3rd etc: at the 1979 tasting the total for the 1971s was 70, and that for the 1970s 64, only a difference of six; while at the 1977 tasting the total for the 1971s was 78, and that of the 1970s 54. If one can go by that at all, it would appear the gap (the 1971s at 78 being well to the fore for preference in 1977) is narrowing. The great wines of 1970 are still very backward; they seem to be losing ground for the time being to the charm of the quicker developing 1971s.

Thus in accordance with their youthful promise of earlier maturity, the 1971s have closed the gap and by 1979 are running the 1970s fairly close. Thinking along these lines it could well be that at a similar tasting in 1981 the 1971s may be in the lead, but not perhaps for long for, apart from the Pomerols of 1971, the 1970s should forge ahead in the long run. Meanwhile the 1971s will have provided considerable enjoyment for a great many people.

These two tastings have demonstrated how good both vintages are. As it happens the 1973s and 1974s have a good role to play in filling the gap until the 1971s are further developed and able to fulfil themselves. They in turn will hold the fort until ultimately the big guns of the 1970s come into action.

The rain continued to fall. I have now been visiting Bordeaux regularly for the past 30 years, longer still if one counts my pre-war visit and in consequence have as many friends there as at home, some more of whom joined us for dinner: Patrick and Titoa Danglade, Daniel Lawton and Jean and Anne Delmas. The 1964 Meursault-Perrières had been so good two nights before that we asked for it again and it met with the same success. The Bordelais greatly appreciate fine white burgundy.

In honour of Jean Delmas, the manager of Haut-Brion, we produced from our cellar a bottle of his 1962 and how good that was, absolutely delightful. That was followed by the best wine in my opinion in the cellar, the 1926 Latour and we all went into raptures over it. Truly superb, it transcends by far the 1929 and the 1928.

On the Friday morning Louis Vialard took us to the premises of Dourthe Frères in Maucaillou to taste some of the 1978s.

23 September 1979 **Crus bourgeois of 1978: blind tasting**	Wine	Characteristics	
	Rigal *Côtes de Bordeaux*	Dark colour, attractive bouquet, medium body, harsh finish.	
	Beauval *Entre-Deux-Mers*	Very dark colour, pleasant bouquet, fuller and of better quality than the Rigal.	
	La Tignerie	Very dark colour, good nose, not a big wine but well made with a delightful flavour and a good finish.	
	La Croix-Landon *Bégadan*	Very dark colour, pleasant nose, good depth of body and some tannin. Prefer to the Labégorce.	
	Maucaillou *Moulis*	Dark colour, pretty very distinctive bouquet, delightful flavour.	
	Labégorce *Margaux*	Very dark colour, good fruit and body and plenty of tannin. Needs time because unattractive at the moment.	
	Tessier *Saint-Emilion*	Colour almost black, good full nose, medium body, quite nice but still some acidity to lose.	
Crus classés of 1978: blind tasting	Wine	Characteristics	
	La Lagune *Ludon*	Dark colour, distinguished bouquet, quite a big wine, sweet and delicious, first rate.	16/20
	du Tertre *Arsac*	Dark colour, attractive bouquet, lighter than La Lagune but good flavour.	14/20
	Rauzan-Gassies *Margaux*	Very dark colour, well bred, plenty of character, good quality. A pleasant surprise.	14/20
	Beychevelle *Saint-Julien*	Good colour, attractive bouquet, good fruit and body but tasting less well today.	13/20
	Lynch-Bages *Pauillac*	Good colour, very good bouquet, has good fruit and body and plenty of tannin. Tasting better today.	16/20
	Calon-Ségur *Saint-Estèphe*	Good colour, very good bouquet, fruit and flavour.	13/20
	Gazin *Pomerol*	Dark colour, attractive but different bouquet with hint of tobacco. Rounded with lots of charm.	17/20
	Cos d'Estournel *Saint Estèphe*	Dark colour, scented bouquet, a big wine with lovely fruit and flavour, plenty of tannin.	16/20

On Sunday Louis and Monique took us to lunch at a restaurant which specialises in sea food at the Pointe de Graves, opposite Royan. The food was excellent but we were warned not to go there in summer time on account of the tourists who swamp the place.

The return journey through the vineyards demonstrated clearly the difference in the topography between the Médoc formerly known as the Bas-Médoc and the Haut-Médoc. It is merely a question of elevation. The former got its name from the flat marshy ground in the northern sector. Certainly there are a few hills, more like rises in the ground and it is on these that the vineyards of the Médoc such as La Tour de By and Roquegrave are planted. As soon as one passes over the brook called Jalle de la Maréchale immediately one reaches much higher ground and it is on this elevation where some of the better known *crus bourgeois* flourish, the more important being mostly close to the river.

Further south there is a break in the altitude caused by the marsh, *le marais de Lafite*, which the vines of Cos d'Estournel overlook from the north towards Pauillac. This marsh winds round separating the first row of hills along the Gironde from the parallel second row on which are planted the vineyards of Cissac, Larrivaux, le Breuil and Lamothe. Incidentally we called on the proprietor of Château Lamothe who proundly showed us his fine new *chai* and his new stainless steel fermenting tanks. Slowly but surely the Médocain proprietors are bringing their wine making up to date.

V USA, May 1979

Washington, D.C.

Strangely enough, I left London in a heatwave, the warmest May weather for many years, and was to find the same sort of temperature awaiting me in Washington D.C. Since my last visit Doug and Gene Burdette have added a new wing to their house in Bowie which with a family of five growing children had been almost bursting at the seams.

For supper that evening we compared two red wines, one very good and the other a little disappointing. The best part of the good one, Pétrus 1959, was its rich bouquet and considering how that vineyard suffered in the frost of 1956 (the worst for 150 years) it is understandable if the flavour was not on quite the same high level. The bouquet of the second, 1971 Volnay *premier cru* Marquis d'Angerville could hardly be described as fragrant, lacking charm, and in addition the finish to the taste was decidedly sharp.

Thursday 17 May

My second day was spent recovering from jet lag but that evening we drove to Washington to meet Ron Fonte at what must be Washington's finest restaurant, the Lion D'Or. Even if the acoustics are bad the cooking is outstanding, and I was delighted to find that great delicacy soft shelled crab on the menu. With delicious veal kidneys we drank the Pomerol Château La Cabanne 1971 and very good it was.

Greatly to our surprise we found a bottle of Croft 1963 was being decanted for us as a present from Jean Pierre, the owner of this already renowned establishment. Not really ready of course but who were we to complain! The Croft is among the top flight of this outstanding vintage.

Friday 18 May

An uncomfortably early rise to drive in to Washington where I was to lunch at the Palm restaurant as the guest of Bill Rice who edits the food and wine section of the *Washington Post*. An old friend, Bill always takes me to interesting places and the Palm, thoroughly American in character, was no exception. With corned beef hash, a favourite dish of mine, we enjoyed a nice bottle of 1976 Simi Chardonnay.

An important tasting had been arranged at the Burdettes home and the guests had come from far and wide, two couples having driven all the way from North Carolina, and that takes about seven hours. The guests' names were Mr. and Mrs. John Gehring, Dr. Hank Escue, Frank Polk, Mr. and Mrs. M. Kennedy, Mr. and Mrs. Paul Fortimo as well as Ron Fonte, the president of Les Amis du Vin. Altogether there were 14 wines and this was to be a blind tasting of 1975 clarets.

Most of the men present had already had some experience tasting the 1975 vintage and it was generally agreed that some of the excessive tannin was less noticeable than on previous occasions. For instance, I myself felt they were

*Les Amis du Vin,
Washington D.C., Ron
Fonté and David
Purseglove (sitting): the
Question . . .*

. . . and the Answer!

showing better than when in October 1978 I had tasted all the great Saint-Juliens at Château Langoa, the house of Ronald Barton. On that occasion they had appeared firmer and more closed up. All the wines had a fine dark colour, especially the Ducru-Beaucaillou, Pétrus, Trotanoy and Léoville-Las-Cases.

The 1975 vintage

Wine	Characteristics	My points
Lascombes *Margaux*	A somewhat plummy bouquet, medium body, but quite a sharp finish, a little disappointing.	9/20
de Pez *Saint-Estèphe*	The bouquet correct, nothing more, plenty of fruit though, if not exciting.	11/20
Gloria *Saint-Julien*	Attractive bouquet and heaps of fruit and tannin. A fine wine.	17/20
Ducru-Beaucaillou *Saint-Julien*	A fragrant fruity bouquet, very good flavour as well.	15/20
Latour-Pomerol *Pomerol*	A rather 'dusty' nose, plenty of fruit, seems to lack some breeding.	12/20
Mouton-Rothschild *Pauillac*	An attractive bouquet, very good fruit and flavour, fine quality.	16/20
Montrose *Saint-Estèphe*	Bouquet nothing special but lots of fruit and flavour, considerable tannin. *Note* As with some of the others, it may not have been showing at its best. When immature, Montrose often presents itself in a poor light. As with Latour and La Mission-Haut-Brion it is slow to develop.	13/20
Latour *Pauillac*	A full rich bouquet, a big well made wine, backward but has a lot of character.	16/20
Lynch-Bages *Pauillac*	Very attractive bouquet, well balanced with a delightful flavour, showing very well now.	18/20
Pichon-Lalande *Pauillac*	Distinguished bouquet, a lovely big wine, heaps of tannin but finishes well all the same.	18/20
Pétrus *Pomerol*	Very good, very rich bouquet, a huge extraordinarily rich wine, great quality.	18+/20
Palmer *Margaux*	Delightful bouquet, heaps of character and style, very good.	17/20
Léoville-Las-Cases *Saint-Julien*	Bouquet undeveloped, medium body, seems somewhat ungenerous.	13/20
Trotanoy *Pomerol*	Delightfully rich bouquet, a huge rich wine which I mistook for Pétrus.	19/20

There have been criticisms of these 1975s but while they may not be of the calibre of 1961 or perhaps even of 1970, they are certainly very good. If correct, the colour of the third and fifth wines were not so impressive as the others. Number eight, Latour, usually has a darker colour than most other red bordeaux and one can only assume that young as they are, these two wines (both called Latour incidentally) are going through some form of growing pains, or perhaps had not recovered completely from the journey across the Atlantic.

Los Angeles
Saturday 19 May

After the five-hour journey to Los Angeles it came as a surprise to see all the summer flowers, particularly after the late spring in Europe. Staying with John and Mary Helen Movius, it was possible to look across the deep valley only a few hundred yards away to the steep hills which had been devastated the previous year by a huge forest fire. The Moviuses had had a lucky escape.

Big John, as he is known affectionately by his friends, had organised a splendid dinner at one of the finest Italian restaurants in Los Angeles, called Florentino and directed by Pierro Salvaggio. Forty-four people were present, each ticket costing 120 dollars! The beautifully cooked Italian dishes provided an excellent foil for a series of the finest vintages of Château Latour. Dom Ruinart 1971 champagne accompanied warm fish hors d'oeuvres, then came quail *farci*, two kinds of delicious pasta, saddle of lamb, cheese and a sweet.

	Wine	*Characteristics*
Eighteen vintages of Château Latour	1975	Colour very dark, powerful bouquet, still brash with youth, masses of fruit. There is still tannin and acidity to lose but a wine of great potential. It was tasting better than the same wine in Washington.
	1974	Dark colour, a smoother bouquet than that of 1975, medium body for Latour, nothing like so great either but more forward. Definitely more masculine than the 1973, but lacks the attraction of the latter. Needs time to develop.
	1973	Quite a good colour, light for Latour, a better nose than the 1974 and has much more charm. This can be drunk now but will of course improve.
	1971	Very dark colour, bouquet still undeveloped, attractive all the same, good depth of flavour and well balanced. Probably needs five more years.
	1970	Unusually dark colour, bouquet closed up, great depth of flavour but still rather aggressive. Masses of tannin. Needs at least ten years but here is a fabulous wine for the future.
	1970 Les Forts	Very dark colour, bouquet more developed than the *grand vin*, fine fruit and flavour and more developed. While it may lack the formidable depth of the *grand vin* it is very good all the same.
	1967	Good colour, an attractive cedar bouquet, lots of fruit, plenty of tannin but far more ready than the 1966. A success in this uneven vintage.
	1966	Very dark colour, an impressive bouquet, still very firm. A massive wine with tannin and some acidity in evidence, although given more time the latter should diminish. It is a shame to drink this now, probably needs at least another five years, perhaps even more?
	1964	An unqualified success in a vintage of numerous failures. Good colour, delightful bouquet, not so big a wine as the 1966 but has a really nice flavour and of course far easier to drink. Possibly the finest wine of this vintage.

1962	Dark colour, very fruity bouquet, a fine deep flavour, has probably reached its top plateau. While many of the delightful 1962s are beginning to fade, this has a good life ahead.
1961	Dark colour, a heavenly 'tobacco' bouquet, delightful mouthful of lovely flavour, not ready yet of course, but truly a wonderful bottle.
1959	Very dark colour, typical Latour bouquet, tremendous depth of flavour, still has plenty of tannin. For me, one of the most attractive wines of the evening.
1955	Dark colour, lovely bouquet, a big wine, packed with fruit. One could almost bite it! Still some tannin, so doubtless will continue to improve.
1953	(Magnum) I had expected a lowering of standard here but was agreeably surprised; the best 1953 Latour I have come across. Good colour, real Latour bouquet, still some tannin but masses of fruit and flavour. What I wonder can be the reason for this?
1949	Dark colour, superb bouquet, in fact the best part. Wonderful taste but spoiled somewhat for me by the evidence of some acidity at the finish.
1945	The only disappointment of the evening. Dark colour, the bouquet showing some age, a big wine of great depth marred by some oxidation, caused no doubt by poor storage.
1928	Colour browning, a fine if old bouquet, showing its age. Yes, it is 50 years old after all, but full of elegance and breeding with even some tannin left. This bottle caused quite a sensation.

Sunday 20 May

John Movius had invited a few friends to taste some California Gewürztraminer – Fred Le Comte, Jim Kronman, Dr. Robert Uller and Dr. Ronald Rich. California Gewürztraminer was a new experience for me, so far as I can remember, never before having assisted at a comparative tasting of this varietal.

At my suggestion a 1977 Alsace from Hugel had been included. Since there were 16 samples to be tasted, they were split up into two groups, and in order to ensure anonymity all the bottles were wrapped up with no capsules showing.

A tasting of California Gewürztraminer

Wine	Characteristics	My points
Sebastiani 1977	Pleasant bouquet on the heavy side, nice but a bit dull.	14/20
Geyser Park 1978	Rather a heavy musty nose, somewhat ordinary with some bitterness at the finish. I appeared to have been at considerable variance with the other tasters.	8/20
Chateau St.-Jean Sonoma 1978	Rather a heavy bouquet on sweet side, also a little dull, another wine with some bitterness at the finish.	13/20
Clos du Bois 1978	An unusual bouquet, rather sweet, no definite character.	11/20

Gundluch Bundscher 1975	Very good, very definite *traminer* nose, rather sweet but good. In view of its bouquet and style I took this to be a wine from Alsace.	17/20
Chateau St.-Michele 1977	An unusual but fresh bouquet. Too sweet for my liking.	12/20
Villa Mount Eden 1977	Average bouquet, again too sweet for my taste.	12/20
Geyser Peak 1978	Clumsy bouquet, medium sweet. (This last wine had the same label as the second one, but must surely have been from a different bottling.)	11/20
Preston 1977	Colour darker, sweet quite fragrant bouquet, very rich almost of dessert wine style.	17/20
Dry Creek Sonoma 1978	Colour quite pale, fragrant bouquet, plenty of character and pleasant, spoiled a little by some bitterness at the finish.	13/20
Stony Hill 1976	Nice pale colour, unusual bouquet and flavour, again some bitterness.	10/20
Navarro 1976	Darker colour, poor bouquet, unattractive, again some bitterness.	9/20
Pedroncelli 1977	Colour too dark, nice nose though, fresh flavour, medium dry and a good finish.	14/20
Hugel 1977	Good colour, elegant bouquet, clean, dry, spicey with good fruit acidity. At least my guess of French origin was correct here!	17/20
Simi Alexander Valley Winery 1978	Pale colour, full bouquet, medium sweet, lacked acidity but pleasant.	15/20
Santa Ynez Valley 1978	Pale colour, good bouquet, pleasant flavour and a nice finish.	12/20

Through lack of experience I had not been aware that one of the weaknesses of California Gewürztraminer is the trace of bitterness that appears occasionally. Our host, John, informed us this is something the local enologists have not so far been able to eradicate as successfully as have the growers of Alsace. I must check this on return; how one learns all the time! I found it fascinating that my colleagues at this tasting had not picked up this hint of bitterness, the reason being possibly that they have become accustomed to it. In fact I reckon I have learned more or at least as much about wine and its making during these journeys to California spreading now over 11 years than I did before I began my annual visits.

Indeed at times in the past I have noticed something similar at comparative tastings of California Cabernets and red bordeaux where some harshness and acidity of the domestic wine have not been picked up simply because the local tasters are used to these characteristics and indeed like them. This is a statement rather than a criticism for as will be seen from my writing my appreciation of California wine is all too evident.

Monday 21 May

My friend Dave Rosier collected me to lunch at his Gourmet Wines at Marina del Rey. Dave has the distinction of being one of the early protagonists of Les

Amis du Vin on the West Coast. Although most agreeable it was in its way a sad occasion for thanks to a serious back injury he is now unable to undertake heavy work. Consequently he and his partner, Dick Crosbie, have sold Gourmet Wines and this was the final meeting together with their stockholders. The sale had been highly successful so that part at least was satisfactory.

Among the many wines offered at lunch the 1975 Château Meyney, Saint-Estèphe, was of particular interest. That it was even opened was surprising for it needs several more years in bottle to show its true worth. The 1975 vintage is already on the shop shelves, and proves once again that the Americans, like the French, are inclined to drink their red Bordeaux earlier than we do in Britain.

The tasting prepared for the Bel Air Club, Los Angeles, was an anonymous comparison between good California Cabernets and red bordeaux. When announcing it was to be a blind tasting John Movius said I was the only British lecturer, in Los Angeles anyway, prepared to do this before an audience. Having done it for some ten years now and in spite of mistakes, I find it amusing as it were 'to have a go'.

Cabernet Sauvignon

Wine	Characteristics	My points
Cheval-Blanc 1970	Very good colour, fine full bouquet, full fruity and very rounded.	17/20
Chateau St.-Jean 1976	A browner colour, varietal bouquet, harsher than the first wine and coarser.	12/20
Lambert Ridge 1976	Brownish colour, pretty bouquet, good fruit but some acidity; mistook this for red Bordeaux!	14/20
Léoville-Las-Cases 1976	Good colour, distinguished bouquet, good quality with fine finish.	15/20
Montrose 1975	Dark colour, fine bouquet, a fine full-bodied wine, plenty of tannin.	17/20
Beychevelle 1975	Good colour, bouquet full and rich, some tannin but a delightful flavour.	18/20
St.-Clement	(Blend 1975/6). Good colour, rather heavy bouquet, a huge wine, with some California harshness, a real whopper.	14/20
Haut-Brion 1976	More brown of colour, lovely full bouquet, rich and full-bodied.	16/20
Chateau Montelena 1974	Dark colour, rich powerful bouquet, a full-bodied rich wine.	15/20
Heitz Martha's Vineyard 1974	Very dark colour, splendid bouquet, very tannic, very distinctive, a well-made wine, excellent quality.	17/20
Mouton-Rothschild 1971	Dark colour, distinguished bouquet, very well made, plenty of tannin.	17/20
Clos du Val 1976	Dark colour, rather clumsy bouquet, full, rich, tannic and too heavy for my taste.	13/20

Among the first flight of four wines I failed miserably but at least gave the highest score to the clarets. In fact I did not distinguish myself at all, getting only seven out of the 12 right. We taste very few California Cabernets in Britain and it is a question of getting used to their style. The second and third flights proved easier as I became more accustomed to the problem. Nevertheless on account of steadily increasing quality of the finer California Cabernets, the gap between them and red bordeaux appears to be narrowing. The 1974 Martha's Vineyard is an extraordinary success and Joe Heitz has really pulled something out of the bag there.

After the event Mr. and Mrs. Roy Ross drove me to Upland where they have a lovely home overlooked by the snowclad San Antonio Mountain. Also with us was Ralph Hutchinson, the director of the Claremont Chapter.

Tuesday 22 May

Besides wine, the Rosses are enthusiasts about coffee and a comparative tasting made our breakfast all the more interesting.

Ralph B. Hutchinson drove Nicki Ross and myself to California State Polytechnic University at Pomona where he is a professor of Economics. He also lectures on wine, a subject which has become so popular among the students that it appears he now spends more time on it than he does on economics!

There is also an important section devoted to gastronomy and the training of young people for the restaurant business, three of whose directors I met during lunch. As may be imagined the food in the restaurant was of a high standard. On the way we had called in at the Claremont Chapter's wine merchant and had picked up the following:

Wine	Characteristics
Andean Chardonnay 1977	(LADV selection of the month.) A varietal bouquet, perhaps a little metallic, not great but one could perhaps mistake this for a lesser class California Chardonnay. Good value at $3.99.
St.-Clement Chardonnay Napa 1976	Pale straw colour, fresh and fragrant, a little sweet perhaps but rather nice. $6.57.
Quady 1977 Vintage Port	Bottled 1979, Rancho Tierra Rejada Paso Nobles. Made from *zinfandel* grapes. An extremely dark colour and while there is a faint resemblance to vintage port it has a heavier and coarser bouquet. This rich almost syrupy wine lacks the finesse of the real thing. In its defence it was still far too young to appreciate properly.

When later on I attended one of Ralph Hutchinson's wine courses for the students I found the subject was Zinfandel.

Zinfandel

Wine	Characteristics
Louis M. Martini 1975	Medium colour, a pleasant though somewhat earthy bouquet, on the light side but very easy to taste. Good value surely at $3.37.
Veedercrest Cask 73/6	87% *Sonoma*, 13% *Amador County*. Medium colour, agreeable bouquet, nicely rounded, slightly sweet and easy to drink.

[103]

Ridge Lytton Springs 1976	90% *zinfandel*, 10% *petite sirah*. Medium colour, somewhat blatant bouquet, a rough harsh taste with some acidity. Unattractive at present, the corners need to be rounded off.

To my European taste this typified some of the less attractive features of some California red wine, a certain degree of harshness and excessive acidity which I notice every now and then. From experience however this is what the locals often seem to like, preferring such wines to those from France.

The tasting of the Claremont Chapter took place at Di Censo's restaurant, noted for its cooking and its list of Italian wines. The owner, Di Censo, who joined us for dinner, is a Château Latour fan and in his private collection are included most of the recent vintages as well as ancients such as 1893, 1890 and 1878. Dick Watrous, a sales manager of Mirassou was with us, so together with the large selection he had brought with him, and those already on the table, the meal turned into quite a wine tasting.

Tasting of the Claremont Chapter

Wine	Characteristics
1978 Mirassou Monterey Chardonnay	Fragrant nose, similar flavour, very dry with a nice clean finish.
1978 Mirassou Johannisberg Riesling	Pretty bouquet and a pleasant flavour.
1978 Mirassou Chenin Blanc	Varietal bouquet on sweet side with a scented flavour.
1974 Chateau St.-Jean Pinot Blanc	Attractive bouquet, delightful flavour, a wine of distinction.
1964 Louis M. Martini Cabernet Sauvignon Private Reserve	A fine dark colour and a delicious taste.
1974 Chateau St.-Jean Cabernet Sauvignon	Very dark colour, nice *cabernet* nose, full-flavoured, also shows considerable elegance.
1975 Château Cos Labory *Saint-Estèphe*	Dark colour, fine bouquet, not a big wine but good fruit. Forward for its vintage.
1977 Mirassou Zinfandel 125th Anniversary	14.5° alcohol, straight from the cask. Very dark colour, fine rich bouquet, rich powerful flavour. This seems more on the lines of a dessert wine.

There was also a 1961 Spanna Castelo S. Lorenzo; it was full-bodied all right but the volatile acidity in it hinted danger. The following wines were presented with their labels showing.

Wine	Characteristics	My points
1977 Puligny-Montrachet, Folatières *Joseph Drouhin*	Distinguished bouquet, good flavour and very dry, with some acidity at the finish. This contrasted with the three California Chardonnays which followed, all of which were richer and more full-bodied.	15/20

1977 Keenan Chardonnay	Some finesse on the nose, quite a good flavour but on clumsy side and too sweet for my European palate. The label was dreadful and could have little shelf appeal.	12/20
1976 Spring Mountain	A fairly full bouquet, good flavour with a very nice finish, good fruit acidity, the driest of the California Chardonnays.	16/20
1975 Chateau Montelena	Excellent bouquet, if a little sweet, of fine quality a good depth of flavour.	18/20
1977 Husch Pinot Noir	Weak colour, strange bouquet, has fruit and tannin but excessive acidity, result hard and severe.	12/20
1976 Carneros Greek Pinot Noir *Napa*	Pleasant rather rich varietal bouquet, good fruity flavour but so rich as almost to be a dessert wine. Some tannin to lose.	13/20
1974 Hanzell Pinot Noir *Sonoma*	Not much bouquet, but good fruit and flavour, for me at any rate of better quality than usual for California *pinot noir*.	14/20
1974 Romanee St.-Vivant *Marey Mange*	Colour barely red, almost rosé, but a lovely well bred bouquet, a well bred distinguished wine but too light in body. One must remember 1974 was not a good vintage for red Burgundy.	15/20

I changed homes again and was driven to a favourite place, Newport Beach, by Steve McAnlis, the director of the Costa Mesa Chapter.

Wednesday 23 May   Steve McAnlis took me to an alfresco lunch at a small place called Paula's where we ate open-faced sandwiches and drank a lot of good Chardonnay. Our host was Chuck Hanson, the owner of Hi Time liquor store; also with us was the chairman of the California Wine Writers, Fred Russell.
These are the Chardonnays we tasted:

Wine	Characteristics
1977 Kenwood	Pleasant bouquet, a full rather lush wine with a clean fairly dry finish.
1977 Robert Stemmler	(New winery) Nice nose, fresh, dry with a slight prickle, seemed rather green and not so good.
1977 Harbor	A different bouquet somehow, clean and dry but still preferred the Kenwood.
1977 Spring Mountain	Attractive bouquet, good fruit and concentration, excellent fruit acidity. The best so far.
1973 Stony Hill	Very good bouquet, easy to drink with a delightful flavour, also excellent.
1973 Freemark Abbey Edelwein	Golden colour, a fairly rich dessert wine.

Steve McAnlis always produces exceptional tastings and the one he had arranged that evening was among the finest I have ever attended. With the addition on this occasion of three extra wines, it was the repeat of an outstanding blind tasting he had organised in the same room of the Newport Beach Yacht Club some four or five years ago.

Thus there were nine wines altogether, five from Bordeaux and four from California, all of top quality and all of the 1970 vintage, a highly successful year for both regions. As we sat down my neighbour at table, Jim Harker, a co-director of the Costa Mesa Chapter reminded me that at the previous tasting my wife, Prue, had put the right name to every wine, as we all know not at all an easy thing to do.

A comparative but blind tasting of California and red bordeaux of the outstanding 1970 vintage

Wine	Characteristics	My points
Lafite	Lovely dark colour, the bouquet of a fine red Bordeaux, medium body but good fruit and still some tannin to lose. Has breeding but not much generosity.	16/20
Spring Mountain	A blend of 1968/9. A wine with a fine reputation and much sought after. Very dark colour but a shade browner, an almost sweet minty bouquet, obviously California, full-bodied, fine quality.	16/20
Figeac	Very dark with a hint of brown, an odd bouquet, fairly full-bodied, but there appeared to be something wrong with this particular bottle.	13/20
Robert Mondavi	Good dark colour, still very youthful looking, an attractive blackcurrant bouquet, lots of fruit and a big wine, has plenty of tannin so should keep well.	15/20
Mouton-Rothschild	Dark colour, lovely bouquet, a big rich well-balanced wine, still backward.	17/20
Mayacamas	Very dark colour, fine rich bouquet, a huge wine almost too massive, still lots of tannin.	16/20
Latour	Dark colour, distinguished bouquet, heavenly fruit and flavour, clearly Latour.	18/20
Beaulieu Private Reserve	Very dark colour, bouquet obviously California, a fine well made wine, heaps of fruit, still rather strong and immature.	15/20
Palmer	Dark colour, a lovely bouquet, a beautiful big wine with still a lot of tannin to lose.	17/20

As I had noticed at the Bel Air tasting the quality gap between the two regions is closing. Now after a few more days in California and becoming more accustomed to the local style I managed to produce a better result (getting only two wines wrong this time, though mixing up Robert Mondavi with the Mouton). It was the blackcurrant bouquet of the Mondavi which at the last minute made me change my mind in spite of the fact that against the Mouton I had pencilled in 'not unlike Latour'. One should always stick to first

Salt Lake City: in Colonel Jack Daniel's cellar

impressions. The wines had been served in three groups of three, so at the end it was impossible to check over all one's findings. On such occasions it is considerably easier when the whole number are all lined up for comparison.

The people around me were saying it was one of the most interesting tastings they had ever attended and with that I agreed wholeheartedly. 1970 has proved its quality as an exceptional vintage both for California and Bordeaux.

Salt Lake City
Friday 25 May

A glorious day and the view from the house of Owen and Barbara Reese is superb. The snowclad mountains all around the plain in which Salt Lake City stands make a romantic background.

Owen drove me up into the Wasatch range of the Rocky Mountains to the noted ski resort called Little Cottonwood Canyon.

Colonel Jack Daniels, the regional director of three Chapters of Les Amis du Vin, had invited about 20 people, all wine lovers, to a delicious meal prepared by his British born wife Julie. Also present were Mr. and Mrs. Steve Robertson; he owns several wine shops and a restaurant in Boise, Idaho. There was a splendid assortment of both California Chardonnay and white burgundy, all from leading growers such as Chalone, Spring Mountain, Freemark Abbey and so on. Included also was an excellent Pinot Blanc from Chateau St.-Jean. The wines followed one another with such rapidity that I regret I failed to make adequate notes.

Saturday 26 May

The weather is unusually warm for the time of the year, 81° by 11 a.m. I went into town with Owen and among other places visited a liquor store, run by the state of Utah.

There has been a big step forward with regard to table wine since my last visit, because Owen Reese has been appointed adviser (unpaid) to the Board and is entitled to import small quantities of better quality. As an immediate result at least in one store it is now possible to find the produce of good California wineries such as Chateau Montelena and Chateau St.-Jean. Since the local tax is 75 per cent there is a limit to French wine except for the less expensive variety.

Although it was a holiday weekend, there was a maximum turnout of 118 for the lecture that evening. The wines tasted were to show the better quality varieties available. Incidentally, the name of the tasting demonstrated Owen's sense of humour, 'The Second Coming of Harry Waugh'.

Wine	Characteristics	My points
Chateau St.-Jean *Cabernet Rouge* 1976	65% *cabernet sauvignon*, 20% *merlot* and 15% *zinfandel*. Very dark colour, a full but rather coarse bouquet, a powerful full-bodied wine with a bit of a bite at the finish. Needs time.	11/20
Château Guibeau 1971 *Saint-Emilion*	Medium colour, well bred nose, rounded, good fruit, easy to drink.	14/20
Beaulieu Vineyards 1975	Medium colour, very young but good bouquet, fairly full-bodied but could have more charm.	14/20
Château Beychevelle 1973 *Saint-Julien*	Remarkably good colour for its vintage. Very pretty bouquet, heaps of breeding and finesse. Excellent for its year.	16/20

Chateau Montelena 1973 *Sonoma*	Dark colour, an attractive grapey bouquet, delightful flavour, fine quality.	16/20
Château Ferrande 1975 *Graves*	A strange vegetable bouquet, hard and disappointing.	13/20
Château St.-Georges 1975 *Montagne St.-Emilion*	Bouquet closed up, plenty of fruit but too backward to enjoy. This needs at least four or five years but will improve. 13/20 on present showing only.	13/20
Château Lynch-Bages 1961 *Pauillac*	Dark colour, a delightful perfumed bouquet but that was all. Clearly this has suffered from poor storage; however one bottle out of the dozen did in fact taste better. (I had a far greater bottle of this wine in Belgium only a month ago. A shame, for this was intended to be the *bonne bouche* of the evening.)	

When comparing the two best wines, the Beychevelle 1973 and the Chateau Montelena 1973 there was all the difference in the world in their style; the Beychevelle elegant and well bred and the Montelena more massive and more obvious. The latter was easily the most popular wine of the evening, but as we discussed at the time, American wine lovers, being more accustomed to the style of their domestic wine, are not unnaturally inclined to give it preference.

Following the tasting the Reeses gave a small dinner party at their home on the hill overlooking the city. The other guests were Jack and Julie Daniels, Steve and Lesley Robertson and Bill Kaufman, who is writing a book on Salt Lake City and the Mormons.

These are the gems Owen opened for us:

Wines	Characteristics
1968 Concannon Cabernet	A big bouquet, full-bodied and robust, a good wine but it could have had more elegance.
1968 Freemark Abbey	Attractive bouquet, lots of fruit and flavour, very good.
1968 Beaulieu Private Reserve	A fine bouquet, well made and well bred.
1968 Heitz Martha's Vineyard	The typical minty aroma of this remarkable vineyard, a beautiful wine with a splendid depth of flavour. Must surely be at its peak.

San Francisco
Sunday 27 May

My arrival at San Francisco was well timed because my hosts Barney and Belle Rhodes both arrived from Fort Worth only a few minutes before. They had been there for what must have been an epic tasting of 37 vintages of Lafite dating back to the beginning of the nineteenth century, in fact to the 1799!

How these wines of California are improving. Our aperitif before dinner was a delightful 1975 Stony Hill Johannisberg Riesling. In the quite recent past wines made from this varietal have usually been too voluptuous and clumsy for my liking, but nowadays one is beginning to come across Rieslings such as this one which have attractive fruit acidity. Our red wine for dinner was the first Cabernet Sauvignon, a 1975, from the Rhodes' own vineyard of Bella Oaks. Considering it had been made from only three year old vines, this vineyard appears to have great promise. The Bella Oaks wine is to be vinified and bottled by Joe Heitz.

Monday 28 May

A splendid day and as warm as in Salt Lake City. The 1977 Chardonnay from the new Rutherford Hill Winery that we enjoyed with our lunch deserves mention because it typified what I can only describe as 'the new look', so fresh, so clean and with more finesse than hitherto.

There appears to be a tendency to get away from the clumsy rather full-bodied wines of the past and to concentrate, as Phil Baxter, the wine maker of Rutherford Hill, is doing on finesse and good fruit acidity.

Through this past decade and very many visits to California I have made countless friends and aware of my pending visit my generous hosts had invited some of them for dinner that evening. Barney Rhodes had even given me a choice of the wines, fine Bordeaux, some great Burgundy or Cabernet Sauvignon from California. Sensibly, I think, I opted for the last named and of the successful 1970 vintage whose wines are already becoming scarce. What better opportunity then to taste some of these anonymously than in the company of authorities such as the following: Mike Robbins, owner of Spring Mountain, Napa Valley, Bill and Lila Jaeger, Freemark Abbey, Milt and Barbara Eisele, vineyard owner near Calistoga, Dr. Bill Dickerson, also a vineyard owner in the Napa Valley, Dr. Robert Knudson, one of California's leading authorities on food and wine, and a superb cook into the bargain, Brian and Jackie St. Pierre. Brian looks after the public relations for the Wine Institute in San Francisco as well as being the highly successful director of the local chapter of Les Amis du Vin.

A blind tasting of 1970 Cabernet Sauvignons

Wine	Characteristics	Group placing	My placing
Martha's Vineyard	Beautiful colour, a delightful scented bouquet, a fine well made wine which when compared with some of the others had quite a dry finish.	3rd	5th
Freemark Abbey Bosche	Dark colour, quite a rich bouquet, a little rich perhaps but a delicious flavour, well made and of fine quality.	= 1st	2nd
Louis M. Martini Special Selection	Medium colour, a fruity but somewhat thinner bouquet, a pretty wine, elegant and charming.	5th	4th
Mayacamas	Very dark colour, a full perfumed bouquet, a big full-bodied wine with plenty of tannin but there was a hint of coarseness at the finish.	7th	6th
Inglenook Cask	Good colour, a rather heavy bouquet, tasted somewhat like port!	6th	7th
Beaulieu Vineyard Private Reserve	Medium colour, fine bouquet, full-flavoured and well made, very good.	= 1st	1st
Mondavi Unfiltered	Good colour, a pretty bouquet, heaps of fruit and flavour.	4th	3rd

The excellent 1977 Spring Mountain Chardonnay, which Mike Robbins had brought with him, was another example of the new look appearing in some California Chardonnays. An attractive bouquet and flavour with good fruit acidity, but above all the finesse for which a number of the growers are now striving. It has already been mentioned that many of the California white wines have been too unwieldy, even clumsy, for my liking, so I was delighted, indeed amazed, to hear Mike Robbins say that much of this recent struggle for elegance, rather than weight, had been thanks to my influence over the past years. If this is really true how proud I shall be.

A tasting such as this was educational as well as enjoyable, but our host had further treats in store. A 1968 Beaulieu Burgundy (so called) had a dark colour, a rich fruity bouquet and a very nice taste. This unusual wine made from *mondeuse, gamay* and *pinot noir* grapes by André Tchelistcheff had caused quite a sensation when first it appeared on the market.

With the birthday cake Gateau Grand Marnier, for Geminis Barbara Eisele and myself, we drank 1976 Johannisberg Riesling Joseph Phelps. Too dark a colour for its age but it had a heavenly flavour.

This was not the end though, because Barney had decanted a bottle of 1931 Rebello Valente! In spite of the fact that 1931 was an outstanding vintage for port, only two or three houses shipped this vintage—the reason being the appalling economic crisis then at its height. While from time to time I have had the opportunity to taste the stupendous 1931 Quinta do Noval, I had heard of, but never previously tasted the Rebello Valente. Quite unlike the dark and rich Quinta do Noval, the colour was fairly pale, indeed for vintage port it was on the light side but with a delightful flavour. Barney told us that when he had decanted the bottle there had been an enormous crust, much more than he usually found with his bottles of Quinta do Noval of the same year.

An interesting snippet of information came from my immediate neighbour at table, Lila Jaeger, who told me that when Freemark Abbey was started in 1967 it was only the twelfth winery in the Napa Valley. Now there are over 70 with 22 new names on the board for launching in 1979!

Napa Valley
Tuesday 29 May

Barney and I set out early for the Napa Valley where Joe Heitz had invited us to taste some of his most recent vintages. The weather was glorious and his home and vineyard in Spring Valley were looking their finest in the lovely sunshine. No sooner had we arrived than the blind tasting of Cabernet Sauvignon commenced:

Wine	Characteristics
1975 Martha's Vineyard	Dark colour, delightful bouquet, medium body, but good fruit, a well made wine with a fine finish.
1974 Martha's Vineyard	A more minty nose, a full rich flavour and heaps of character. The origin easy to detect.
1975 Fay Vineyard	A good bouquet, slightly fuller than the first wine, very good body but the finish less good.

Both Barney and I recognised the second wine as Martha's Vineyard but I did not recognise the first as such. Joe explained that this wine, still in wood, needed 'polishing' a bit before bottling later this year.

In spite of the high cost, the second wine of the famous 1974 vintage, it had sold out immediately at 20 dollars a bottle. When I told Joe I had had difficulty in deciding which was the better of the two wines he was delighted because he thinks highly of his 1975 Martha's Vineyard. It looks as though it will be a repetition of the success that has been made with his 1974. Poor Joe had been in hospital at the time the 1974 vintage was gathered in, so it speaks well for the skill of his son David who had actually vinified this excellent wine.

More Cabernets followed, this time from the Rhodes' own vineyard, Bella Oaks in the Napa Valley, the grapes being bought by and the wine made by Joe Heitz. Considering it was only planted in 1972, this vineyard would appear to have a fine future.

Bella Oaks Vineyard	Wine	Characteristics
	1976	Colour purple, attractive bouquet, heaps of fruit and body with a pleasant underlying richness.
	1977	Medium colour, fine bouquet, good fruit and an attractive flavour.
	1978	Medium colour, very young nose, plenty of fruit but the lightest of the three.

Since I had to get back to be in time for my lecture in San Francisco, Alice Heitz had prepared an alfresco meal. Indeed it was so warm it was nice to sit in the shade. To accompany the food, Joe had assembled the following Cabernets:

Wine	Characteristics
1973 Napa Valley	Very good flavour, finished well.
1973 Martha's Vineyard	A wealth of flavour and finer than the Napa Valley label.
1974 Martha's Vineyard	A huge wine of splendid quality.
1975 Martha's Vineyard	Still too young but clearly has a great future.

As Joe pointed out, the 1973 tasted wonderfully well until we tasted the 1974 and 1975 vintages, both of which overshadowed it. Already it is too late for the opening price of the 1974, but I shall certainly put my name down for the 1975!

A tasting of California Chardonnays with Les Amis du Vin	Wine	Characteristics	Group placing	My placing
	1977 Sonoma Vineyards	Pleasant bouquet, medium body, watery and of no great character.	7th	7th
	1977 Dry Creek Sonoma	Interesting bouquet, good body and an attractive flavour with quite a dry finish.	4th	2nd
	1976 Joseph Phelps Napa	Lovely bouquet, plenty of fruit, excellent quality.	1st	1st
	1977 Lambert Bridge Sonoma	Fuller bouquet, a little sweeter, fatter and less elegant.	2nd	4th

1976 Roudon Smith *Santa Cruz*	Full rather perfumed bouquet, different from the rest full flavoured but quite good fruity acidity.	5th	3rd
1977 Villa Mount Eden *Napa*	Signs of fermentation, sweetish, full-bodied.	3rd	5th
1977 Conn Creek *Napa*	Good bouquet, medium dry, rather nice.	6th	6th

The retail price of these varied between 7.50 and 10 dollars.

Stanley and Ruth Burton who sponsored my initiation for the Knights of the Vine had invited us to dine with them in a private room at the Stamford Court Hotel. Among the other guests were Dr. and Mrs. Ronald Light with whom Prue and I had made friends on the first Call of the Vintage cruise in 1977.

Stanley had prepared quite a feast for us in the way of the wine, 1971 Chassagne-Montrachet, Embrazées, *Morey et fils*, a wine of considerable distinction and delightful flavour. This was followed by something totally different, the 1974 Stony Hill Chardonnay, sweeter but with good fruit acidity. Then came a range of Côte de Beaune made by a friend of the Burtons, Dr. Jean-Louis Laplanche who, with his brother, owns the Château de Pommard near Beaune.

Château de Pommard

Wine	Characteristics
1973	There was something about the bouquet we did not like and the wine was rather dull.
1969	A better colour, lovely bouquet and flavour.
1967	Fine bouquet, with a depth of flavour, better than I had expected of this vintage.
1966	Quite a good bouquet but the wine tired.
1964	Fine bouquet, more depth than all the others, a wine such as this helps to restore one's faith in red burgundy.

Finally there came a bottle of Niepoort's 1945 vintage port, very dark colour, lovely bouquet, quite sweet but absolutely delicious. The Portuguese school makes its wine a little sweeter than the British but with such a bottle who were we to complain.

Rutherford Hill Winery
Wednesday 30 May

When I arrive in California it is gratifying to find winery owners inviting me to give an opinion on their new wine. Thus it was with Joe Heitz, and so it was today with a range from the Rutherford Hill Winery.

Situated on the hillside to the east of Rutherford this architectural embellishment to the already beautiful Napa Valley scenery is an extension of the numerous vineyard holdings of the partners of Freemark Abbey. Phil Baxter, the wine maker, is endeavouring and seemingly succeeding in producing Chardonnay with the new look, i.e. lighter in style and with more finesse.

Although not outstanding, 1978 was quite a good all round vintage while in 1977 the wines were more uneven, with the whites better than the reds.

Wine	Characteristics
1977 Chardonnay	Pale golden colour, a nice varietal bouquet, light, crisp and attractive with just a touch of sweetness on the palate. In this wine Phil Baxter has found some of the lighter style he is seeking.
1978 Dry White Riesling	Very pale colour, made specially dry for the eastern market, a definitely fragrant bouquet, good flavour but a touch of bitterness at the finish. I am informed the Californians themselves prefer a fuller Spätlese style.
1978 Johannisberg Riesling	Pale colour, a more distinguished but not so obvious a nose as the Dry White Riesling. A fuller more luscious flavour but on account of good fruit acidity appears to be almost as dry. A good example of this varietal.
1978 Gewürztraminer	Good and typical varietal bouquet, good flavour too, could be mistaken for a wine from Alsace, first rate.
1978 Pinot Noir Blanc	Rose colour, quite a fresh bouquet, full flavour indeed quite plump and very easy to drink. It appears this is popular with the public.
1976 Pinot Noir	A full almost plummy bouquet, plenty of fruit and flavour but the finish was disappointing, there is a strike of something difficult to define.
1975 Cabernet Sauvignon	Fine dark colour, a decided *cabernet* bouquet, good fruit, medium body and a lot of tannin, some harshness.

Anchorage

In spite of the very long journey, the prospect of going to Alaska was exciting—the total distance was just over 2,000 miles. After Portland, Oregon, we flew over hundreds of miles of apparently uninhabited snowfields and snowclad mountains—the highest being St. Elias at 19,000 feet. Then suddenly from the wilderness, we descended to the civilisation of Anchorage, bathed in summer sunshine. In such an extremely northern latitude one would expect to find permanent ice and snow, but the reason for the equable climate is warm currents from Japan, similar to our Gulf Stream at home.

Bob Warren and Bob Gonze were there to meet me and at once whipped me off on a minor sightseeing tour, past the Potter Game reserve where it was possible to see a wonderful variety of wild fowl—this place must be a paradise for bird watchers. I was given a view of Mount McKinley, at 20,000 feet America's highest mountain, and clearly visible from some 250 miles away.

My host, Bob Warren, had invited one or two friends in for a blind tasting of California wines but I was really too tired to make much sense. Among those present were Shawn Beck, director of the local L.A.D.V. Chapter, and Bob Gonze, who works for Brown Jug Inc. which has no less than 18 local outlets. I was past noting all the wines we tasted but among them were 1977 Chateau St.-Jean Chardonnay, 1974 Martha's Vineyard Cabernet Sauvignon, 1970 Ridge Zinfandel Montebello and 1970 Mayacamas Cabernet.

Thursday 31 May

Shawn Beck drove me to the offices of the *Anchorage Times* for an interview and then for a little sightseeing, including the small but excellent museum which displays the history of Alaska from the era of the Russian fur traders to the earthquake of 1964. While at the museum gift shop I bought a minute, but exquisite, example of Eskimo art carved in ivory by a famous craftsman called E. Mayac. At 67° the temperature came as a relief after the heat of the Napa Valley and Salt Lake City. Shawn Beck took me to two or three branches of Jug Wine Inc., where it was impossible not to be impressed by the exceedingly good variety of wines in stock—especially all the best from California. How different from and how much better than what is to be found in many a controlled state further south.

This was to be a crowded day because a lunch had been arranged at the Crow's Nest restaurant at the top of the first class modern hotel aptly named the Captain Cook—who discovered Alaska. Decorated within on the lines of Captain Cook's ship, the 'Discovery', many of the artifacts or copies therof relating to Captain Cook had been collected from England.

The Crow's Nest is directed by an outstanding Dane, Jenz Hansen, and a fine chef. At lunch we had the pleasure of his company together with that of Jean Felix, his 'maitre D', originally from Algiers, and his head *sommelier* called Chip. Also with us were Micki Koblyk, a remarkable girl who started and runs successfully a retail store in a nearby town, Shawn Beck, my host Bob Warren, Bob Gonze and two congenial importers Tom Snowbeck and Gary Fournier.

Unhappily for me the famous Alaskan crab was out of season. Nevertheless Jenz had prepared for us a salad of the frozen variety followed by really fresh halibut caught only that morning.

Commencing with 1969 Bollinger R.D., very dry and of great finesse, there followed with the fish a 1976 Meursault Clos du Cromin, *Morey Rocault*. After these came an impressive range of vintages of Château Latour, details of which have already appeared in these notes; however, the following comments on them may be pertinent: (a) how ready to drink is the 1973 and how nice is it? and (b) a further comparison between those two great years for Latour, 1959 and 1961.

As happened in Los Angeles, the 1959 is much the nicer of the two for present drinking, the 1961 is still really too powerful and should be far better in a few years' time.

With fresh strawberries came that masterpiece Château d'Yquem 1967. Searching my distant memory, this must surely be as great as the now historic 1921 vintage when I drank it just before the war. I remember at that time the retail price at 15s. a bottle was considered a phenomenal sum. Not to be outdone by the sheer nectar of the Yquem, or even to be compared on account of the difference of style, came the 1977 Château St.-Jean Johannisberg Riesling Late Harvest Belle Terre Vineyard, the flavour strongly resembling an essence of apricots.

The Alaskans pride themselves on their smoked salmon, and during the meal my neighbour at table, the thoughtful Mickie Koblyk, telephoned her father to send some in time for me to take home to London. (These duly arrived and were much enjoyed.)

The theme of my lecture in the Captain Cook hotel provided an interesting comparison of vintages of Châteaux Léoville-Las-Cases and Langoa-Barton and gave me a further idea of the wide range obtainable in the wine shops of this outflung part of the United States.

Wine	Characteristics
Château Langoa-Barton 1975	Youthful bouquet. Has a nice fruity flavour but very immature. Needs from five to ten years.
Château Léoville-Las-Cases 1970	A beautiful colour, but something not right about the nose, not fragrant as a 1970 should be, good depth of flavour but a question mark. Needs four to five years. Maybe it was a poor bottle.
Château Léoville-Las-Cases 1969	Medium colour, attractive bouquet, easy to drink now, very light and it faded away rapidly on the palate.
Château Léoville-Barton 1969	Medium colour but turning a little brown. More backward than the Las-Cases but a deeper and better wine.
Château Léoville-Las-Cases 1967	Distinguished bouquet, body between light to medium, attractive with a pleasant finish, one of the better 1967s.
Château Langoa-Barton 1967	A fuller bouquet and has more body and tannin than the 1967 Las-Cases and was generally preferred to it. Another good 1967.
Château Léoville-Las-Cases 1966	A fine dark colour, a delight, quite rich, very well made and almost ready. First rate and the best wine of the evening.

This was to be a long day and it was past 10.0 p.m. when the lecture ended. But it was still quite light out of doors and the view of the snow topped mountains in the evening light almost bowled me over. From our private room, which looked out over the Sound, I was able to watch the red sunset magnificently outlining Mount McKinley a good 250 miles away. Indeed the sun never seemed to set and it was still light when I went to bed at 1.0 a.m. Although it was such a long day the King Salmon, prepared personally by Jenz Hansen, was as good as I had been led to expect. Served with a light hollandaise sauce it was as tender as could be.

Oklahoma City
Friday 1 June

What one does in the cause of wine? I got up at 5.30 a.m. for my flight from Anchorage at 7.0 a.m. To cut a painful story short I did not arrive in Oklahoma City until 10.0 p.m. local time, and by the time Bob and Kay Baron got me home I was in a state of collapse.

Saturday 2 June

Awoke feeling rather dazed after some ten hours' sleep but thanks to the kindness of my hosts slowly recovered through the day.

Terry Smith owns the wine store connected with the Oklahoma City Chapter of 'Les Amis', and he had invited us to dine with him and his wife, Caroline, one of the most accomplished cooks in Oklahoma City.

As a rule I have found the shrimps served in America to be tough and rubbery, but these were as fresh and tender as one could wish and made all the more delicious by an excellent somewhat piquant mayonnaise. These were set off by 1971 Heidsieck Silver Label.

The really outstanding part of the meal however was the red bordeaux that accompanied the steak, namely 1961 Latour-Pomerol in half bottles. I had expected it to be good from its performance some six weeks previously when I had been invited to a kind of international tasting of no less than 26 1961s in Belgium. The Latour-Pomerol had come fourth, surpassed only by Mouton,

Pétrus and Palmer. Served as it was on this occasion in half bottles it seemed even better; thus like so many of this spectacular vintage, that particular wine in bottle should continue to improve.

This is my third visit to Oklahoma City and the tasting took place in the Quail Creek Country Club, the subject being the 1974 vintage from Bordeaux. When I heard this, I became quite excited because not having tasted the 1974s for some time I was interested to see how they were developing. Unhappily on account of the predominance of acidity the outcome proved to be educational rather than pleasurable. As was generally agreed afterwards 1974 is not a vintage for present consumption; in fact, if one can judge from these particular wines, it would be wise to wait three or four years to give them a chance to become palatable. Their main asset at the moment is that they are relatively inexpensive.

1974 red bordeaux	Wine	Characteristics	My points
	Ducru-Beaucaillou	Good colour, very good Saint-Julien bouquet, good fruit but still very immature, astringent even, with excessive acidity.	13/20
	Pape-Clément	Medium colour, an attractive typically Graves bouquet, very light though. The flavour was pleasant but again the finish was sharp. More ready to drink than the Ducru, but has less depth.	13/20
	Cheval-Blanc	Medium colour but oh dear what a disappointment from this great vineyard. The bouquet was hard to find and although the acidity was less apparent than in the first two wines, the general impression was thin and meagre.	12/20
	Haut-Brion	Quite a dark colour, a nice well bred bouquet and a good flavour with quite a long finish. Still some acidity and probably needs four to five more years.	17/20
	Mouton-Rothschild	Medium colour, good bouquet with a nice berry taste. Not too much tannin but some acidity to lose.	17/20
	Latour	Deep colour, a fine powerful bouquet, not as big as usual but there is plenty of flavour. Some acidity as well as some tannin to lose.	18/20
	Pétrus	Medium colour, bouquet fair, a light even thin wine with an unattractive sharp finish.	

Happily for me the Latour emerged head and shoulders above the rest, another example of Latour doing well in an off-vintage. It was generally agreed that the successful 1973s are more attractive than the 1974s. That may not be the case in, say, five years' time.

Memphis, Tennessee
Saturday 3 June

Took the 9.30 am to Memphis which gave me time to lunch with the Barons at a restaurant called Les Caveaux, where the cooking was excellent. Also I visited again the Cowboy Hall of Fame, especially to see the first rate paintings of the wild west by Charles M. Russell and Frederic Remington, paintings which have become immensely valuable. On reaching Memphis I found that I had missed a dinner given for me by The Last Friday Club which included Châteaux Pétrus and Haut-Brion, both of 1961, and a fine 1919 Chambertin!

I stayed with Arthur and Maggie Halle and it is Arthur who has over 70 vintages of Château Latour in his cellar! At breakfast we ate the first raspberries of the year, picked from his garden.

Lunch at the Petroleum Club in Memphis proved to be an epic event, the food very simple, just one course, but the wine truly memorable. Together with my host, Walter Armstrong, Clifford Pierce, A. G. Burkhart, Benno Friedman, Ben Baer and Ron Perel, we began with a mystery wine as an aperitif. Since the bottle was brown and flute shaped and since the wine was Germanic in style, I asked if perhaps it came from the Rhine. When Arthur said no, I wondered if possibly it could be English and by golly it was: 1976 Lamberhurst Priory Müller Thurgau. I had never dreamed of finding an English wine in America and apparently this had been brought over as a present for Arthur by Michael Broadbent. There were three red wines:

Wine	Characteristics
Corton 1865	Colour a pale red, the bouquet definitely old but pleasant, the flavour old yes, but amazingly it had lots of fruit together with all its faculties and even some sweetness. It did not last long in the glass though, only about 15 minutes at its best but how fantastic for a wine of 114 years! 1865 incidentally was an exceptional vintage for red burgundy.
Latour 1877	The same pale colour, but no sign at all of great age on the nose. By now a light wine, but completely sound. How well this had held up and it lasted all the time in the glass. According to André Simon in *Vintagewise*, Latour and Margaux and Haut-Brion were the best wines in what he said was a good, if not great, year.

The third bottle (according to Christie's a pre-phylloxera of an unknown vintage) was dark brown in colour and virtually dead, but to find two good centenarians out of three was a remarkable achievement. It is needless to say that they had all come from my host's cellar.

The 1973 Tokay Essence was easily the finest Tokay I had ever tasted. Dark golden colour with a very rich raisiny flavour, fresh and delightful.

Benno Friedman, a devotee of vintage port, had, bless him, saved half the decanter of Taylor 1912 from the night before and told us it had been almost too powerful then. What a tribute to such an old bottle! The colour was dark, the bouquet excellent, no sign of age, full, rich, rounded and sheer nectar, superb wine.

Here in Memphis there was a change of allegiance: instead of Les Amis du Vin I was in the hands of the International Wine & Food Society. In a previous book I have mentioned the remarkable cellar of this group which over the years has had the foresight to collect wine. Valuable under any circumstance, to amass such a cellar under the present era of risen and still rising prices would be virtually impossible.

The highlight of my visit was the dinner held at the Summit Club. The turnout was the largest since my previous visit two years ago, and although I would like to take credit for this, a look at the menu will explain much of the reason.

Aperitif: Steinberger Kabinett 1975 or Guy Beauregard Champagne, Epernay; fresh *Bisque* of Crayfish followed by *Paupiette de Sole*, sauce *Albert*, both of which were first rate. With these two courses we drank Corton Charlemagne 1973, *domaine* bottled Duchet, lighter than Louis Latour but nice all the same. The delicious sweetbreads Lucullus were covered with chopped truffles, and that was all I could manage, so had to pass the main course of stuffed leg of veal Nesselrode. The rest of the wines at this Lucullan feast were as follows:

Wine	Characteristics
1957 La Mission-Haut-Brion	A very dark colour, the bouquet reluctant at first expanded well later on, a delightful Graves flavour and very soft, perhaps too soft, with masses of fruit. I have usually drunk this wine at the *château* where it has in fact been more lively.
1961 La Mission-Haut-Brion	A magnificent colour, a rich powerful bouquet, a heavenly mouthful simply packed with fruit and in all its splendour. Fine as it already is, it should continue to improve.
La Tâche 1957	Colour rather pale, great breeding on the nose but pointed at the finish, the flavour is lovely of course but there is a lack of warmth. A nobleman with a rather severe if not grim appearance.
1933 Richebourg	Pale colour, old yes, but first rate, still some sugar, still some depth, a splendid rich wine. Another aristocrat but of a more generous school. These two exemplified perhaps the difference between the style of post-war and pre-war burgundy.

In spite of all these treasures the *pièce de résistance* had been reserved for the end, a superlative magnum of vintage port, Dow 1955. A dark colour, a beautiful nose, huge, rich and powerful with many a year before it. A great bottle and how we enjoyed it.

Knoxville
Tuesday 5 June

For British readers, it seems the length of Tennessee is about as great as the distance between Lands End and John O-Groats in Scotland. I also found I had lost an extra hour, so by the time I arrived at the country home of Professor Norman Gailar and it was almost time for lunch. There I met Fred and Raisa Killifer and Dick Reizenstein, the director of the Knoxville Chapter of L.A.D.V. A glass of 1966 Dom Pérignon was more than welcome for a tired man. The Professor then set about grilling some shrimps and with these we drank a couple of Chardonnays. The 1977 from the Keenan Winery was too clumsy for my personal taste but any defects there may have been were admirably made up by a 1975 from Freemark Abbey.

I had forgotten what an attractive place Knoxville is. Fred and Raisa Killifer live in beautiful surroundings on the bank of the broad Tennessee river and it was there that the tasting was to take place. Beforehand, however, we had been invited to supper by Mr. and Mrs. S. Becker and it was in their house that we drank two superlative bottles of Mouton-Rothschild.

Wine	Characteristics
1961 Mouton-Rothschild	Dark colour, wonderfully complete bouquet and a heavenly rich flavour, still some tannin of course but oh so good.
1945 Mouton-Rothschild	A remarkable bouquet, Mouton at its best, a huge mouthful of superb flavour, almost sweet and truly delicious. Just a little tannin was noticeable in the perfect finish. A very great bottle. It is seldom one has the opportunity to drink together two such gems as these.

This confirms the result of my visit to Belgium in March where we had tasted not less than 26 wines of the famous 1961 vintage and we had all placed the Mouton on top, with Palmer and Margaux just behind (Latour was not present on that occasion but doubtless it would have presented itself with dignity!)

Back at the Killifers' house the following tasting was educational. The dinner in Los Angeles, based on many vintages of Château Latour, had given me the impression that perhaps the 1970s would after all turn out to be slightly superior to the very good 1975s. However if one can judge from the *châteaux* we tasted on this occasion, the 1975s appeared to have more depth and thus perhaps more future.

With considerable perspicacity, Dick Reizenstein had picked out for comparison three fairly recent successful vintages but all of which are quite heavily endowed with tannin, 1975, 1970 and 1966.

Château Ducru-Beaucaillou

Wine	Characteristics	My points
1975	Very dark colour, a youthful rather 'plummy' bouquet, very immature of course, but heaps of fruit and very good.	17/20
1970	Very dark colour, still full of tannin, appears to have less depth than the 1975 and is drier.	16/20
1966	Dark colour, dryish bouquet, very good fruit though and still extremely hard.	15/20

Château Lynch-Bages

1975	Colour almost purple, attractive full bouquet, rich and sweet, not too much tannin.	17/20
1970	Very dark colour, that lovely cedar (eucalyptus) smell (peculiar to Lynch-Bages and Mouton-Rothschild) a fine well made wine. This 1970 Lynch-Bages has acquired a well deserved reputation.	17/20
1966	Dark colour, good bouquet and flavour but there is still some acidity to lose.	15+/20

Château Cheval-Blanc

1975	Very dark colour, full sweet, also rather plummy bouquet, a delightful wine, so rich and so fruity. Heavy tannin of course but surely a success.	18/20
1970	Medium colour, not so much bouquet as expected nor so big a wine. Good of course but overshadowed by the 1975.	16/20
1966	Very dark indeed, a delightfully fruity bouquet, a fine well made wine, still just a little acidity to lose.	17/20

As it transpired the Cheval-Blanc should have been kept for the last because its abundance rather overwhelmed the Haut-Brion which had to follow immediately afterwards.

Château Haut-Brion

1975	Medium colour, even pale for its vintage, a very attractive Graves bouquet and flavour.	17/20
1970	Good dark colour, a rather dry nose, the wine firm and undeveloped and it needs some years to present itself at its best.	16/20
1966	Dark colour, a fine well bred bouquet, very good flavour with a slightly dry finish.	18/20

Indianapolis
Wednesday 6 June

5.45 a.m. and another painfully early start to the day – two in succession begin to tell on one. Nevertheless I had an opportunity to recuperate in the woodland home of Charlie and Jill Thomas outside Indianapolis.

Dr. Thomas has a fine cellar which includes over 20 vintages of Château Gruaud-Larose but he also makes his own wine with grapes which come from California. He is currently drinking a blend of hybrid and *cabernet*, but the one now maturing in an oak barrel is pure *cabernet*.

Bob Simburger had flown over from Detroit and we had all been invited to dine at the Highland Country Club where the lecture and tasting were also to be held. Our hosts Dr. and Mrs. Richard Dick produced two interesting 1973 Chardonnays to compare from Stony Hill and Freemark Abbey and finally completely fooled us with a red wine which we took to be a red bordeaux. In fact it turned out to be the 1935 Simi Cabernet, one of the epics of California. I have once had the good fortune to own a bottle of this wine myself and remember producing a similar result among some *cognoscenti* at home in London.

The tasting for about 80 people consisted of eight clarets, all of the 1970 vintage. The result for me personally was a little disappointing, for I had expected most of them to be better than they actually showed.

1970 red bordeaux, tasted blind

Wine	Characteristics	Group placing	My points
Lafon-Rochet *Saint-Estèphe*	Good colour and a pleasant bouquet, tannic still but has a nice depth of flavour with, however, too much acidity for my liking	7th	13/20
Malartic-La Gravière *Graves*	Good colour, nothing special about the bouquet, on light side, again with too much acidity.	8th	12/20

[121]

Duhart-Milon *Pauillac*	A darker colour, a good bouquet but altogether too astringent, still some tannin	6th	14/20
Ducru-Beaucaillou *Saint-Julien*	Medium colour, distinguished bouquet, medium body with an excellent finish.	2nd	17/20
Fourcas-Hosten *Listrac*	Medium colour, attractive bouquet, plenty of fruit but too sharp, the bouquet the best part.	5th	14/20
Palmer *Margaux*	Medium colour, fine bouquet, fairly robust with lots of fruit.	3rd	16/20
Léoville- Las-Cases *Saint-Julien*	Very good colour, fine bouquet, good flavour, somewhat light.	4th	15/20
Lynch-Bages *Pauillac*	Dark colour, lovely bouquet, delicious flavour with a fine finish.	1st	18/20

At this particular tasting the Lynch-Bages and Ducru-Beaucaillou came out easily above all the rest. Clearly I must try some of these again in London, for instance the Palmer and the Leoville-Las-Cases because this result from such a fine vintage was disturbing. Also the Lafon-Rochet for I seem to remember that in the early days that wine was awarded a gold medal.

Thursday 7 June

From great heat and humidity it has turned to heavy rain, and the cooler weather is a relief. There is little to report except for the arrival of the May-June issue of *Wine Magazine* in which there is an article about me by Pauline and Sheldon Wasserman entitled 'The Million Dollar Palate'!

The main feature of the day was a splendid dinner at the Glass Chimney where Dieter Puska, the chef and owner, has the reputation of being the best cook in Indiana. An Austrian by birth, he produces delectable dishes, and considering there were 24 of us the result was highly successful. The quite remarkable selection of wine had come from Charlie Thomas' own cellar.

Wine	Characteristics
Talbot 1949	Good dark colour, an attractive bouquet, good flavour but too much acidity at the finish. This must have been better a few years ago.
Gruaud-Larose 1949	Darker colour, lovely bouquet, very good fruit and flavour. Has kept better than the Talbot.
Talbot 1961	Dark colour, attractive bouquet, but the delightful flavour was marred a little by just a trace of acidity, a good bottle nevertheless. It is doubtful whether it will improve any more and should be drunk up now.
Gruaud-Larose 1961	Very dark colour, the bouquet became better and better, a wonderfully rich flavour in divers dimensions, the taste went on and on. A lovely bottle.

Lansing, Michigan
Friday 8 June

Dick Scheer and Bob Simburger picked me up at Detroit Airport and we drove to the university town of Lansing, Michigan. Dick Scheer is the owner of the Village Corner at Ann Arbor, another university town in the same state and the wine list must surely be the finest in the Mid-west. When I asked him whether he had a problem financing so large an inventory, he assured me that thanks to the inflation of the past year or so, he had on the contrary been able to make an appreciable profit; an example of one man's evil being another's gain.

My hosts were Steve and Marylyn Sheffel. Steve is the wine merchant (Goodrich) for the local chapter, so at dinner that evening I was able to meet some of the leading lights, Lyle Brown, the chapter director, Jim and Hattie Behemeyer, Steve's assistant, Bob Haun, Martin Ricard, an enthusiastic if somewhat eccentric wine consultant, as well as Roger Lamothe, the chapter director from nearby Jackson. Our venue was the Beggar's Banquet, seemingly an immensely popular place to eat and drink; in fact the bar was so packed all the evening it was almost impossible to pass through.

There were the three Chardonnays we drank with a main dish of sole New Orleans:

Wine	Characteristics
1976 Chateau St.-Jean *Sonoma Valley*	Clean and very good but as always a characteristic nose and flavour, it finished well.
1976 Burgess *Sonoma*	Good bouquet, an altogether fuller wine, but more attractive than many Chardonnays, a well made wine.
1977 Edna Valley *Sonoma*	Made, so I was told by Dick Graf, of the noted Chalone Vineyard. A delightfully fresh bouquet and a delightful flavour, excellent fruit acidity. There was unfortunately a heavy tartaric acid deposit in each bottle but for those who understand wine this did not detract in any way from the enjoyment.

The final bottle, the delectable Freemark Abbey Edelwein Gold, made a fitting conclusion to our enjoyable evening.

Tasting at the Kellogg Centre
Saturday 9 June

My birthday, three-quarters of a century, oh dear! oh dear! I slept until 9.0 a.m. – the fatigue of this journey must be catching up on me.

Mr. and Mrs. Beyer Mayer joined us for brunch when we had: Jeanmaire 1970, Cuvée Elysée Champagne, tiny bubbles and finesse; and Meursault 1941, Francois Martenot, from the Dr. Barolet Collection. Steve Sheffel had been apprehensive but it turned out better than expected for so ancient a white burgundy. After the bottle stink had worn off the bouquet came through. It was old of course but the fruit was there and it finished well. We had also Beaulieu Vineyard 1970, Private Reserve; twice already on this journey I have had an opportunity to taste this wine, but have never had a chance to drink it. A good full bouquet, a mouthful of delightful flavour, in fact an excellent wine.

The tasting took place in the Kellogg Centre where, apart from the 1974, all the wines had been carefully decanted.

1974 Réserve de la Comtesse de 'L' (second label of Pichon-Lalande)	Colour rather pale but a pleasing bouquet, the body medium to light, with a nice finish. Good value one would say at $5.00

[123]

1970 Haut-Marbuzet *Saint-Estèphe*	Fine dark colour, bouquet questionable to begin with but it improved. Lots of fruit with good acidity even a touch of sweetness. Could perhaps have more breeding, the tannin has all gone, consequently this Haut-Marbuzet is well forward.
1971 Les Forts de Latour *Pauillac*	Medium dark colour, delightful bouquet and a delicious spicy taste, nearly ready.
1971 Latour *Pauillac*	Dark colour, a full but closed up nose, grander, more important and with more depth than the 1971 Les Forts but of course more backward. Needs four or five more years.
1970 Les Forts de Latour *Pauillac*	Good dark colour, a fuller but more withdrawn bouquet than the 1971 Les Forts. A big rich full-bodied wine. Much of its essential quality is still overshadowed by tannin, acidity and immaturity. Quite a contrast to the more forward 1971. This can hold its head up with any of, say, the second growths of 1970 and could turn into a really fine bottle by, say, 1985.
1967 Latour *Pauillac*	Dark colour, typical bouquet and flavour, showing very well, a proven success for this erratic vintage. This comparative tasting emphasised very well the difference between the *grand vin* of Latour and Les Forts in the same vintage as well as the difference between the two vintages 1970 and 1971.

The tasting completed, I discovered that Bob Simburger and Dick and Sally Scheer had brought along with them a birthday cake and a bottle of 1971 Climens.

Rochester, New York State
Sunday 10 June

Another hot and very steamy day, a day which proved to be considerably longer than desirable. We returned to the Beggar's Banquet for a Sunday brunch and with it drank a nice 1976 Sonoma Chardonnay made by Burgess, the new kind combining fine quality with finesse. Bob Adler, the enterprising owner of this popular if unusual establishment constructed from two old barns, also presented us with a half bottle of the 1976 Freemark Edelgold.

Meanwhile a thunderstorm had broken and there my troubles began. Luckily I managed to catch a plane to Detroit but then found my connecting plane had been cancelled on account of the weather. Instead of arriving at Rochester, New York State, I was diverted via Toronto, Canada, where I had to go through the rigmarole of passing through customs and suffered two miserable hours in appalling heat and humidity. When I finally arrived in Rochester at 10.0 p.m. my luggage was missing and I felt more dead than alive.

Monday 11 June

All along the line on this journey the theme has been either California wine or red bordeaux so a session on red burgundy came as an agreeable change.

I have mentioned my host, Sherwood Deutsch, in previous books; he is the owner of an important and thriving store called Century Liquors where the sale of fine burgundy is one of his specialities. It was refreshing to find his view differed somewhat from that of other storekeepers with whom I had discussed the matter. Whereas the average store proprietor has the opportunity of only occasional visits to the Côte d'Or, Sherwood is able to go there at least once a year. With this advantage he claims he is able to find better wines than through normal channels available within the U.S. Being a specialist he finds he has a ready market for wines of top quality but there are nevertheless some drawbacks.

While he is convinced that to find the best value it is necessary to search for it on the spot, he has found that in order to succeed he often has to place orders from 200 to 300 cases of some lesser wine, otherwise the grower in question will not release his better quality. In fact while in Burgundy only two weeks before, in order to secure 80 cases of older vintages, he had to place an order for 450 cases of other wines, and until the shipment arrived he was still uncertain as to how many of those 80 cases would be included in the consignment.

The morning tasting was held in the home of Terry Faulkner, the chapter director of L.A.D.V. and selfishly it was a relief to find only three or four people participating. It is difficult to concentrate when there are a number of people milling around.

An anonymous tasting of fine burgundy of the 1971 and 1972 vintages

Wines	Characteristics	My placing
1972 Echézeaux *Gustave Gros*	Medium colour, a well bred but somewhat meagre bouquet, the flavour good but the wine rather light with excessive acidity at the finish. In fact the whole thing had a sharpish overtone.	9th
1971 Corton, Renardes *Marius Delarche*	Medium colour, an attractive fairly full bouquet. Again on the light side, but this had decidedly more body and a much better finish. Fine quality and delightful.	6th
1971 Morey St.-Denis *Amiot*	Good colour, distinguished bouquet, good fruit and well made, even so an example of the modern style.	7th
1972 Richebourg *Gustave Gros*	Dark colour, splendid bouquet, a fine powerful wine with heaps of breeding, some tannin to lose but super quality.	2nd
1971 Clos Vougeot *Henri Gouroux*	Medium colour, bouquet suspect, unattractive with a poor finish.	10th
1971 Gevrey-Chambertin *Louis Trapet*	Medium colour, fine bouquet, an attractive depth of flavour and a good finish.	4th
1971 Latricières-Chambertin *Louis Trapet*	Medium colour, a fragrant distinguished bouquet and a fine, big, well made wine, still some tannin to lose, excellent.	3rd
1972 Chambertin, Clos-de-Bèze *Pierre Dannoy*	Medium colour, very good bouquet, a rather ungenerous wine though, there was a strike of acidity and it finished poorly.	8th
1971 Chambertin *Pierre Dannoy*	Distinguished bouquet, a fine full-bodied wine with excellent depth of flavour, needs time to mature.	1st
1971 Hospices de Beaune *Cuvée Guigone de Salins*	Good colour, nice complete bouquet, some acidity but good fruit and a delightful flavour; apart from the acidity it would have been placed higher than 5th.	5th

After such a selection it was difficult to believe yet more was to come: an opportunity to taste a whole vintage of the Domaine de la Romanée-Conti, and a very fine one at that, is a rare treat. Assembled to enjoy the wines with us at the Genessee Valley Club were Warren Doremus (C.B.S.), Bob Simonson (Kodak), Joe Bourey (Kodak), Jack Bremetter (banker), Robert Prisch and Woody's manager, Jack Ryan. The latter had also been tasting the 1971/2 burgandies with us.

	Wine	Characteristics	Group placing	My placing
Tasting of the 1971 vintage of the wines of the Domaine de la Romanée-Conti	Echézeaux	Quite a dark colour, good depth of bouquet, lovely flavour and a nice finish, very good and ready now.	=4th	4th
	Grands-Echézeaux	Medium colour, great finesse of bouquet, a wine of considerable distinction but spoilt for me by too much acidity. Clearly this had greater breeding than the Echézeaux but it was in fact less attractive.	=4th	5th
	Romanée St.-Vivant	A paler colour but a delightful full bouquet. Lovely fruit and flavour with an excellent finish. An aristocrat of super quality.	2nd	2nd
	Richebourg	Good dark colour, a bouquet full both of depth and elegance, superb solid flavour, the only wine it would seem with a long life before it.	1st	1st
	La Tâche	Unfortunately both the bottle as well as the one held in reserve were corked. Later on that afternoon we tried a third bottle, happily in perfect condition. While the colour was somewhat pale, both the bouquet and flavour were excellent, in fact it tasted delicious. This could easily have emerged either first or second.	–	–
	Romanée-Conti	Good colour, heavenly bouquet and a lovely after taste. Spoilt for me though on account of lack of substance and more acidity than desirable.	3rd	3rd

All these wines left a delicious taste in one's mouth, more than customary.

By the evening it was back again to red bordeaux with about 260 people present, some of whom had flown in from Canada. The 1976 Pavillon Blanc of Château Margaux served as an aperitif reminded me of the good news that Pavillon Rouge has been restored at Château Margaux. This means that instead of being included in the *grand vin* the less good *cuves* will henceforth be sold under the label of Pavillon Rouge. This should help to improve the quality of the *grand vin*.

Some wines of the 1975 vintage

Wine	Characteristics
La Tour-du-Pin-Figeac *St.-Emilion*	Medium colour, pleasant typical St.-Emilion bouquet, an attractive rounded wine, still immature and probably needs three to four years, perhaps more.
Les Ormes-de-Pez *St.-Estèphe*	Good dark colour, very fruity bouquet, a delightful flavour packed with fruit. Still has plenty of tannin and needs four to five years. Clearly has a good future.
Durfort-Vivens *Margaux*	Rather pale for a 1975, but a well bred if somewhat withdrawn bouquet, pleasant flavour. Four years?
Beychevelle *St.-Julien*	Good colour, bouquet still closed up, attractive all the same. Very good fruit and flavour with tannin still in evidence. Again four to five years.
Gloria *St.-Julien*	Fine dark colour, full fruity bouquet, seems a stronger wine at the moment than the Beychevelle, also of excellent quality; ready, say in 1984 or thereabouts.
Latour-Pomerol *Pomerol*	Dark colour, a rich bouquet reminiscent almost of chocolate, a delightful rich seductive flavour. What a wine to have in one's cellar and how much more attractive these pomerols are than the Médocs when they are young.
Latour *Pauillac*	Very dark colour, tremendous bouquet, a huge wine packed with fruit and of course with tannin. Tasting really well. It is doubtful whether this will be ready to drink until the late 1980s.

This really good tasting had an interesting finish, because while walking round the tables to talk to individuals I met a young wine maker called John Engels who, with a partner, has established a new winery called Heron Hill. Afterwards we opened a half bottle of his 1977 Johannisberg Riesling – with a nice varietal bouquet and flavour it was surprisingly good, the best I can remember tasting from the East Coast area.

Atlanta, Georgia
Tuesday 12 June

Humping my bags between the Allegenney terminal at Philadelphia and Delta seemed about a mile although probably it is less than half that distance. Jim and Sue Hinsdale were at Atlanta airport to meet me and drove me to their attractive house in the country where we were able to take full advantage of the glorious weather.

A new and very successful restaurant has recently been opened here in Atlanta and is named Pano's and Paul's after the two owners.

The wines had been donated by some of those present, the 1966 Krug and the cognac by Jim Hinsdale, the sherry by Parks Redwine, an excellent 1975 Chappellet Chardonnay by Clive Howe, 1966 Montrose, very good too, by Stuart Wood, the 1964 Margaux, as expected, disappointing, by Dr. Milton Bryant and an Austrian Trockenbeerenauslese, 1971 Langenloiser Mandelgarten, presented by John Mozley, a wine merchant. I see I have omitted the wine for the cheese, a very good 1959 Château Lascombes.

Stuart Woods, an author, gave me a copy of his book, not yet published, on English and Irish Inns, which he informed me had taken four enjoyable months to write. When published in England this will be useful for us at home.

A light lunch with Parks Redwine, the L.A.D.V. chapter director, at the Marriot hotel where the tasting was to take place.

Our supper before the tasting was purposefully light and notable for the excellent bottle of 1953 Trottevieille, St.-Emilion. It was in fine condition – congratulations to the wine maker, Emile Castéja.

Parks Redwine had clearly taken trouble to find the right wines for a comparison of the great 1974 vintage for California Cabernet Sauvignon and suitable good wines from Bordeaux. The wines presented anonymously were served in pairs.

Wine	Characteristics
First Pair	
1975 Beychevelle	Good colour and bouquet, delightful flavour, still youthful with plenty of tannin, has a good future.
Robert Mondavi 1974 Cabernet Sauvignon	Regular bottling. A richer bouquet, heaps of fruit and flavour, rounder than the Beychevelle but lacking its elegance. A very good bottle needing four to five years.
Second Pair	
1971 Château Lafon-Rochet	Dark colour, lovely bouquet, rich and fruity, quite a special flavour, good quality.
1974 Stag's Leap Wine Cellars Cabernet Sauvignon	Medium colour, a more refined bouquet than the 1974 Mondavi, good fruit, still very young. Fine quality.
Third Pair	
1974 Beaulieu Vineyard Private Reserve	Dark colour, very good bouquet, heaps of fruit, still rather rough with signs of a lot of oak. Plenty of tannin.
1971 Brane-Cantenac	Pale to medium colour, distinguished bouquet, not a big wine, in fact a typical Margaux, fine quality.
Fourth Pair	
1974 Sterling Cabernet Sauvignon Private Reserve	Dark colour, full *cabernet* bouquet, a huge wine and of remarkable quality.
1971 Château Latour	Dark colour, lovely nose, splendid depth of flavour.

Possibly because by now I have had plenty of practice it was fairly easy to detect which was bordeaux and which California among these pairs. When I asked the members present almost invariably I found they preferred the California wine to that from Bordeaux. As I have found frequently elsewhere, the American wine lover has become accustomed to the style of his own domestic wine and likes better the heavier bouquet and the stronger flavoured wine to the lighter and more distinguished from Bordeaux.

The glass of 1960 Cockburn port was so good that Jim Hinsdale dashed home to decant a bottle of his Dow 1945 from the same shipper. This, in the company of Bill Graves, we polished off in fine style. It was a magnificent bottle.

Washington, D.C.
Thursday 14 June

The weather has been treating me splendidly towards the end of this visit. Here at my last stop in Washington D.C. it is equally warm with, thank goodness, no humidity. I am staying with Marvin and Phyllis Stirman from whom I gather the fuel shortage is every bit as acute as on the West Coast.

Therefore to get into the city for the evening tasting we were given a lift by my old friend Henry Greenwald, the founder and president of Club des Cents Chevaliers of Washington D.C. and of which I have the honour to be a Charter Member. In fact, contrary to customary practice, the tasting was a combination of the Club des Cents, the Chaine de Rotisseurs and Les Amis du Vin, all splendidly organised as usual under the expert aegis of Doug Burdette.

Having had no knowledge of the subject to be discussed I had brought no notes with me but since it was one after my own heart, vintage port, no great difficulty was involved. In fact there were no less than eight vintages from the house of Sandeman. By a happy coincidence Frank Visconti, a U.S. director of this illustrious house was in Washington, and his presence added greatly to the success of a delightful evening.

	Wine	Characteristics
Eight vintages of Sandeman's port	1975	Rather pale for so young a vintage, naturally tasting immature and on the light side.
	1970	Dark colour, noticeably more mature, however still has some of the fierceness of youth. As this disappears it should turn into a lovely wine.
	1967	Dark colour, youthful bouquet, quite rich and delightful. Almost ready to drink. As a vintage 1967 was not generally shipped, I seem to remember Cockburn and Martinez were two of the other shippers to do so. This would be a nice wine to drink at home when one does not wish to open a great bottle.
	1966	Medium colour, fine bouquet, has greater depth and flavour, more majestic in fact. Fine quality.
	1963	Dark colour, a splendid bouquet, a big rich wine of exceptional quality. Still too strong and powerful for present consumption, drinkable possibly yes, but a shame to do so for several years. No wonder the authorities say 1963 is the finest vintage since 1945.
	1962	Medium colour, pleasant nose, good flavour and very easy to drink. Another off-vintage as it were, but useful to have in the house.
	1960	Good colour, a delightful bouquet not of massive calibre but has a delicious flavour with a lovely finish. Probably at its best now. If not absolutely in the top flight like 1963 or 1955, 1960 has proved to be a highly successful vintage.
	1953	Another 'off vintage' and one entirely new to me. The style and flavour was different from the others, pleasant but not spectacular.

Thanks to Doug Burdette this evening provided just the right kind of finale for a lecture tour of this description.

VI Bordeaux, Autumn 1979

Our normal route is via Newhaven–Dieppe but this time we took the Portsmouth–St.-Malo Ferry. With no tourists about, St.-Malo in the early morning is an attractive place. Although on the map the journey had looked shorter as well as more attractive than that from Dieppe, it was both tiring and tiresome, having narrow roads with interminable trucks to pass.

On arrival finally at La Mission-Haut-Brion our flagging spirits were revived by the most splendid pick-me-up of all time, a bottle of old landed Pol Roger Champagne. Besides our hosts at dinner, Francis and Françoise Dewavrin, was a fellow guest, Alain Gagnez, a talented photographer who is helping with the preparation of a new brochure for the *domaine*.

Although I was reasonably close I was really too tired to guess the vintages accurately but this is what we had.

Wine	Characteristics
Château Laville-Haut-Brion 1960	Pale colour, nice fresh bouquet, pleasant flavour. 1960 was not a great vintage for the white wines of Bordeaux.
Château Laville-Haut-Brion 1952	(Half bottle.) Slightly darker colour, a fuller more assertive flavour, fine quality.
Château La Mission-Haut-Brion 1962	Good colour, nice bouquet, not a big wine but the flavour was delicious. Surely at its best now.
Château La Mission Haut-Brion 1952	The colour a little brown at the edge, fine well developed bouquet, a good flavour too but marred a little for me by some acidity at the finish.

Thursday 5 October

An important tasting had been arranged by Patrick Danglade and Jean-François Moueix at Duclot. When we arrived we were delighted to find present some of our London friends, Robin Kernick and John Armitt of Corney & Barrow and Eddie Penning-Rowsell of the *Financial Times*. The bulk of the tasters, however, were the leading brokers of the Bordeaux area.

There has been much discussion concerning the relative merits of the 1973/4 vintages and several tests have been made. As the matter was still in doubt our hosts had prepared a further blind tasting of the 1973/4 vintages, i.e. a bottle of each vintage from eight or nine leading *châteaux* and on this occasion La Mission-Haut-Brion had been included among the great growths.

As I have written, before these two vintages, while not exactly in the top class, provide an interesting contrast. The light charming 1973s which in so many instances suffered from over abundance, versus the more masculine 1974s which have a promise of longer life.

[130]

Château la Mission Haut-Brion.

A blind tasting of the 1973 versus the Vintage 1974

Wine	Characteristics	My points
Latour 1973	Pleasant fruity nose, not a big wine but well made and has an attractive finish.	3/5
Cheval-Blanc 1974	Good nose, a bigger wine, more depth of body than Latour 1973 but with less finesse.	2/5
La Mission-Haut-Brion 1974	Good bouquet, an attractive well made wine, still has plenty of tannin. Good potential.	2/5
Pétrus 1973	Good bouquet, a fine wine with both style and quality.	4 plus/5
Haut-Brion 1974	Plenty of fruit, somewhat severe with a sharpish finish.	1/5
Margaux 1974	For me an unattractive wine with excessive acidity.	1/5
Mouton-Rothschild 1973	Good bouquet, plenty of fruit and flavour, but spoilt perhaps by too much wood.	2/5
Lafite 1974	Good bouquet, good fruit and in spite of some acidity a delightful flavour.	4/5
Ausone 1974	Nice bouquet and flavour with some tannin to lose, guessed to be a Pomerol!	4/5
Latour 1974	Good bouquet, lots of fruit and body but some acidity to lose.	1/5
Cheval-Blanc 1973	Good nose, good quality with heaps of character (guessed as St.-Emilion).	3/5
La Mission-Haut-Brion 1973	Nice nose, plenty of style and character but could have more middle.	2/5
Pétrus 1974	Fine bouquet, fruity and full bodied with a lot of tannin, a big wine easy to drink in spite of a little acidity.	4/5
Haut-Brion 1973	Good fruit, some acidity, could have more charm.	2/5
Margaux 1973	Quite a nice bouquet, on light side, fair quality only.	2/5
Mouton-Rothschild 1974	Good bouquet, a big full-bodied wine, rather nice.	2/5
Lafite 1973	Nice bouquet, good fruit, has plenty of style.	3–4/5
Ausone 1973	Good bouquet, a fine full-bodied wine which I guessed incorrectly as a Pomerol.	4–4/5

The final result was as follows:

1st	Pétrus 1973	10th	Latour 1973
2nd	Lafite 1973	11th	Pétrus 1974
3rd	Cheval-Blanc 1973	12th	Mouton-Rothschild 1973
4th	Lafite 1974	13th	Latour 1974
5th	Haut-Brion 1973	14th	Margaux 1973
6th	Ausone 1974	15th	Ausone 1973
7th	Cheval-Blanc 1974	16th	La Mission-Haut-Brion 1973
8th	Haut-Brion 1974	17th	Margaux 1974
9th	Mouton-Rothschild 1974	18th	La Mission-Haut-Brion 1974

If one can judge from a tasting such as this the 1973s are still showing better than the more resistant 1974s. This is perhaps to be expected because the light 1973 vintage has always had more immediate attraction than the backward

1974. In my notes on the 1974s, in at least four instances out of the nine wines, there is mention of acidity, not excessive acidity, of course, but sufficient to detract from immediate charm. This acidity infers keeping power and in four or five years' time at a similar tasting the result could be very different. If my memory is correct, at a similar tasting some three years ago of these two vintages the then youthful 1974s, admittedly of the second and third growths etc., showed relatively better than on this occasion.

Returning to Château La Mission to lunch with Alain Gagnez we drank the following.

Wine	Characteristics
La Mission-Haut-Brion 1971	Good dark colour, attractive bouquet, a delicious sweet taste and ready now.
La Mission-Haut-Brion 1936	A developed bouquet, delightful flavour. Such an attractive flavour that I took it for either a 1953 or a 1947, an unexpected surprise from such a poor vintage!

For dinner that evening we had three really nice wines, in fact so good were they that I called them *Les Trois Glorieuses*.

Wine	Characteristics
1967 La Mission-Haut-Brion	A pretty, attractive Graves bouquet, showing finesse. A delicious flavour, a super 1967 which is just beginning to reach its plateau.
1961 La Tour Haut-Brion	An unusually dark colour, a fine full bouquet, a splendid rich wine with quite a sweet finish. Only recently has this become drinkable and it will last for a good ten more years.
1945 La Mission-Haut-Brion	Beautiful colour only just a shade *tuilé*, a glorious bouquet, glorious underlined, and a heavenly rich taste, a fabulous wine.

Friday 6 October ·

Through his enthusiasm and ability Henri Woltner has raised La Mission-Haut-Brion to be one of the leading wines of Bordeaux so there is little left for his successors to do other than, were it possible, to improve even further the quality of the *grand vin*. As we know to our cost at Latour, this rigorous selection of the best *cuves* (only the wine from the best parts of the vineyard) results in less wine to be sold at the higher price and more at a lesser one. Such is the search for perfection.

Three out of the last four vintages of the *grand vin* have been highly successful and their wines made the poor 1977, as it were the runt of the litter, looking somewhat forlorn!

Tastings of recent vintages
White Wine

Wine	Characteristics
Laville Haut-Brion 1978	A clean bouquet, still undeveloped and the same for the flavour. It was only bottled at the end of April so from now on we should begin to see a difference.

1977	The bouquet more developed and in spite of the vintage there appears to be plenty of fruit and flavour.
1976	A delightful honeyed smell, like a flower garden. On account of the extra ripeness of the grapes after that especially hot summer there was less acidity than usual so this may not last so long.
1975	A fine yet more subdued bouquet, a fine full-bodied wine with a good future. There seems to be a resemblance here to the 1976s and 1975s from the Moselle in Germany. On account of the heat that summer, the 1976s are more obvious and flamboyant than their immediate predecessors, the 1975s.

Red Wine

La Mission-Haut-Brion 1978	Fine dark colour, a splendid bouquet, very complete, a wine with a fine future. No wonder 1978 is known as the 'miraculous vintage'.
1977	Light to medium colour, bouquet a little thin but pleasant, a light very typical Graves taste. Should develop fairly early. Will make a nice lunch wine.
1976	Good colour, attractive distinguished bouquet, delicious taste and finishes well. An aristocrat.
1975	Splendid colour, a lovely deep bouquet, a rich wine with a delightful flavour, so big one can almost eat it. Long after-taste. Will make a great bottle.

After lunch Francis drove us to several vineyards, beginning with the lovely Château Carbonnieux where Anthony Perrin told us all his white grapes had been gathered in well and he was now picking his *merlot*. The grapes going into the press certainly looked very healthy. His white wine fermenting in stainless steel tanks was being kept at under 18°.

Wine	Characteristics
White Wine	
1978 Carbonnieux Blanc	A fresh *sauvignon* bouquet, fresh clean and dry. The *sauvignon* taste comes through more at this early stage.
1975 Carbonnieux Blanc	Fine bouquet and attractive flavour, still a trace of the *sauvignon* to lose but this is a fine wine.
1970 Carbonnieux Blanc	Well developed nose, a good wine but slightly heavier and more full-bodied.
Red Wine	
1978	Dark colour, attractive bouquet, not a big wine but distinctive flavour, touch of bitterness at the finish.
1975	Medium colour, pleasant bouquet, attractive flavour and a nice finish.
1970	Good colour, delightful bouquet, a well made wine, good depth of flavour with a dryish finish.

We then went on to Château La Tour-Martillac where there is indeed an attractive old tower. There Monsieur Jean Kressman, a fine looking man, let us taste the following reds.

Wine	Characteristics
1978	Medium colour, an attractive nose, good fruit with some acidity to lose.
1975	Good colour, well bred bouquet, medium body, well made, plenty of tannin.

Our drive ended on a high note at Château de Fieuzal where with Gérard Gribelin we visited the vineyard to see the *merlot* grapes being picked under very good conditions and in a healthy state. He only makes about 500 cases but all his white grapes had been gathered in and as elsewhere he is expecting to make a white wine of better quality than usual.

Here are the results of an instructive tasting.

de Fieuzal Blanc

Wine	Characteristics
1978	Fine nose and flavour, this should make a very good bottle.
1977	Pleasant bouquet with the *sauvignon* in evidence but not excessive, a clean dry wine with some acidity to lose. The *sauvignon* taste will also diminish in time.
	There followed a range of seven vintages of red de Fieuzal but similar notes were recorded on a previous visit.

Chateau de Fieuzal is a *château* to follow, because each time we come here the wine seems to be even better. With Professor Peynaud to help him, Gérard Gribelin appears to be on the way to achieving his ambition to make the finest wine possible from his property.

Lunch with Claude Ricard
Saturday 7 October

Monsieur Claude Ricard had invited us to taste his wine and lunch afterwards at Domaine de Chevalier, one of the finest estates in the Graves district. The morning was not auspicious for there was a hint of rain in the air. As we arrived we saw the *merlot* grapes being picked. Not much white wine is made here but what there is is of top quality. Many a respected authority will claim Domaine de Chevalier to be the finest white wine of Bordeaux, others prefer the more honeyed flavour of Haut-Brion and the Laville Haut-Brion.

Our host informed us that it is both more difficult and expensive to make white wine rather than red so it is done almost as a labour of love. This is probably the reason why only two and a half hectares, roughly six acres, are planted here with *sémillon* and *sauvignon blanc* vines. Only about 500 cases were produced from the 1978 crop and in order to bring in the 1979 the pickers had had to go through the vines four times in order to cut the bunches of grapes at their ripest. Such meticulous work could not be considered with a larger number of vines.

Thanks to favourable weather the crop for white wine here appears to be considerably larger than last year and the quality excellent, although one could not tell much from the cloudy glass of must which Claude Ricard showed us. Anyway the 12° of alcohol and 5° of acidity is all one could wish for.

Wine	Characteristics
1978 Domaine de Chevalier Blanc	From the cask. A fine pale colour, finesse on the nose and a delicious taste. Monsieur Ricard says it is not yet sufficiently developed and so will be bottled around April/May 1980.
1978 Domaine de Chevalier Rouge	From the cask. A good dark colour, a lovely Graves bouquet and an excellent taste. Our host told us it resembles his successful 1976 vintage and if anything seems a bit better.

At lunch, the first course, consisting of all kinds of clams and shrimps, was ideal to show off good white wine. Of these there were three and as we had been told which vintages to expect, I thought it would not be too difficult to decide which was which, but I was wrong. The third, and very different, of course, was the Corton Charlemagne.

Wine	Characteristics
Domaine de Chevalier Blanc 1964	A pale colour and a wine of enormous elegance, both for nose and palate, a joy to drink!
1962	More straw coloured with a lovely honeyed and more pronounced bouquet and similar flavour.
	Of these two, we all preferred the 1964.
1953 Corton Charlemagne *Rapet Frères*	A lovely developed bouquet and of splendid quality. It has kept remarkably well.

We felt honoured for this burgundy was our host's last bottle, which he had been keeping for years for a special occasion. This unusually fine bottle ended in a blaze of glory.

Guy and Nicole Tesseron had invited us to spend the weekend with them at Château Pontet-Canet, a *château* of which I have happy memories from my earliest visits to Bordeaux.

They had taken the trouble to invite a number of old friends for dinner that night, and the wines Guy spoiled us with were the Lafon-Rochet 1964 and the Pontet-Canet 1945. I managed to get the vintage of the first but not the second. The 1945 Pontet-Canet was one of the successes of that outstanding vintage.

On Sunday morning we went for a walk among the vines and here like everywhere else they are in a splendid state of health. The *merlots* were all safely in and we watched the first loads of *cabernets* being crushed.

Two *château* proprietors came to lunch, namely the Castejas of Batailley and the Casteleins of St.-Pierre and that evening the Aymer Foulds invited us to Château Beychevelle for a drink.

Château Latour

Lunch at Château Latour
Monday 8 October

The anxiety concerning the result of continuing high prices in Bordeaux is not unfounded. The ordinary wines had reached 2,000 francs a *tonneau,* far too high for comfort. On account of the possibility of the large crop the sales of the cheap wine had stopped early in September. Whether the price of fine wine will be reduced is another matter. So far as one can see, the weather has been conducive to good if not exceptional quality.

At Château Latour we tasted the new wine with Clive Gibson, and later lunched with him and his wife at the *château*. The two wines were the 1966 Les Forts de Latour, which without excessive tannin will certainly continue to improve, and the delightful 1960 Latour, at its very best now. There can be few of the 1960 vintage which are still so good.

There can be little doubt that 1978 is a fine vintage, unexpected as the result may have been.

Wines at dinner that same evening at Château La Mission (in half bottles) were:

Wine	Characteristics
1964 La Tour Haut-Brion	Very dark colour, a rich bouquet, a good mouthful of wine, fine and full-bodied. Ready in a half bottle but will improve.
1966 La Mission-Haut-Brion	Dark colour, nose still closed in, a heavenly flavour, really fine, with a delightful finish.

Château Batailley
Tuesday 9 October

After settling in at the Hotel de Sèze in Bordeaux, Emile Castéja picked us up to drive us to dine at Château Batailley with his family, where our fellow guest was George L. Watt, the president of Frederick Wildman, the well known importers in the U.S. As we drank the still delicious 1953 Batailley, Emile reminded me that this was the wine of which I had bought a huge quantity for Harvey's. The 1960 Trottevieille which followed was an equal surprise; except for wines like Mouton and Latour, most of the 1960s gave up years ago, but this with its very dark colour was robust, full-bodied and altogether delightful.

Tasting of crus bourgeois
Wednesday 10 October

While the better wines of 1978 are fine, I had been told the lesser ones such as the *crus bourgeois* were more irregular. This fact we were unable to confirm at Delor where Bernard Duten had prepared a range of 18, none of which could be described as irregular but of course all these wines had been carefully selected. In order to avoid prejudice they were tasted anonymously, except for the Château Clarke-Rothschild in its rather awkward bottle resembling a British half pint of brown ale!

Wine	Characteristics	My points
1978		
Château St.-Bonnet *Médoc*	Good colour, fruity nose, perhaps a little coarser than the others but with good fruit and flavour.	8/20
Château Terre Rouge *Médoc*	Dark colour, nice bouquet, more breeding than No. 1, good flavour.	9/20
Patache D'Aux *Bégadan*	Good colour, different style of bouquet, of much finer quality and will make a nice bottle.	12/20
Château Segur *Haut-Médoc*	Medium colour, pleasant bouquet, good fruit but more severe.	10/20
Château Verdignan *Haut-Médoc*	Darker colour, nice nose, good fruit and less acidity than some of the preceding samples, has tannin.	11/20
Château Coufran *St.-Sevrin*	Very dark colour, rounded bouquet, good fruit and flavour and well balanced.	13/20

Château Bon Dieu des Vignes *Graves*	Quite a good colour, attractive bouquet, good fruit and flavour with a nice finish.	12/20
Château Chantegrive *Graves*	Good colour, very nice bouquet, not a big wine but has a pleasing flavour.	12+/20
Château La Tour-Carnet *St.-Laurent*	Good colour and bouquet, plenty of fruit, some tannin and a distinctive flavour.	14/20
Château Camensac *St.-Laurent*	Good colour, a slightly different bouquet, well made with a nice taste.	14+/20
Château Clarke-Rothschild *Listrac*	Medium colour, fruity bouquet, has fruit and some acidity or is it 'greenness'?	12/20
La Tour-de-Mons *Soussans*	Good colour and bouquet, a distinctive flavour, some acidity as well as a lot of tannin. Still very young.	11/20
Château Chasse-Spleen *Moulis*	Dark colour, very nice bouquet, attractive flavour, first rate.	18/20
Château du Glana *St.-Julien*	Good colour, very fruity bouquet, good flavour but some acidity to lose.	14-15/20
Château Croizet-Bages *Pauillac*	Dark colour, elegant bouquet, plenty of fruit and flavour but some acidity.	14/20
Château Les Ormes-de-Pez *St.-Estèphe*	Dark colour, attractive bouquet, a nice well made wine, good quality, has tannin to lose.	17/20
Château Lafon-Rochet *St.-Estèphe*	Good colour, nice full bouquet, good fruit and flavour, still has acidity and tannin to lose, but has style.	18/20
Château La Pointe *Pomerol*	Good colour, attractive bouquet, rounded and full flavoured but could have more middle.	16/20

Lunching with two of Bernard's partners we drank the 1971 Château La Dominique, St.-Emilion and 1971 Brane-Cantenac, both very good indeed.

Prue and I had an excellent meal that evening at Chez Philippe in the old part of the city of Bordeaux which now that many of the 18th-century houses have been cleaned up is well worth a visit.

Until some years ago the restaurants in Bordeaux were rather a dull lot but now with the St. James, the Chapon Fin and Chez Philippe which specialises in fish one can feed very well indeed. The wine Château Pessan-Cadillac was new to me but both good and inexpensive. The white wines of Bordeaux have improved almost out of recognition.

Libourne
Thursday 11 October

A delightful day in Libourne with the Moueix family gave us an opportunity to further our acquaintance with the 1978 vintage.

Saint-Emilion

Wine	Characteristics	*My points*
Chateau Canon *Canon-Fronsac*	Fine dark colour, good nose, plenty of fruit and well balanced, a wine to buy.	10/20
Château Fonroque *St.-Emilion*	Dark colour, full bouquet, rich round and fruity and finishes well. Attractive but could perhaps have more finesse.	14/20
Château Moulin du Cadet *St.-Emilion*	Dark colour, distinguished bouquet, medium body.	14/20
Château Magdelaine, *St.-Emilion*	Good colour, attractive bouquet, a delightful flavour, almost like velvet,	18/20

Pomerol

Wine	Characteristics	My points
Château La Grave-Trigant	Good colour, distinctive bouquet, not a big wine but good flavour.	13/20
Latour-Pomerol	Very dark colour, full bouquet, rich, rounded and very good.	15/20
La Fleur-Pétrus	Dark colour, fine bouquet, a huge mouthful of lovely flavour.	16/20
Trotanoy	Dark colour, fine bouquet, lovely taste with an excellent finish, has tremendous breeding.	17/20

The Three Kings

Wine	Characteristics
Ausone	Fine dark colour, attractive nose, delicious flavour, great finesse. Will make a fine bottle. A perfect example of the 'Prodigal Son'; after many years in the wilderness, once again Château Ausone is producing wine worthy of its name.
Cheval-Blanc	Fine dark colour, lovely bouquet, a huge rich wine of great quality.
Pétrus	Dark colour, rich bouquet, not so massive as the Cheval-Blanc but with more elegance and finesse. A heavenly rich flavour with heaps of style.

Our fellow guest at lunch was General Katz, now retired but famous for his handling of the Algerian problem and clearly most knowledgeable about wine. Among the splendid wines we drank during lunch were the famous 1967 Château Pétrus and a quite remarkable 1948 Château Lafleur, very dark of colour and with a tremendous concentration.

After lunch Christian Moueix drove us to Pétrus, Trotanoy and Latour-Pomerol. Normally the harvest is safely gathered in before the picking begins in the Médoc, so at Pétrus it was a surprise to see all the grapes still on the vines. This year all the grapes are extremely healthy as they have thicker skins than usual, so there is little risk of *pourriture* even if it does rain. The plan according to Christian was to pick the following week commencing 14 October when the grapes would have reached maximum maturity. There is no risk at Pétrus, for if the worst were to occur the crop could be gathered in during a couple of afternoons by means of a *blitzkrieg*.

This year in spite of cloudy skies and rather unsettled conditions there has been little or no rain, so no one is worried. It has been a late harvest, however, with all the attendant risks of bad weather setting in. (*Note*. The weather remained reasonably good, and the rest of the crop was gathered in under satisfactory conditions.)

While it has been a splendid year for the *merlot* grapes some of the *cabernet-sauvignons* are still a little short of sugar and producing from only 9.5° to 10.5° of alcohol. This is why a number of owners are waiting, hoping for further maturity. Nevertheless the vintage has been in full swing all this week in the Médoc.

In 1977 the climatic conditions had not been favourable on account of poor weather during the summer. The quality was saved by fine weather in August, September and during the vintage. However, on account of serious spring frost the crop was small. Similarly in 1978 the weather had been dreadful until 12 August. All hope had almost been abandoned and one of the worst vintages ever anticipated. Suddenly the weather changed and wonderful day after wonderful day succeeded each other until long after the grapes had been gathered in – hence the name 'The Miraculous Vintage'. While not of course superlative, the general quality of the 1978s is highly satisfactory, a fine dark colour, a good bouquet and good flavour. Some growers are comparing their 1978s with their 1976s, so it is not for us to complain about that.

Regardless perhaps of the quality, the great thing abour these 1979s now being gathered in is their relative abundance after two small crops. The price of the Bordeaux *rouge* etc. had become dangerously expensive, detrimental to the image of Bordeaux not only in the export markets but also at home in France. This extra quantity is badly needed to reduce the price of the generic wine.

The vintage in 1977 had commenced around 5 October and in 1978 on 8 October. This year in 1979 I had first heard of 1 October as the date for beginning the harvest and it was disturbing to learn it was not to be until around the 9th. Usually that means the *cabernets* are still backward and this was admitted by some of the growers.

Normally the harvest begins around 25 September and it is a coincidence that there have now been three very late harvests in succession. According to the records in Bordeaux it is seldom that good quality is obtained after a late harvest.

Friday 12 October

Since I had to write a report on the 1976 vintage I had asked Patrick Danglade if he would be kind enough to arrange a tasting of wines from his own district, the Fronsadais.

Some ten years ago now I wrote an article on this district calling it 'The Cinderellas of Bordeaux'. And so they still are. In good vintages the wines from the Fronsadais can be most attractive and what is more, they are relatively inexpensive.

Briefly from the point of view of nomenclature there are two regions, the Côtes de Fronsac and the Canon-Fronsac, the latter normally being bigger wines and of greater importance. Nevertheless most attractive ones are produced in both areas and as elsewhere the difference usually depends on the human element, the man who owns the property and makes the wine.

[141]

A tasting of some 1976 Fronsadais, 12 October 1979

Wine	Characteristics	My points
Gaby *Fronsac*	Colour on light side for this vintage, a pretty bouquet, light fruity and attractive. A pleasant lunch wine, ready now but not for keeping.	10/20
Arnauton *Côtes de Fronsac*	Very good colour, full bouquet, altogether a bigger wine, considerable tannin, needs another two years.	12-13/20
Dalem *Côtes de Fronsac*	Good colour, fruity bouquet, good fruit, attractive flavour, better than the Arnanton.	14/20
Rouet *Côtes de Fronsac*	Very good colour, nice nose, good fruit but considerably harder.	13/20
Canon de Brem *Canon-Fronsac*	Good colour, attractive bouquet, well made with a lot of charm, a little tannin.	17/20
La Dauphine *Côtes de Fronsac*	Medium colour, attractive bouquet, good flavour with a nice finish, ready fairly early.	17/20
Moulin de Pey Labrie *Fronsac*	Very good colour, pleasant bouquet, a nice rounded wine, attractive.	16/20
Mayne-Vieil *Côtes de Fronsac*	Good colour, very good bouquet, fairly full-bodied, fairly forward.	14/20
Tessendey *Fronsac*	Good colour, and attractive full flavour, quite forward.	14/20
Canon *Canon-Fronsac*	Good colour, a rich attractive wine, heaps of fruit, will make a lovely bottle.	15/20

There were naturally variations but those were all satisfactory. Some were more forward than others but even those with most tannin should make good drinking over the next five years.

During these two weeks in the Bordeaux area, I had the opportunity to taste a wide range of the lesser Médocs, the Caves Co-Operatives and *pétits château*, many of which were decidedly disappointing. The colour was too pale and there was excessive acidity. Much of this I was informed later was caused by over-production.

For the sake of brevity, some notes on a few of the more successful 1978s are included here.

Some more 1978s from the Médoc

Labégorce-Zédé *Margaux*	Dark colour, fruity bouquet, medium body, but good fruit and flavour and finishes well.	14/20
Gressier, Grand-Poujeaux *Moulis*	Dark colour, nice nose, good fruit and flavour, well made.	15/20
Poujeaux *Moulis*	Dark colour, good nose, medium body, quite nice.	14/20
La Fleur-Milon *Paulliac*	Good colour and bouquet, a big wine with heaps of fruit, good quality.	15/20
Fonbadet *Paulliac*	Good colour, deep bouquet, good fruit and flavour and finishes well.	15/20

Lanessan *Cussac*	Good colour, quite a nice nose, no definite character and not showing well.	13/20
Pibran *Paulliac*	Good colour, nice bouquet, medium body, a little coarse perhaps, but well made.	13/20
Gloria *St.-Julien*	Medium colour, good bouquet, full flavoured with a pleasant finish.	15/20
Les Ormes-de-Pez *St.-Estèphe*	Good colour and bouquet, masses of fruit and plenty of tannin, very good.	15/20
Picard *St.-Estèphe*	Good colour and bouquet, nice flavour, well made, good quality.	15/20
Fourcas-Dupré *Listrac*	Medium colour, quite a nice bouquet, plenty of style, good quality.	16/20
de Pez *St.-Estèphe*	Good colour, average bouquet, has fruit and body, is full bodied in fact, but backward on account of considerable tannin.	15/20
Rauzan-Gassies *Margaux*	Good colour, average bouquet, medium body, easy to taste but nothing special.	14/20
Croizet-Bages *Paulliac*	Good colour, medium bouquet, perhaps a little rough still, but a big fruity wine. Masses of tannin and quite a mouthful.	17/20
Mouton-Baronne-Philippe *Paulliac*	Good colour, medium body and bouquet with tannin. Well made.	16/20

A blind tasting of the 1978 vintage crus classés

Please note the points out of 20 bear no relation to those given to the other 1978s which were tasted on different occasions. The colour of this vintage is excellent, so even those marked as medium at this tasting would be quite good for average vintages.

Wine	*Characteristics*	*My points*
Montrose *St.-Estèphe*	Not dark but quite a good colour, the bouquet not very pronounced but pleasant, not a big wine but has fruit. Some acidity to lose.	14/20
Clerc-Milon *Pauilliac*	Medium colour, average bouquet, if still a little rough has fruit and body and plenty of tannin.	10/20
Grand-Puy-Lacoste *Pauilliac*	Darker colour, an attractive bouquet, some tannin evident but has good fruit and body as well as breeding.	11/20
Brane-Cantenac *Margaux*	Good dark colour, attractive scented bouquet, different style and flavour from those of the first three, medium body, some acidity to lose, good quality.	14/20
Haut-Batailley *Pauilliac*	Good colour, quite nice bouquet, nothing special but should be easy to drink.	12/20
Lynch-Bages *Pauilliac*	Good colour, a deep bouquet, good fruit and well made and well bred. Less acidity than some of the others, best so far.	16/20
Pichon-Lalande *Pauilliac*	Dark colour, a pretty bouquet, not a big wine, has plenty of character and definitely attractive.	16/20

Les Forts de Latour *Pauilliac*	Dark colour, a full fruity bouquet, much more fruit and body than the predecessors, good flavour, good quality. N.B. I should I suppose have recognised this, but failed to do so.	16/20
Pichon-Baron *Pauilliac*	Dark colour, bouquet hard to find. Has good fruit but quite a lot of acidity. Quality appears only fair.	13/20
Beychevelle *St.-Julien*	Dark colour, nice fruity nose, good fruit, good flavour, a nice well balanced wine.	15/20
Ducru-Beaucaillou *St.-Julien*	Dark colour, bouquet average, good fruit but at the moment could have more charm.	14/20
Léoville-Las-Cases *St.-Julien*	Very dark colour, nothing special to say about the bouquet but the fruit and flavour more impressive, some acidity.	15/20
La Mission-Haut-Brion *Graves*	Very dark colour, a bouquet showing considerable finesse, plenty of fruit but some acidity to lose. A well made wine.	15/20
Pétrus *Pomerol*	Fine dark colour, pleasant bouquet, a more rounded wine, softer more like a fine St.-Emilion!	17/20
Ausone *St.-Emilion*	Very dark, almost purple, pretty, sweeter bouquet, more severe perhaps than the preceding wine but well made and of similar quality.	16/20
Margaux *Margaux*	Very dark colour, lots of fruit on the bouquet, more depth of flavour, well made with plenty of tannin. More finesse here with return to a Médoc?	17/20
Haut-Brion *Graves*	Very good colour, fine fruity bouquet, fuller and rounder than the preceding wine, plenty of breeding and easy to taste. Fine quality.	17/20
Cheval-Blanc *St.-Emilion*	Very good colour, very fruity nose, a huge wine, has style as well as character, most attractive.	19/20
Mouton-Rothschild *Pauiliac*	Good colour, a fine full bouquet, lots of character as well as breeding but the charm masked by a streak of acidity.	16/20
Lafite *Pauiliac*	Good colour, a fragrant scented bouquet, a fine well made wine, great quality.	19+/20
Latour *Pauiliac*	Very dark colour, an impressive but undeveloped bouquet, fine fruit and flavour, *un vin solide*, lots of tannin, clearly Latour.	19/20

In the cellars at Ch. Lafon-Rochet

VII   The Sleeper at Château La Tour Haut-Brion

If it were a question of 'time and place' to commence writing about one of the products of the Domaine La Mission-Haut-Brion, where could be more appropriate than in a wing of the *château*? As I was beginning this on 4 October 1979, through the wall I could hear the regular thud of the pump as it forced the juice of the freshly crushed white grapes of 1979 up into a vat. There it would remain for about 24 hours to get rid of excess deposit before being transferred to ferment in oak casks. This operation was, as it were, the birth pangs of the 1979 vintage of Château Laville Haut-Brion, a part of the domaine of Château La Mission-Haut-Brion. The bulk of the grapes, *semillon* and *sauvignon blanc*, had already been gathered in under cloudless skies and the potential of the white wine about to be made appeared to be excellent.

This is not however an essay on white Bordeaux, but about the second and relatively unknown red wine of the Woltner estate, Château La Tour Haut-Brion, a real 'sleeper', whose vineyard adjoins that of La Mission-Haut-Brion, and where the vine has been cultivated through the centuries. In order to avoid confusion, it may be better perhaps to explain early on that La Mission-Haut-Brion lies on the border of the *communes* of Pessac and Talence, while La Tour Haut-Brion is in Talence. This latter wine deserves to be better known both in Britain and the United States.

Long ago, during the English occupation of Aquitaine, the royal forest of Talence provided excellent hunting, enjoyed both by King Edward I and the Black Prince. An early building of the same period and owned by the noble family of Roustaing was a small fortress known as *La Vieille Tour* and in a document dated 1547 Louis Roustaing is described as Equerry Lord of La Tour.

Some time before the Revolution, the whole property, including the vines of La Tour Haut-Brion, passed into the hands of Monsieur de Cholet, an attorney to the King with the title of Admiral of Guyenne. The latter lived in a house (now a nursing home) no further than 200 metres from the present château. In turn Monsieur de Cholet must have sold part of the original property to a Monsieur Chapelle, whose son Jérome was a general exporter who peddled his wares, as well as his wine, to the French-speaking inhabitants of the State of Louisiana and in particular those of New Orleans. In the park of the *château* there are two fine redwood trees which he is reported to have brought back and planted after one of his journeys. Since the redwood is, I believe, indigenous to California, is it possible his travels could have taken him even further afield?

Incidentally, in 1785 there were seven or eight hamlets in the *commune* of Talence with a total population of only about 1,800 people, but a 100 years later this had increased to 3,604. At the present time there are over 33,000 inhabitants, excluding the University of Bordeaux with its 45,000 students!

According to the first edition of William Franck (1824) a descendant named Chapella (the correct spelling is Chiapella) was producing 38 to 40 *tonneaux* in Talence, and his neighbour the *domaine* Royal Cholet 30 to 35; and Monsieur Chapella is mentioned as producing ten to 12 *tonneaux* in Pessac. (*Note.* A *tonneau* is the equivalent of roughly 100 dozen bottles.)

The first edition of Cocks et Feret 1850, now the bible of Bordeaux, lists La Tour Haut-Brion as being the property of Jérome Cayrou and producing 25 *tonneaux*, Cholet, also the property of Jérome Cayrou, 28 *tonneaux*, Chapella 28 *tonneaux* in Talence, but also 18 in Pessac, the latter specifically listed as La Mission Chapella. At that period La Tour Haut-Brion of Chapella was considered the finest wine of Talence.

By 1868 (Cocks et Feret, second edition) Château La Tour Haut-Brion had changed hands again and here is an extract from the third edition of 1874: 'La Tour Haut-Brion belongs to Monsieur Louis Uzac who built anew the château, the agricultural buildings and a magnificent *cuvier-modèle* which can claim to be one of the most remarkable in the whole countryside. This vineyard has a very old reputation and includes eight hectares (roughly 20 acres) where the soil is very dry and composed of heavy gravel. . . .'

There is also a tower dated 1873 which was built at the same period slightly apart from the house. The same edition of 1874 mentions that in Talence there were 25 vineyards whose production was more than five *tonneaux* and 20 which produced under five. Apart from the vineyards of La Mission and La Tour Haut-Brion, the greater part of that area has since succumbed to bricks and mortar.

Later on, both vineyards must have been acquired by Monsieur de Constans, the head of the Bordeaux *négociants* Schröder et de Constans. An employee of that firm during the 1890s was the young Frederic Woltner who quickly appreciated the potential of the unexploited *domaine*. This story has already been told in Chapter 3.

At the same time as the purchase of La Mission, Frederic signed a ten-year contract to buy the total crop of La Tour Haut-Brion, but since both the *cuvier* and the *chai* at La Tour had for long been inoperative, the wine would actually be made in the cellars of La Mission, as indeed it had been in the past.

In 1926 the owner of Château Haut-Brion, a Monsieur Gibert, had brought a suit against all vineyard owners who, with the exception of La Mission-Haut-Brion, were incorporating the name Haut-Brion on their labels. Monsieur Gibert won his case against the following *châteaux*: Brivazac, Les Chambrettes, L'Hermitage, Fanning-la-Fontaine, Phénix and Laburthe. He failed however with a few which were authorised to continue as before namely: Les Carmes Haut-Brion, La Mission Haut-Brion, La Tour Haut-Brion and Candau Haut-Brion. Nevertheless in order to avoid confusion, La Tour Haut-Brion was no longer permitted to sell its produce as Château Haut-Brion La Tour as had frequently happened in the past.

The soil of La Tour Haut-Brion must be richer than that of La Mission because the wine is quite a bit fuller than that of the *grand vin*; it may nevertheless lack some of the latter's elegance and finesse. Château La Tour Haut-Brion is in fact fruity and full bodied with an attractive Graves bouquet. The colour is a deep ruby and as will be seen in fine vintages its quality can be really surprising.

While staying at the *château* in the autumn of 1979, I had the opportunity to taste and drink a whole range of vintages of La Tour Haut-Brion and was thus able to form an opinion of its specific style. Tasting a wine is all very well but much more can be ascertained through actual consumption. In spite of the definite Graves character, had I not known the origin of them at all, at times I could easily have imagined I was drinking one of the better growths from the district of Pomerol. These wines of La Tour Haut-Brion are particularly deep and full-bodied and are best enjoyed on a winter evening with roast game. They are especially appreciated by people who like a big wine; for example they are extremely popular in Belgium where the wine lovers are enthusiasts for the wines of Pomerol.

Here are my impressions of some of the vintages tasted.

La Tour Haut-Brion

Wine	Characteristics
1978	A fine dark colour, deep bouquet, a huge rounded wine with a fine future.
1977	Medium colour, typical of its year but with fruit and body.
1976	Colour almost purple, a full fruity bouquet, heaps of fruit and full-bodied. (*Note.* Very little was made, merely two *tonneaux* for the record.)
1975	An even darker colour, very full bouquet, masses of fruit and lots of tannin.
1974	Very dark colour, good bouquet, a big full-bodied wine, a success for its year, needs from four to five years.
1973	Medium colour, plenty of fruit and still undeveloped.
1970	Very dark colour, a full fragrant bouquet, a huge wine, finishing well. Should be excellent by 1983, perhaps even later.
1967	Good dark colour, has both fruit and body, is still closed up though, should be better in say two or three years.
1966	Dark colour, well developed bouquet, a huge rich wine, super quality. Will continue to improve.
1964	Dark colour, a rich bouquet, a good mouthful, big and full-bodied. Ready in half bottle, but even that will improve.
1961	An unusually dark colour, fine full bouquet, a splendid rich wine with quite a sweet finish. Has only become drinkable recently and should last another ten years.
1959	Dark colour, fine bouquet, very rich and very full-bodied, a proper mouthful, even finer than the 1966.
1955	Good colour, full bouquet, a big rounded wine which like so many of its vintage finishes a little flat, has some tannin still to lose.
1947	A lovely colour, if a little *tuilé*. Fine rich bouquet and a heavenly rich wine, super quality. A rare bottle.

The normal procedure has been to blend the less good *cuves* of La Mission in with those of La Tour Haut-Brion, to the advantage of course of the latter. Since the death of her father, Fernand Woltner, Françoise Dewavrin, the new director, determined to make her *grand vin* even finer if possible and this could only be achieved by even more ruthless elimination of the less good *cuves*. Consequently as from and including the 1978 vintage, the result has been a reduced quantity available of La Mission-Haut-Brion.

As a result of this policy, there should be a larger quantity available of La Tour Haut-Brion and of even better quality than hitherto. In fact it may not be so much a matter of quality, but of style, that is if some of the added elegance of La Mission comes through.

In this striving towards perfection, the inevitable loss of some revenue is considered worthwhile, but in these days of lowered standards, how refreshing this is. One can think of quite a few well known vineyards around Bordeaux where a similar practice could be beneficial to us all. Anyway it will be fascinating to watch how the new policy of extra selectivity will affect the quality and style of these two fine red Graves.

La Mission Haut-Brion

VIII   Burgundy and the Rhône Valley, March 1980

This enjoyable journey took place at a felicitous moment. 1978 had been a successful vintage both for Burgundy and the Rhône Valley and as it transpired March 1980 was a good moment to assess some of its attractive produce. My companions Dick and Sally Scheer are well known in the Mid-west as the owners of that fine business, The Village Corner, at Ann Arbor, Michigan, and Bob Simburger is a newspaper man and lecturer from Detroit. Unfortunately, on account of domestic problems, Prue was not able to join us until we reached Avignon.

As so often happens our plans for the Côte d'Or proved too ambitious so we found ourselves pressed for time. At Moillard in Nuits St.-Georges, Henry Thomas had prepared an excellent range of the 1978 vintage reds for us and these were beginning to show quite well. Among those I liked best were:

Wine	Characteristics
1978 Beaune Grèves	A fragrant bouquet and a delightful flavour.
1978 Nuits St.-Georges	A fruity bouquet and a big well made wine.
1978 Vosne-Romanée, Malconsorts	Fine bouquet, a well bred wine with some tannin to lose.
1978 Nuits Clos de Thorey	Distinguished bouquet, full-bodied and good quality, will make a nice bottle.

It was a pity we arrived so late at Auxey-Duresses, for there we found Mme. Bise-Leroy had prepared a tremendous tasting for us, most of which had to be postponed until the afternoon. I have heard complaints in England that this firm's wines are expensive and so they may be, but the result of this tasting confirmed the quality to be on a very high level.

Thus we only had time to try one or two wines before lunch, one of which, a 1978 Nuits les Perdrix, should make a splendid bottle. The two red 1955s we enjoyed with the meal prove how outstanding really good burgundy can be, a faultless Volnay, Santenots and the Chambertin, truly *un grand seigneur*. Later we drove to Rully where the main cellar lies and there began one of the most important Burgundy tastings I can remember and since there were over 30 wines, the notes have to be confined to some of those we liked best. There were some interesting 1974s and 1973s, but no room for comment.

Wine	Characteristics
1976 Savigny-les-Beaune	Dark colour, fragrant bouquet, fine flavour which needs about five years to develop.

In the Côte d'Or

1976 Chambertin	Fascinating complex bouquet, a lovely mouthful of flavour, should make a great bottle one day.
1972 Beaune, Les Suchots	Lovely bouquet, another large mouthful of wine, still needs several years to be at its best.
1972 Chambolle-Musigny, Les Charmes	Lovely aromatic bouquet, complete and delicious, more forward than the previous wine.
1972 Gevrey-Chambertin, Lavaux St.-Jacques	Well bred bouquet, still closed up but given time will make a fine bottle. (These three 1972s were all in the fine Burgundian style.)
1971 Nuits-St.-Georges, Les St.-Georges	Wonderful rich bouquet, full, rounded and superb, lovely now but will improve.
1971 Chambertin, les Cazetières	A full almost aggressive bouquet, a huge wine which should be magnificent around 1885 or even later.
1971 Mazis-Chambertin	Perhaps more finesse of bouquet than the Cazetières, heaps of breeding, a delightful taste and further developed.

Two fine 1969s followed, Chapelle-Chambertin and Chambertin, both of exceptional quality but neither really ready to drink. There were some 1967s and no less than eight 1964s, among which the Nuits St.-Georges, poulettes had a fabulous flavour, resembling purple velvet in the mouth, if that conveys any meaning. For those of us who have become increasingly disillusioned with the general run of red wine from Burgundy, a tasting such as this provided welcome reassurance.

While in the Beaujolais we stayed at the Hôtel les Maritonnes, in Romanèche, and called on three merchants. At Les Caves de Champclos, Robert Felizzato told us that while some 1979s were good, about 20 per cent were terrible! In general they lacked colour and had more acidity than desirable, but the white 1979s are perhaps better than the 1978s.

Georges Duboeuf specialises in wine from individual growers and there was a marked difference between some of the 16 1979s he showed us. Among those we liked best were Brouilly (Nervers), Juliénas (Pistoresi) and Moulin-à-Vent (Charvel). The third call was at that fine firm in Villefranche, Jacques Depagneux, where we tasted two delightful white wines, their Mâcon-Villages and Pouilly-Fuissé. Outstanding among the reds were the Beaujolais Villages Château de Lacarelle, which had won a gold medal, as well as a nice Morgon.

We spent the next night at the delightful Beau Rivage at Condrieu, a useful centre when visiting the growers of the northern part of the Rhône Valley. Naturally we had to try a 1979 Condrieu for dinner, with so unusual yet so delightful a taste. The red wine was the 1976 Côte Rôtie La Viaillière from Dervieux-Thaize, a youthful bouquet, a rich wine but still too young and aggressive.

The first call the following morning was on that splendid family Guigal in Ampuis whose wines are always a revelation. Monsieur Guigal told us he had only produced a very little Condrieu in 1978, but his 1979 was fresh and full of flavour.

Wine	Characteristics
1978 Hermitage Blanc	Clean bouquet, totally different in style from the Condrieu, fairly full-bodied and very good.
1978 Hermitage red	An unusually dark colour, a splendid bouquet and a superb flavour, truly a masterpiece.
1978 Côte Rôtie (Côte Blonde)	This wine had about 10% *viognier* added, a fine fragrant bouquet with plenty of fruit; there was however the slightly bitter finish from the *syrah* grape, which of course will disappear in time.
1978 Côte Rôtie (Côte Brune)	A rich bouquet, a huge very rich wine, still full of tannin. These two from Côte Rôtie were still in wood and perhaps will be blended in due course; the quality was so good anyway, I have ordered some cases for my own cellar.
1976 Côte Rôtie (Côte Brune)	Matured in new wood, but now in bottle. A remarkable bouquet and a great rich wine which should make a fine bottle in a few years time.

The 1979 harvest was quite prolific in this area, producing some wine of very good quality and some very poor. 1978 on the other hand was only a small crop, but of very high quality.

Later on we visited Paul Jaboulet Ainé in Tain, l'Hermitage-where Monsieur Louis Jaboulet told us there had been such a demand for their 1978 red wines there was nothing left for sale. In their place he produced such a large range of his 1979 vintage; but there is no space for all the notes here.

Wine	Characteristics
1979 Crozes-Hermitage, La Mule Blanche	White, and a winner of a gold medal in Paris. A generous fresh wine with good fruit acidity. Made from *marsanne* and *rousanne* grapes.
1979 Gigondas	Almost black colour, a fine bouquet and a lovely rich taste, will make a good bottle.
1979 Châteauneuf-du-Pape, les Cèdres	Rich bouquet, a full, rounded wine, like crimson velvet, plenty of distinction as well.
1979 Hermitage, La Chapelle	Extremely dark colour, a fine bouquet, has great power as well as elegance, a delightful flavour.

The *vin d'honneur* offered to us by our host was an astonishing bottle of 1966 Hermitage, La Chapelle, a heavenly bouquet, rich and silky.

Further south we stayed at that nice hotel, Le Prieuré, just outside Avignon. Our first call was on Monsieur Bouachon at Les Caves St.-Pierre in Châteauneuf-du-Pape, and it was he who provided the invaluable introductions to some of the leading growers in and around Châteauneuf-du-Pape. With some exceptions such as 1963, most of the vintages here in the southern region are reasonably good, but of course all with their various nuances. 1978 was excellent throughout and 1979 while more copious, varied in quality from some very good to quite a large proportion of poor wines. Among the wines Monsieur Bouachon had set out for us were two very good Côtes du Rhône:

Wine	Characteristics
1978 Château de Bastet	An attractive bouquet and a fine powerful wine.
1978 Château d'Aigueville	Very good bouquet and super quality for a wine of this *appeletion*.

Some of the leading growers of Châteauneuf-du-Pape

Paul Coulon of the Domaine de Beaurenard

1979	A pretty colour, quite easy to taste and a good finish.
1978	Darker colour; a fine well bred wine with good depth of flavour.
1976	Charming bouquet, well developed, rich and full-bodied combined with elegance. Still plenty of tannin, so needs at least two more years.

Paul Avril, whose family have been making wine here for 300 years, is one of the few who continues to make his Clos des Papes in the traditional style.

1979	A blend of five different varieties of grape, of which 80% was *grenache*, 10% *mourvèdre* and 5% *syrah*. A full but distinguished bouquet, a lovely flavour; this should make a good bottle.
1978	90% *grenache* and 5% *mourvèdre*, a splendid 'solid' wine with a great future ahead of it.
1976	Same proportion of grapes, a huge, but delicious wine with masses of tannin.
1970	A spicey bouquet reminiscent somewhat of truffles with a wonderfully rich flavour. It was not surprising to hear this had won a gold medal.

Monsieur Abeil of the Domaine de Mont Redon.

1979 White Châteauneuf-du-Pape	A very attractive wine and winner of a silver medal in Paris.
1978 Red	A lovely well balanced wine, another *vin solide*, with a fine finish.
1977	Fragrant bouquet with plenty of fruit but a harder finish. The production was large in 1977, but for quality it could only be considered as an off-vintage.
1976	Beautiful colour, rich bouquet, beautifully balanced and of super quality. A good example of the style they like to produce at Mont Redon, not too big, not too powerful, but with lots of elegance.

Monsieur Perrin of the Domaine de Beaucastel.
Here only about 50% *grenache* is used in the blends, but all of the other 12 varieties of grape are included. The *Appelation Controlé* for Châteauneuf-du-Pape demands that the wine has at least 12.5% alcohol. The *grenache* provides most of that alcoholic strength; however from his blend, it is obvious that Monsieur Perrin does not like to have too strong a preponderance of the *grenache* grape.

1978	Still in wood, almost black colour, a fine big wine which will need several years to develop.
1978 White Châteauneuf-du-Pape.	An attractive bouquet and flavour and very easy to taste. Made from 80% *roussanne* and 20% *grenache* blanc.

We had our disappointments though; the Cave Co-Operative at Beaume de Venise was just as commercial as it had appeared on a previous visit and the Cave Co-Operative at Gigondas seemed even worse.

Happily our journey ended on a higher note in the village of Vacqueyras with the Lambert family. Our introduction to Monsieur Lambert and his son had come through their London agent, Colin Fenton. We tasted from quite a number of vats and bottles, but there were two wines which struck me particularly:

Wine	Characteristics
1979 Côtes du Rhône Cuvée 19	Very dark colour, a pleasing bouquet, rounded and full-bodied, a gold medal winner at Orange.
1979 Vacqueyras	Very dark, lovely fruity bouquet, a fine full-bodied wine with an attractive finish.

Tain l'Hermitage on the bend of the Rhône

IX Château Pichon-Longueville, Comtesse de Lalande

From time immemorial most of the Médoc was an undeveloped area of forest and swamp. There were of course certain parts which were inhabited hundreds of years ago, for instance when a few years ago the foundations of a garden house were being excavated close to the church at Cissac, a number of eighth-century graves were uncovered. Château Cissac itself built in 1769, possibly stands on the site of a former house owned by the poet Ausonius. The latter had a friend, another poet named Theon, who lived not far away at Soulac, at that time an island, and they had to visit one another by boat.

Other local villages also have a long history, but it was not until skilful Dutch engineers came to undertake the drainage of the marshes that habitation and agriculture became possible over a wider area. Thus the laying out and planting of the important Médocain vineyards did not begin until around the middle of the 17th century, and by some 50 years later they had already established their reputation.

Among the early landowners in the Haut-Médoc was the Baron de Pichon-Longueville, first president of the Bordeaux parliament as well as the official keeper of the city's keys. He became a vineyard proprietor through his marriage in 1700 to Thérèse de Rauzan whose dowry included the important property of Saint-Lambert in Pauillac. This fine vineyard was situated with the village of Saint-Lambert as the northern boundary, extending southwards as it does today, with the present Pauillac-Bordeaux road as the eastern border.

For 150 years it remained intact, but after the death of Joseph de Pichon in 1850, it had to be divided on account of the French law of inheritance: two-fifths going to his son, the Baron Raoul de Pichon, and the remainder allotted to the latter's three sisters, the Comtesses de Lalande, de Lavaur and Sophie, the painter who eventually became a nun. None of this family had any offspring. For some time the two vineyards remained as it were in the family, but became entirely separate entities, subsequently known as Pichon-Baron and Pichon-Comtesse. Through the course of time, both have passed into other hands.

The classification of the wines of the Médoc became official in 1855 some five years after the partition of the property and the importance of these two vineyards was duly recognised when they were included among the second growths.

In common with Château Latour, Pichon-Comtesse lies alongside the southern limit of the *commune* of Pauillac; in fact it is not generally known that about one-third of the vineyard of La Comtesse is actually in Saint-Julien. Those particular vines are much prized by the owners, for their grapes add finesse and subtlety to the final product.

What was known as the golden age for the Médoc commenced around 1858 and lasted until the incidence of the phylloxera, which began in earnest after the vintage of 1878. At last vineyard owners had been able to make some money and in consequence newly built *châteaux* cropped up like mushrooms, many of them rather sugary but smaller replicas of some of the Loire *châteaux*. The *château* of Pichon-Longueville, Comtesse de Lalande, however, had been built around 1830 during an earlier period of architecture, and with its elegance and fine proportions must be among the more attractive houses in the area.

Almost immediately across the road stands the romantic looking Château Pichon-Baron, built in 1851 by Raoul de Pichon and a faithful example of the architecture of that period. The older house was apportioned to the three sisters, one of whom, endowed with considerable artistic talent, worked in Paris for five years in the *atelier* of Gérard, the well known painter. Evidence of her work is to be found in the *salon* of the *château*, namely a good oil painting of her brother-in-law, the Comte de Lalande, dated 1821, together with other portraits and landscapes.

There is a romantic if somewhat confused story that after the death of her husband, the Comtesse became the mistress of one of the owners of Château Latour who presented her with the land on which to build her *château* and where it is said he used to stay during his visits to his own vineyard. Certainly from the terrace of Pichon-Comtesse there is a splendid view over the vines of Latour towards the river and beyond.

Whatever the truth of the story concerning the Comtesse de Lalande may be, it is certainly a fact that the *château*, the *chai* and about a hectare of precious vines abut into the boundary of the Latour property.

An old Médocain legend runs somewhat like this: 'To make the best wine, the vines must be able to see the river.' Vines thrive particularly well in a gravelly soil and all the finest Médocain vineyards are situated on gently rising ground close to the Gironde. In the distant past, the river was considerably wider than today and as the water receded it left a broad deposit of this gravel so suitable for the cultivation of the vine. Situated in this favoured area, the vineyard of Pichon-Comtesse comprises some 60 hectares (about 150 acres) and the production averages roughly 20,000 cases a year.

In 1926 this part of the original estate was taken over by the *Societé Civile du Château Pichon-Longueville*, Comtesse de Lalande and since then has belonged to the Miailhe family. During the past few years it has been managed by General and Madame Hervé de Lencquesaing, the latter formerly a Mademoiselle Miailhe, and the effect of their husbandry has already become evident. Incidently, the General, one of the Knights of Malta, fought with the Free French and was stationed in England after the fall of France.

The rise and fall of the Médocain vineyards affords a fascinating study, because ultimately the finer points of quality depend upon the human factor. There are for example some *châteaux* even among the second growths bearing famous names, whose quality does not by any means match their potential. Others such as Ducru-Beaucaillou, formerly not too successful, for the past 20 years have produced splendid quality time after time.

Pichon-Comtesse appears to be emerging into this latter category; while the produce over the past decades has been reasonably good, it has not been at all exciting. Now, thanks to new direction and the help of the well known oenologist, Monsieur Emile Peynaud, who acts as a consultant, there has been a definite improvement of quality which is now obtaining general recognition. Once again, it is the old story of the prodigal son – how delighted everyone is when a vineyard returns to grace!

I have had the good fortune every year to taste the latest vintage in Bordeaux when it is both six months and a year old. These tastings are always anonymous and as the years go by one has become accustomed to finding the same *châteaux* among the leaders. Pichon-Comtesse had not normally been among them and I can remember the surprise at finding it so near the top when tasting was it the 1975 vintage? I queried my choice, wondering whether I had been mistaken, and I heard the magic words – a new wine maker! Every year since including the 1979 vintage, that success has been repeated.

When I received an invitation to go to Bordeaux to attend a special tasting of the recent vintages, I accepted with alacrity. Accordingly, on 8 July in the company of Jean-François Moueix, Patrick Danglade, both of the firm of Duclot, the broker, Max de Lestapis, our hosts, the General and his wife and their manager, Monsieur Godin, we tasted the following vintages.

	Wine	Characteristics	Average points
Tasting of recent vintages	1979	Very dark colour, delightful bouquet, a full, fruity well made wine. Should mature relatively quickly and undoubtedly will make a good bottle.	17/20
	1978	A dark colour and a lovely bouquet which is just beginning to settle down. Good fruit, a nicely balanced well bred wine, firmer and with more tannin that the 1979 and may ultimately make a finer bottle.	18/20
	1977	Medium colour, a pleasant but rather thin bouquet, the flavour agreeable, but without the depth of either the 1979 or the 1978. One must not expect too much of this off-vintage, but doubtless this will make an acceptable bottle for not too serious occasions.	14/20
	1976	Medium colour, an attractive bouquet, a charming rounded wine with a delightful finish. In the not too distant future, this will also make a very nice bottle.	18/20
	1975	Very dark colour, a fine distinguished bouquet, although still closed up, a splendid full-bodied wine. Much of its quality is still masked by the tannin. This may need some eight or ten years to develop.	19/20
	1971	Good colour, a well developed bouquet, not a big wine and is ready now. Reasonably good, but not great.	15/20
	1970	Dark colour, an excellent bouquet. A little disappointing when first opened, but developed into a fine wine with plenty of fruit and flavour and should continue to improve.	17.5/20
	1967	Good colour, an attractive bouquet, the flavour a little dry, has some of the acidity of its vintage.	16/20
	1966	Dark colour, delightful bouquet, a well made wine with heaps of flavour. Fairly forward for a 1966, in fact almost ready now.	18/20

1964	Good colour, pleasant bouquet, the flavour a little dry with some signs of acidity. Doubtful whether this will improve.	14/20
1962	Good colour, the distinctive bouquet of its year with an equally nice taste. This must be at its best and should be drunk and enjoyed before it begins to decline.	18/20
1961	Very dark colour, the splendid rich nose of the 1961s. A lovely full-bodied wine, probably at its best.	19/20

The points given represent the general consensus of opinion.

In order to give a rough idea of the relative quality of the 1976 and 1977 vintages mentioned above, at blind tastings held in Bordeaux for leading wine brokers, the 1976 vintage came easily first and among the 1977s equal first with Ducru-Beaucaillou.

The modernisation being carried out is impressive. Among other things, a whole range of stainless steel fermentation tanks with thermostatic control was about to be installed and these should help even further with the improved quality of the wine. In addition, a new *chai*, covering roughly 1,000 square metres had just been completed. This houses an up-to-date bottling plant and provides storage for a further 520 casks for maturing wine.

The policy is to make Pichon-Comtesse ready to drink reasonably early; therefore in order to avoid excessive tannin only some 50 new casks are used for the young wine. This percentage varies of course in accordance with the tannin of the vintage in question. The present constitution of the vineyard is roughly 45% *cabernet sauvignon*, 35% *merlot*, 12% *cabernet franc* with about 8% *petit verdot*.

Recently this vineyard has been known as Pichon-Lalande, but according to the wish of the present owners, it is once again to be known as Pichon-Comtesse. Thanks to their influence, the quality of this *château* may now be considered as among the very best of the second growths.

X   The wines of the Pacific Northwest

With one notable exception, the wine producing regions of the world have a long history behind them. One of the oldest established outside Europe must be South Africa, followed later on by other countries i.e. the Hunter Valley in Australia, California in the United States and so on.

The quality of the wine made in France and Germany has long been recognised and appreciated, but it is really only during the last 20 years, one could almost say the last decade, that there has been such a profound improvement in quality among the later developed areas. The English vineyards could also perhaps be included in this category, because although the vine had been cultivated during the Roman occupation, the production of wine, except in rare incidences, had been virtually discontinued until after the last war.

The notable exception to these well established wine regions is of course the Pacific Northwest, an area which vinously includes the states of Washington, Oregon and Idaho. My first introduction, and a brief one, was when I visited Portland, Oregon, some four years ago and had the opportunity to see the relatively freshly planted vineyards of Eyrie and Knudson Erath. My main recollection was the possibility, owing to the cooler climate, of making a better *pinot noir* perhaps than in California where it has never yet really succeeded.

Vines had in fact been planted in eastern Washington before the war but at that time there was little or no public interest in table wine. It was not until the early sixties (as also in Oregon) that European vines were planted more seriously but only on a minor scale. Thanks possibly to the lively interest which has developed in table wine all over the United States, production has increased enormously throughout the past decade and in Washington State alone, there are now some 5,000 acres already under vines, with new areas still being prepared.

Among the leading wineries in this state are Associated Vintners, Bingen Wine Cellars, Hinzerling Vineyard, Preston Wine Cellars, Chateau Ste. Michelle, Snohomish Valley, Puyallup Valley Winery and Manfred Vierthaler Winery. The greater part of these vineyards lie some 150 miles east of the city of Seattle on the foothills of the Cascade mountains. This range virtually divides the state of Washington into two distinct climatic regions. On the western side, which of course includes the city of Seattle, the climate is not dissimilar from that of Britain, fairly mild winters but generally wet and unpredictable summers, unsuitable anyway for good varietals because the grapes such as *chardonnay* or *cabernet sauvignon* would never ripen sufficiently.

For this reason the vineyards have been planted on the eastern side of the mountains in what could be described as reclaimed desert. The rainfall is limited, so these vineyards are nourished by irrigation which is essential both here as well as in California. The water comes from the Columbia river and its use is carefully controlled, usually by the drip method.

Whatever disadvantages a sandy soil may have for vines, and after all on account of its proximity to the river Gironde there is more sand than one would imagine in the vineyard of Château Latour, this opens up an interesting situation. That dreaded scourge the *phylloxera vastatrix* does not thrive in a sandy soil and, as an authority informed me, it needs relatively poor drainage together with cracks and crannies to exist.

If one studies the disastrous history of the devastation of the Bordelais vineyards during the closing decades of the last century, one discovers that the areas where the vines suffered the least were those where they had been planted in a sandy soil. Now we come to the crux of the matter: on account of this sandy soil in eastern Washington, it has been possible to plant the original European vines and not the usual grafts onto American root stocks. It would appear that this planting of original vines is to continue because the incidence of phylloxera is not expected.

What a prospect this raises! When these Washington vines have reached proper maturity, how fascinating it will be to compare their produce with that of the same varietals from grafted stocks!

The same situation applies to the vineyards of Oregon, where apparently there is only one grower who is planting grafted vines, and only on an experimental basis. It is hoped that the well drained slopes of the Oregon vineyards, together with a kind of sandy loam soil, will also provide immunity. This is not unique, of course, because one or two wineries such as Callaway in California have been planted with ungrafted French vines. There is no space here to mention the names of all the 27 Oregon wineries but among those which exhibited at the 1980 Festival were Amity, Cote des Colombe, Elk Cove, Eyrie, Hillcrest, Knudson Erath, Oak Knoll, Ponzi, Siskiyou, Sokol Blosser and Tualatin.

The bulk of the wine from the Pacific Northwest now on the market has been made from young vines of under ten years and, as is well known, under normal circumstances vines do not begin to produce really good grapes until they are at least seven years old, and thereafter the quality continues to improve. Thus as the vines mature over this decade, the progress of the produce of these states of the Pacific Northwest should be worth watching. What a challenge it must be to the growers where the future of the vine is still to be revealed!

No one with such a brief acquaintance as mine can write with authority on the wines of the Pacific Northwest, but as I had the honour to be invited to act as one of the judges at the 1980 Festival, I did at least have an opportunity to taste quite a wide range of presumably the best of them.

The Festival was held under the auspices of the Enological Society of the Pacific Northwest, the brainchild of the remarkable Dorothea Checkley. Founded only six years ago, there are no less than 3,500 members mainly from the state of Washington, a good example of the refreshing enthusiasm for wine which has developed in the U.S.A.

As this wine growing region has increased in stature and production, the number of wines to be judged has increased annually and at this sixth festival in 1980 a record figure of 57 examples was reached. The varietals included *sauvignon blanc*, Late or special Harvest *riesling*, dry and medium *riesling*,

Open White, *merlot*, Open Red, *pinot noir*, *cabernet sauvignon*, *gewürztraminer* dry and medium and of course *chardonnay*.

The other judges were Professor Maynard Amerine, Professor Walter Eggenberger from Wadenswil, Switzerland, Joseph Heitz, wine maker, Robert Finigan, editor of his *Private Guide to Wines*, Mary Ann Graf, wine consultant and wine maker, and Charles Olken, co-editor *Connoisseurs Guide to California Wine*. The tasting was held in the Faculty Club of the University; from where the superb views proved almost too great an attraction – San Francisco may be more spectacular, but the general scenery of Seattle is surely more impressive.

The actual Festival took place in the ideal setting of the Pacific Science Centre, originally constructed for the World Fair of 1962, and although the weather in Seattle may be no better than that of London, it certainly did its best for us on the evening of 25 August. No less than 30 different growers and/or merchants were displaying their wares and generously providing tastings. The tasting was followed by an excellent buffet supper, and when one considers that virtually 2,000 visitors had to be organised and fed, the mind boggles at the efficiency of the administration which managed all this entirely with the aid of volunteers.

It is impossible here to comment on all the medal winners, even those which won a gold, but there were one or two which were particularly impressive, primarily perhaps the 1978 Ice Wine of Chateau Ste. Michelle, good enough to stand up proudly against its counterparts from Germany. Another outstanding effort from the same winery was the Blanc de Noir Brut sparkling and how refreshing to find it was not called champagne!

A disappointment for me personally were the *pinot noirs*, in view of what has been written earlier on in this article, I had expected more of them. By contrast, the *chardonnays*, of which there were 13 entries, were so good, the judges had to retaste some in order to sort them out more thoroughly. Two which gained gold medals came from the Ste. Chapelle winery, a 1978 made from Washington grapes and a 1978 made from grapes from Idaho. Besides the two golds, these *chardonnays* also gained six bronzes. This result leads one to wonder if the *chardonnays* could be one of the more successful varietals of this region. All is so new here, the growers are still assessing which vines to plant and where.

Over the past 15 years I have been in the happy position to witness the change in northern California from in most instances pretty ordinary quality to the remarkable results of the present day. With the same technical advantages available and certainly the same drive and enthusiasm as their Californian contemporaries, there appears to be no reason why these vineyard proprietors of the Pacific Northwest should not succeed equally well. There is of course a difference of soil and climate, both of supreme importance, but perhaps the cooler climate in the north could ultimately prove more favourable. Who can tell. Only time and experience will provide the answer!

XI Bordeaux, October 1980

It had been raining, but the sun was shining at Merignac airport, although that was more or less the last we were to see of it for almost two weeks, not a good omen for yet another late vintage. Our home for the next two weeks was to be the 'pavilion' at La Mission-Haut-Brion and there for lunch besides our hosts Françoise and Francis Dewavrin, was the editor of the Bordeaux newspaper, *Le Sud Ouest*.

With ripe figs and Parma ham, we enjoyed a nice bottle of 1968 Laville Haut-Brion; the bouquet was well developed and while not a big wine it had a pleasant flavour. It was a surprise to find anything so agreeable from such a deplorable vintage. The red wines were the 1969 La Tour Haut-Brion, fairly full-bodied and not at all bad for this somewhat ordinary year, followed by a first-rate bottle of the 1959 La Mission-Haut-Brion.

Our hosts had arranged what they called a light supper, but even so there were three courses! The 1966 Laville Haut-Brion was definitely finer than the 1969 served alongside, having more depth and personality. This was followed by two red wines. The first, 1969 Simard, Saint-Emilion (for comparison with the 1969 we had had for lunch), provided another pleasant surprise, for generally speaking 1969 was only a mediocre year for Saint-Emilion. The second wine, the 1962 La Tour Haut-Brion, was remarkable and has kept better than most 1962s, many of which, sad to relate, are now on the decline.

Tasting with Henri Lagardère
Tuesday 7 October

Wine	Characteristics
1978 Laville Haut-Brion (bottled April 1979)	A fresh youthful bouquet and although very young shows considerable promise. We did not try any of the 1978 reds for owing to recent bottling they had not recovered from the disturbance.
1979 La Tour Haut-Brion	A fine dark colour, the bouquet rich and deep. A delightful full, rounded wine with plenty of tannin. This should be ready to drink around 1988 and by then should make an attractive bottle.
1979 La Mission-Haut-Brion	Good dark colour with an elegant bouquet, more distinction than the 1979 La Tour. A fine well bred wine, less robust perhaps than La Tour Haut-Brion, but with more finesse and breeding. This too should make a good bottle in due course.

It seems 1979 is turning out to be a good all-round vintage for the red Graves, whereas the same cannot be universally said of 1978. In 1978 it was mainly the leading vineyards which were successful; they were helped by the mass of pebbles (such a notable feature in the finer Graves vineyards) which had retained the heat of the sun during the night, whereas among the lesser ones where there are relatively few stones, the cold earth did not assist the ripening in the same manner. This fact may partly account for my disappointment when tasting the Médocain *petits châteaux* a year before, but another important reason in that particular case was over-production.

A tasting of three vintages each from Châteaux Cos d'Estournel, Lynch-Bages, Léoville-Las-Cases, Petit-Village, Figeac and Domaine de Chevalier was being planned for November for the Circle of Wine Writers at the Ritz Hotel in London, as well as for the Masters of Wine and the Guild of Sommeliers. Bruno Prats, the owner of Cos d'Estournel and for this year the president of the C.I.V.B., had invited Madame Jacqueline Duffour (public relations) Thierry Manoncourt (Figeac), Monsieur Delon (Leoville-Las-Cases), and Jean-Paul Cazes (Lynch-Bages) to lunch to discuss the arrangements. These are two of the wines he offered his guests.

Lunch with Bruno Prats

Wine	Characteristics
1934 Cos d'Estournel	A good dark colour, nice fruit on the nose and if on the dry side, as is not unexpected for this vintage, it had kept remarkably well.
1921 Cos d'Estournel	Here was a real surprise. We were asked to guess the vintage and I felt I managed a fair bracket with either 1924 or 1920. The bouquet certainly showed some age, but this wine was delicious, altogether attractive with the lovely sweetness so typical of its vintage. It is so long since I had tasted a 1921 that I had forgotten the special charm.

While discussing the 1977 vintage, the opinion expressed was that it was better than expected, on the light side of course and with an occasional trace of bitterness caused by unripe grapes. At best 1977 could be of a quality similar to 1973, but that may be over-optimistic. The 1977 La Mission-Haut-Brion which I tasted later had quite a pretty colour and although correct, was on the weak side; the taste was agreeable none the less. It should be ready for drinking around 1983 or 1984.

The Dewavrins had invited some friends for what transpired to be a *grand diner*. The Bruno Prats, Alexis Lichine, and Eugène and Monique Borie of Ducru-Beaucaillou. The prospects for the 1980 vintage were of course mentioned and the outlook was gloomy. 1980 was to be the fourth late vintage in a row; good weather was needed more than ever because the grapes were more unripe than usual, especially the *cabernet sauvignons*. In any case, the sap was no longer rising so freely in the vines and that also hindered further maturity.

Francis said he intended to commence picking his white grapes on 9 October, just as well in view of the downpours of rain that were prevailing. If nothing else, the grapes were at least healthy and since the weather was so cool, under such circumstances there was less fear than usual of the dreaded *pourriture*.

The wines at that meal were splendid. First of all we compared two successful vintages for white Bordeaux.

Dinner with the Dewavrins	*Wine*	*Characteristics*
	1966 Laville Haut-Brion	A lovely pale colour, youthful both on the nose and palate, astonishingly fresh for a 14 year old.
	1959 Laville Haut-Brion	A pale golden colour, a softer and perhaps sweeter bouquet, older of course, but great quality, great breeding and we found it difficult to decide which we liked best.
	1961 Ducru-Beaucaillou	(In honour of the Bories.) A fine dark colour, that lovely and so distinctive bouquet of 1961 and a delightful flavour. When younger I remember this particular wine had had its ups and downs, perhaps too much had been expected of it. Anyway, having sown its wild oats, it has now settled down splendidly into aristocratic maturity.
	1959 La Tour Haut-Brion	Dark colour, a full bouquet and a full-bodied wine, but for me its perfection was marred by a little acidity at the finish.
	1955 Cos d'Estournel	(A compliment to the Prats.) A good dark colour and a big fruity wine. This is clearly one of the good 1955s and that cannot be said for all of that vintage which did not really live up to original expectation.
	1947 La Mission-Haut-Brion	(Magnum.) Not dissimilar from the Cheval-Blanc 1947, one of the great wines of this century, a dark colour, a superb Graves bouquet, with a truly remarkable rich flavour, words cannot do justice to this masterpiece.

Wednesday 8 October

It rained all night – oh dear, oh dear! And it went on raining most of the day. Before leaving England we had arranged a rendezvous with Eddie and Meg Penning-Rowsell at the office of Jean-Pierre Moueix at Libourne. This meeting was to compare the 1978 and 1979 vintages for the districts of Saint-Emilion and Pomerol and from a first glance it was evident that the 1979s had a better colour. The colour of the 1978s was quite good, but that of 1979 much, much darker, in fact almost black.

Wine	*Characteristics*	*My points*
Saint-Emilion 1979		
Fonroque	Very dark colour, pleasant bouquet, medium body, a lack maybe of some generosity, not bad though.	13/20
Moulin du Cadet	Very dark colour, nice nose, a fuller, rounder wine than the Fonroque, will make a nice bottle.	16/20
Belair	Colour dark purple! A full attractive bouquet, medium body with plenty of breeding, but preferred the Moulin du Cadet.	15/20
Magdelaine	Very dark colour, a fine well bred bouquet, delightful flavour, excellent quality, this stood out from the others.	17/20
Pomerol		
La Grave Trigant de Boisset	Colour almost black, an attractive bouquet, medium body, but plenty of fruit. Well made with a pleasing finish and may be ready relatively early.	15/20

It has been fascinating to watch how the quality of the wine from this *château* improves as the vines grow older. For a long time La Grave Trigant had been neglected, and it was in a poor state when Jean-Pierre Moueix bought the property some years ago. He gave it to his son Christian who had to undertake extensive replanting. Rehabilitation of a vineyard takes a very long time, but now that good husbandry is assured all that is needed are older vines, which only time can provide. The potential is there for I remember with nostalgia the lovely wine this particular vineyard produced in 1929, 1945 and 1947.

Wine	Characteristics	My points
1979 vintage		
Latour-Pomerol	Colour black, a full fruity bouquet, altogether more full-bodied than the La Grave Trignant, with more power and more stuffing.	16/20
Clos l'Eglise	A full fruity bouquet, a different flavour, but attractive none the less. A big wine with plenty of character.	14/20
La Fleur-Pétrus	Black colour, a fine well bred bouquet, still very closed up, but underneath well rounded and full bodied. Still plenty of tannin to lose.	16 plus/20
Certan de May	Black colour, attractive bouquet, a decided but very pleasant taste, lots of character and a different style of wine. Should make a delightful bottle. Some tannin but not excessive.	16/20
Trotanoy	Very dark colour, fine well bred bouquet, still very backward, nevertheless rich and rounded, excellent quality.	17/20
1978 vintage		
Saint-Emilion Fonroque	Good colour, nice bouquet, sound but lacks the charm of the 1979 and has a relatively poor finish.	12/20
Moulin du Cadet	Good colour, nice nose, not a big wine, good flavour and finished well.	14/20
Belair	Good colour, nice nose, medium body, nothing special.	13/20
Magdelaine	Good colour and bouquet, well bred, attractive flavour and a wine of some distinction. All the same not so good as the 1979.	15/20
Pomerol		
La Grave Trigant de Boisset	Medium colour, agreeable bouquet, much lighter than the 1979 and with less depth.	12/20
Latour-Pomerol	Fairly dark colour, more bouquet here and a fuller and more rounded wine, rather good.	15/20
Clos l'Eglise	Dark colour, nice bouquet, not a big wine but well bred and well balanced.	13/20
La Fleur-Pétrus	Medium colour, nice nose, not a big wine and could be richer, attractive nevertheless.	14/20
Certan de May	Dark colour, a different but attractive bouquet, medium body, richer than the others, a well bred wine.	15/20

Trotanoy	Very dark colour, not quite so big as in the great years but attractive and well balanced.	16/20
	N.B. The points given to all the above had to be somewhat restrained in order to allow room for the greater wines to follow.	

Les grands seigneurs 1978 vintage

Ausone	Colour almost black, delightful bouquet, very good fruit and flavour, fine if not exceptional quality.	17/20
Cheval-Blanc	Black colour, splendid bouquet, a lovely lingering smell and a huge mouthful of flavour. Still considerable tannin.	18/20
Pétrus	Very attractive bouquet, not such a big wine as usual, but has heaps of flavour.	18 plus/20

1979 vintage

Ausone	Lovely dark colour, a delightful bouquet, not massive but elegant and well-bred nevertheless.	17 plus/20
Cheval-Blanc	Lovely dark colour, fine bouquet, a big mouthful of wine. This will make an excellent bottle.	18 plus/20
Pétrus	Colour almost black, delightful nose but still a little closed up, full-bodied though with a glorious flavour.	19/20

This experience confirmed an impression gained from previous tastings that for Saint-Emilions and certainly for Pomerol the 1979s are superior to the 1978s.

We had all been invited to Château Videlot for lunch where Jean-Pierre Moueix thoroughly spoilt us with, just as a starter, a magnum of the already fabulous Château Pétrus 1971, followed by the same wine but of the 1961 vintage, a very rare bird indeed. The colour was beautifully dark, the bouquet superb; what a wonderful wine – no wonder it is considered one of the very best, if not indeed the best, of this magnificent vintage. We all felt greatly honoured.

Château Cissac
Friday 19 October

At Château Cissac Louis Vialard and his son Pascal had prepared an extensive tasting of the *crus bourgeois* of the 1979 vintage. Unlike the previous vintage of 1978 when so many of the *crus bourgeois* and *petits châteaux* were disappointing, compared with the finer growths, whatever weaknesses the lesser growths of 1979 may have they appear to be more regular.

Les crus bourgeois of 1979: blind tasting

Wine	Characteristics	My points
Landat *Haut-Médoc*	Quite a pretty bouquet, like a whiff of good tobacco, fairly light, but quite pleasant, marred by a trace of acidity, but should develop early.	11/20
Lamothe *Cissac*	A nice clarety nose, considerably more fruit and body than the Landat.	13/20

Patache d'Aux *Médoc*	A pleasantly scented bouquet, good fruit and flavour, still considerable tannin.	14/20
Phélan-Ségur *Saint-Estèphe*	Medium colour, good bouquet, a rounded wine with a hint of sweetness and a decidedly individual taste.	14/20
Lanessan *Haut-Médoc*	Deep colour, bouquet slightly different but good nevertheless. Heaps of flavour and body, excellent quality, should make a good bottle.	19/20
Malescases *Haut-Médoc*	Deep colour, pleasing bouquet, good fruit and body with a slightly different flavour.	13/20
La Tour-du-Mirail *Cissac*	Pleasant bouquet, lighter than some of the others with some tannin.	13/20
Cissac *Cissac*	Deep colour, full bouquet, not a big wine, well made though and a nice taste.	16/20
Capbern Gasqueton *Saint-Estèphe*	Attractive bouquet, good flavour, well balanced and finished well.	14.5/20
Les Ormes-de-Pez *Saint-Estèphe*	Deep colour, very fruity bouquet, medium body, but lots of flavour and a good finish.	18/20
Potensac *Médoc*	Good colour, good bouquet, a serious wine with heaps of fruit and flavour, first rate quality for this category.	18.5/20
Tronquoy-Lalande *Saint-Estèphe*	Dark colour, bouquet with plenty of character, full of charm. Less tannin than some. Also first rate.	18.5/20
Gloria *Saint-Julien*	Dark colour, very good bouquet, a different style and flavour, plenty of tannin and well made.	16/20
Maucaillou *Moulis*	Medium colour, bouquet good but still closed up, full and fruity with quite a distinctive character, good.	18/20
Chasse-Spleen *Moulis*	Good colour, fine bouquet, an attractive well made wine, plenty of tannin.	16/20
Poujeaux *Moulis*	Deep colour, fine bouquet, a well made, attractive wine with a lot of tannin.	17/20
Labégorce *Margaux*	Medium colour, and elegant bouquet, light and charming.	17/20
La Tour-du-Mons *Margaux*	Medium colour, good nose, plenty of fruit and well made.	16/20

The general impression was good, better than that obtained from a tasting of similar wines of the 1978 vintage in October 1979. Even the lesser wines such as Landat had their attraction. The colour in general was good and on the whole these *crus bourgeois* of 1979 have plenty of fruit and flavour. With no sharp points, they should mature reasonably early and be useful commercially. Of course the Lanessan stood out, but the Potensac and Tronquoy-Lalande were not far behind, likewise the Maucaillou and Les Ormes-de-Pez.

As elsewhere the picking of the 1980 vintage had started at Château Cissac, so with the Vialards we ate the same food as the *vendangeurs* and how good it was!

Château Cissac

Later while we were having tea with the Tesserons at Lafon-Rochet, Eddie and Meg Penning-Rowsell arrived in the pouring rain. The weather had deteriorated steadily throughout the week and this had been a day of veritable downpour. Finally in spite of their heavy waterproof clothing even the grape pickers were driven in. We went into the *chai* to taste the following.

Wine	Characteristics
Lafon-Rochet 1979	A fine dark colour, the bouquet almost sweet, good fruit and flavour and not too much tannin, so should develop fairly early.
Lafon-Rochet 1978	Good colour, nice nose and a pleasant flavour, but like so many 1978s was not showing at its best owing to recent bottling; nearly all proprietors seem to have bottled their 1978 vintage within the previous two months. It should nevertheless make a nice bottle some years hence.

We dined quietly at Pontet-Canet where we were to spend the weekend with Guy and Nicole Tesseron. The first wine was the light but attractive 1973 Pontet-Canet and it was followed by the 1960 Lafon-Rochet, the first wine Guy had made after he bought the vineyard. He said he had been ruthless in his selection when he assembled it and that probably accounts for how well this particular 1960 has lasted when most of that vintage began their decline some time ago. It was not of course a big wine, but there was lots of charm and elegance.

Guy Tesseron comes from a family of vineyard owners and distillers which for centuries has been established in the Cognac district. He is not 'a front man' but, based on Châteauneuf in Charente, he supplies the great cognac houses whose names are household words. There must be thousands of casks of the finest cognac lying in his widely distributed cellars.

Guy's guests have the rare privilege of tasting fabulous cognac which kept in barrel has never left his cellars, and that evening was no exception. Merely for comparison we were asked to compare two very famous vintages for cognac, the *Grande Champagne* of 1906 and 1900! They were different of course, but both utterly superb. Although the system had been abused, it was a sad day for the English connoisseur when the sale of vintage cognac was abolished.

Since it became a branded article, much of the fun has gone out of the search for fine cognac. When in the past *Grande Champagne* cognac was shipped in cask for maturing and eventual bottling by the leading British merchants, there used to be some expertise in deciding whether Avery's *Grand Champagne* 1934 was better than say Harvey's, for one could have come from Hine and the other from Delamain and so on. But now that has all gone and English early-landed cognac has become a *rara avis*.

I have known Guy for over 30 years and he has always been an ultra enthusiast for the wines of Bordeaux, especially those of the Médoc. At what must have been one of our first meetings I remember him saying his ambition was to be the owner of a *château* in the Médoc and now he has not one but three! Being a fanatic for quality, proprietors like him can only act as a good influence for the future of Bordeaux.

As usual, it had rained all night and was still coming down in torrents. Later on in the day, the wind got up in force, but did not drive off any rain. These must be some of the worst conditions during vintage time since the disaster of 1964. When rain is as heavy as this and is interspersed with warm spells of sunshine, there is always the danger of *pourriture*, especially among the *merlot* vines. This year the sunshine and warmth were conspicuous by their absence so, as a poor consolation, the risk of rotten grapes was lessened. Indeed whatever else one could say of the inclement weather, at least the grapes remained in a sound condition.

In spite of the adverse conditions, the picking had started at Pontet-Canet and elsewhere, and we watched the first loads of *merlot* grapes being brought in to the press. It came as a surprise to see them looking so well, but of course the unripe bunches had been discarded out among the vines. When there is *pourriture* around it can be detected when the tubs are tipped over into the press, and a kind of smoke arises from them; happily there was no sign of that!

Our lunch that day was a special occasion because Edouard and Jeanne-Marie Cruse had been invited. Now retired, Edouard always represented the very best of the Bordeaux trade. I first met him before the war and renewing the acquaintance in 1947 had led to a firm friendship ever since. At the risk of repetition, it was he who in 1947 opened my eyes to the possibilities of the wines from the Pomerol district, wines which before the war were little known and little appreciated in Britain.

Perhaps one of the reasons for the lack of interest in these wines (which regrettably seems still to persist) may lie in the fact that the traditional firms which had supplied the British market over the centuries, were more interested in the Médoc, where some of them also owned *châteaux* whose produce they were naturally anxious to promote. The house of Cruse was a case in point, for at that time they were the owners of both Rausan-Ségla and Pontet-Canet as well as lesser vineyards such as Laujac and Taillan. Another promising supplier to the English market had been Barton & Guestier, responsible for the distribution of both Léoville and Langoa-Barton.

Cruse however had also built up an important outlet for Pomerol in the Scandinavian countries, a style of wine popular in those cold climates. Another source of supply for the wines of Pomerol was Hanappier Peyrelongue, now also no longer independent, and they and Cruse formed a useful source of supply while I was endeavouring to build up the name of Harvey's for table wine. When I joined that firm at the end of 1945, Harvey's was known only for port and sherry, especially the former; it took me a good 15 years to establish a reputation for table wine as well, but it was worth the effort!

So far as I know Pétrus did not appear on the lists of English merchants in pre-war days. I had of course heard of this legendary wine (as one had of *Salon* champagne) and later tried hard to buy some of the 1947 vintage, but failed because all my sources of supply were based on Bordeaux and not Libourne, and I was insufficiently well informed in those days to know where to look! Finally, I managed to lay my hands on the 1949 vintage, but had no exclusivity because I found that our Bristol competitor, Ronald Avery, had done the same thing. It may seem strange now when Pétrus is so well known, but I believe those were the first two firms to import any after the war.

To return to the Médoc, a famous wine of this century was the 1929

[171]

Pontet-Canet, one of the best if not the best of that outstanding vintage, and according to my recollection better than any of the first growths – even Latour! Many are the memorable bottles I have shared with the hospitable Christian or Edouard Cruse during my annual visits to the *château*. One of Guy Tesseron's good natured complaints, since his purchase of the property, is that Edouard had drunk up all the 1929. But who could blame him? I know I can't because I had the privilege to share some myself! Even so, for that lunch Guy produced two gems from the private cellar.

Wine	Characteristics
Pontet-Canet 1961	A fine dark colour with that heavenly and so typical 1961 bouquet, a wonderful flavour and a glorious bottle, still at its very best.
Pontet-Canet 1945	Dark colour, another splendid bouquet and what a taste that wine had! It must be at its summit now because all the excessive tannin of its vintage had disappeared. A joy to drink.

The bouquet of the two above wines almost bowled one over when they were poured. When Pontet-Canet is good, it is very, very good.

Sunday 12 October
At long last the storms had subsided and a strong north wind was drying the grapes. It was sufficiently fine to walk through the vineyard, which must be one of the largest in the *commune* of Pauillac, and although we looked for signs of *pourriture* we could find no traces of it. In spite of the weather the grapes were still in good condition.

Other interesting wines tasted over that weekend were:

Wine	Characteristics
1970 Lafon-Rochet	Good colour, bouquet and flavour. The tannin has all gone but there is still some acidity to lose.
1939 Pontet-Canet	Medium colour, pleasant bouquet, elegant with some finesse. Considering how light the 1939 vintage had been and with no pretensions to great quality, it was astonishing how well this bottle had kept.
1971 Lafon-Rochet	Good colour and bouquet with a nice flavour, tasting much better than the 1970 at the moment.
1964 Pontet-Canet	Medium colour, attractive bouquet, not a big wine and ready to drink now, but not I imagine with much future!

Monday 13 October
At last a fine day! The strong wind had dried up the grapes so the growers were facing the *vendange* with renewed confidence. It is not often that one encounters a group of young English people picking grapes, but apparently about a hundred of them had arrived on vacation work.

We called on Alexis Lichine at Le Prieuré-Lichine to taste his 1979 vintage; it showed considerable promise and he had every right to be pleased. From there we returned north to Ducru-Beaucaillou where we had been bidden for lunch. We found Eugéne Borie in his cellar tasting his latest vintages together with Professor Emile Peynaud, the oenologist who has done so much to improve the quality at many a Bordeaux *château*.

Eugéne now has no less than five properties under his wing. One of them, belonging to his wife Monique, had always sold direct to the Co-Operative of Listrac, but henceforth was to be marketed under its own label, Duclausean. Another is the small vineyard he had recently purchased in Saint-Julien and named Borie-Lalande. Then of course there is his sister's well known Haut-Batailley, his recently purchased Grand-Puy-Lacoste and the admirable Ducru-Beaucaillou. There should be plenty to keep him and his two sons fully occupied!

The 1979 Duclausean, Listrac was of lighter calibre than the others, but in Eugéne's opinion that wine and his Borie-Lalande have both been more successful in 1979 than in 1978. But the three classified growths were better in 1978.

The 1976 Ducru-Beaucaillou at lunch was unexpectedly forward, another proof of how early it is possible to drink this charming vintage. Whether the 1976s will eventually make 'old bones' is another matter, but many of them are already very nice to drink. Then followed the 1961 Ducru-Beaucaillou which was as delicious as it had been a week before at La Mission-Haut-Brion. 1955 Haut-Batailley was served with the cheese, a nice well made wine and better than usual for its vintage. Eugéne's second son Bruno, who is at present doing his *service militaire*, joined us for lunch, having been given special leave to help his father with the harvest.

Château Latour
Tuesday 14 October

As usual there had been rain during the night and when we arrived at Château Latour we saw all work among the vines had been discontinued although this was to resume later when eventually the sun emerged from the clouds.

An important tasting of the 1979 vintage had been prepared for us and the scene was enlivened by the presence of Lord Snowdon who, accompanied by a team of photographers, had come from England to capture the aspects of the vintage at Latour.

1979 red Bordeaux, tasted October 1980

Wine	Characteristics	My points
de Pez	Very good colour, nice nose, medium body, good flavour.	14/20
Les Ormes-de-Pez	Very good colour, quite a good nose, plenty of body.	13/20
Gloria	Very good colour, nose not developed, but delightfully round wine.	16/20
Lanessan	Very good colour, very fruity bouquet, good body and a nice finish.	14/20
Poujeaux	Very good colour, very good nose, delightful flavour, special character, some tannin.	14/20
Chasse-Spleen	Very good colour and bouquet, rounded and well made.	14/20
Bel Air, Marquis d'Aligre	Medium colour, fine nose, full of charm and character.	14/20

Labégorce-Zédé	Medium colour, nice nose, plenty of fruit but not showing well.	11/20
Meyney	Medium colour, very good bouquet, plenty of fruit and charm.	14/20
Talbot	Colour very dark, very good full nose, has plenty of fruit and rather good.	15/20
Palmer	Very dark colour, a most attractive bouquet, a big rounded wine, best so far.	16/20
Brane-Cantenac	Medium colour, distinguished bouquet, well bred but rather sharp finish.	13/20
Rauzan-Gassies	Medium colour, distinguished nose, quite a good flavour.	13/20
Malescot	Dark colour, full fruity nose, good fruit and flavour, lot of tannin.	14/20
La Lagune	Very dark colour, delightful bouquet, a lovely full wine, packed with charm.	17/20
Montrose	Dark colour, attractive bouquet, attractive and well bred.	15/20
Cos d'Estournel	Very dark colour, a fuller bouquet and a lovely full wine tasting of blackcurrants.	17/20
Calon-Ségur	Medium colour, quite a nice nose, good fruit but thinner.	13/20
Lynch-Bages	Very dark colour, good bouquet, good fruit and well made.	15/20
Pichon-Comtesse	Very dark colour, good full bouquet, pleasantly full-bodied, good quality.	17/20
Pichon-Baron	Dark colour, full fruity nose, good fruit.	14/20
Grand-Puy-Lacoste	Very dark colour, nice bouquet, a big rich, complete wine.	16/20
Clerc-Milon	Very dark colour, well bred nose, good fruit, well made but lacks charm.	13/20
Léoville-Las-Cases	Very dark colour, distinguished bouquet, good fruit and flavour, well bred.	16/20
Léoville-Poyferré	Dark colour, full bouquet, quite full-bodied, quality fair.	15/20
Les Forts de Latour	Very dark colour, quite a pretty nose, medium body, some acidity to lose.	15/20
Ducru-Beaucaillou	Good colour, deep bouquet, not a big wine but lot of character.	16/20
Beychevelle	Very dark colour, deep bouquet, medium body, but good flavour.	15/20
Gruaud-Larose	Dark colour, full bouquet, not a big wine but has plenty of charm.	16/20

The top growths

Latour	Lovely dark colour, nice nose, full bodied, good flavour, lot of tannin, very good.	18.5/20
Lafite	Lovely colour, fine scented bouquet, good fruit, full-bodied but some acidity to lose.	17.5/20

Tasting Ch. Latour 1979

Mouton-Rothschild	Very dark colour, very nice nose, masses of fruit and flavour, also some acidity to lose.	17/20
Margaux	Very dark colour, not much bouquet yet, rounded and packed with flavour, trace of acidity, some tannin.	18.5/20
Haut-Brion	Very dark colour, very nice bouquet, full-bodied delightful flavour.	18.5/20
Pétrus	Dark colour, different very nice nose, full-bodied and round with a nice finish.	18/20
Ausone	Dark colour, very good bouquet, full-bodied lots of fruit and flavour.	17/20
Cheval-Blanc	Dark colour, full fruity bouquet, rounded, smooth and delightful.	18/20

Lunching afterwards with Clive Gibson, the President of the *domaine*, we had three interesting wines.

Wine	*Characteristics*
1973 Les Forts de Latour	It has always been the policy to give this second wine from the estate some age in bottle before releasing it to the public. The 1973 had only recently been put on the market so it was interesting to see how it was faring, in fact it was the first time I had tasted it since 1974 when about a year old. The colour was good for the vintage and although still a little firm, the flavour was fairly full and typically Pauillac. It can be enjoyed now but will continue to improve.
1962 Latour	When so many of the formerly delightful 1962s have begun to go downhill, this Latour, a splendid example of its vintage must be at its best now.
1952 Latour	Good colour, beautiful well developed bouquet, a magnificent full-bodied wine. Here is an example of a really late developer. Many years ago, I had bought two or three cases, but fearing it would never come round had sold them and worse still it seems had advised Clive Gibson's father to do likewise, *mea culpa*!

Château d'Issan

Marguerite Cruse had invited Prue and me to spend the night at Château d'Issan in the *commune* of Margaux. I think it is safe to say the two most beautiful houses in the Médoc are those of Beychevelle and d'Issan, but the latter with its moat is of an earlier period. A salient feature of this property is the old *chai* whose roof is supported by splendid wooden beams, reminiscent of some of the famous 16th-century buildings still surviving in England.

Between the wars this whole estate had been sadly neglected and during the 1939/45 war the vineyard had been allowed to dwindle to the equivalent of about 12 acres. The house, a historic landmark built in the 17th century, had become almost a ruin. This may be the reason why one so seldom encounters old vintages of Château d'Issan. The property was purchased after the war by Emanuel and Marguerite Cruse, through whose foresight and painstaking effort the vineyard had been replanted to its present size of 60 acres.

Marguerite and her son Lionel had invited an attractive couple to meet us for dinner, the recently appointed English Consul-General and his wife, Mr. and Mrs. Glaize, and as may be expected the wine was very good.

Wine	Characteristics
Château d'Issan 1973	Dark colour for its year and with much more body and depth than usual. This is recognised to be one of the successes of this light and variable vintage.
Château d'Issan 1961	Dark colour, a wonderful bouquet and equally fine flavour. This 1961 has probably reached its best now, but should remain on its plateau as it were, for some time to come.

Lionel had reserved another *bonne bouche* for the end of the meal, the fabulous 1937 Château Climens. Although the colour was now a dark amber and the wine had lost some of its sugar, it was still a gem and altogether enjoyable. 1937 was an outstanding vintage both for Sauternes and Barsac, and the 1937s were probably at their best in the immediate post war period continuing until around the middle sixties. I always found it difficult to make up my mind which one I preferred, the 1937 d'Yquem or the Climens – the elegant but lighter Barsac or the richer Sauternes. Both of them had a great reputation and each its own adherents.

Wednesday 15 October

For almost three-quarters of a century the Bordelais growers had suffered from adverse conditions. In consequence the vineyards had become run down and the wine making equipment was years out of date. So much so, that few businessmen wished to outlay capital in a money-losing vineyard which would constitute a drain on resources no matter how glamorous it might sound.

The tide did not really begin to turn until around 1960 and it has taken a long time for the result to become visible. Possibly the most spectacular example of the change was the rehabilitation of Château Latour in 1964 with, at that time, the controversial installation of thermostatically controlled stainless steel fermenting vats. Since then other properties in the Médoc have followed suit and it is encouraging to see how up to date some of the leading *châteaux* are becoming. Pichon-Comtesse is but one example where modern equipment has been installed and here at d'Issan a whole range of thermostatically controlled stainless steel vats were being used for the first time with the 1980 vintage.

With justifiable pride, Marguerite and Lionel also showed us the splendid new *chai* for housing the wine in barrel – instead of being merely functional, as so many were in the past, this is a place of beauty.

Wine	Characteristics
1979 Château d'Issan	Good colour and an attractive bouquet, medium body with a very nice taste. This well bred wine should make a nice bottle in the fairly near future.

1978 Château d'Issan (bottled late June)	Very nice nose which is beginning to develop, firm full-flavoured and good quality.
1977 Château d'Issan	Quite a good colour, pleasant bouquet and plenty of fruit, but still some acidity to lose.
1976 Château d'Issan	Good colour, delightful bouquet, good fruit and flavour, also some acidity to lose. May therefore need another two or three years to develop.

Emile Castéja and his son Philippe were awaiting us at Borie-Manoux in Bordeaux where they had arranged an extensive tasting of their 1978 and 1979 vintages. Apart from their own considerable range of *châteaux* whose produce they distribute themselves, this firm has a worldwide sale of a house red and white wine called Beau Rivage. Since wine has become so expensive in French restaurants when travelling, these are what I usually drink myself!

Wine	Characteristics
1979 Chapelle de la Trinitè *Saint-Emilion*	Good colour and bouquet with plenty of fruit.
1979 Baret *red Graves*	Good colour, a nice bouquet, medium body, still a little acidity to lose.
1978 Baret *red Graves*	Good colour and bouquet and a very nice flavour, preferred this to the 1979 vintage.
1979 Haut-Bages-Monpelou *Pauillac*	Good colour, bouquet and taste but also a trace of acidity.
1978 Haut-Bages-Monpelou *Pauillac*	A pretty colour, a rounder firmer wine than the 1979 and seemed better.
1979 Batailley *Pauillac*	Very dark colour, a delightful full bouquet, pleasing fruit and flavour.
1978 Batailley *Pauillac*	Good dark colour, a fine bouquet, quite a big wine with lots of fruit and body, preferred this to the 1979.
1979 Domaine de l'Eglise *Pomerol*	Good colour, attractive bouquet, what a flavour too, packed with charm. Although the 1978 was also good, I preferred the 1979.
1979 Trottevieille *Saint-Emilion*	Medium colour, pleasant bouquet, not a big wine but has plenty of fruit and flavour.
1978 Trottevieille *Saint-Emilion*	Very dark colour, a lovely rich nose, a fine big wine full of fruit, a wine I would certainly buy.

Here was a further confirmation that the Saint-Emilions and Pomerols are finer than those of 1978.

By the time we had got back to La Mission-Haut-Brion, the Peppercorns, David and Serena, had arrived for what was to be a memorable lunch. Apart from the fine food, these were the wines – 1971 Pol Roger, Chardonnay was the aperitif.

Wine	Characteristics
1970 Laville Haut-Brion	Colour a pale golden, a delightful mature bouquet and it tasted equally well. Indeed it was so good I thought it must have reached its best, but our host Francis Dewavrin insisted it has still a long way to go!
1945 Laville Haut-Brion	The colour was a deep golden and although the bouquet was showing some age, it tasted very well. It is remarkable how well these fine dry white wines will keep.
1976 La Tour Haut-Brion	Very good colour, typical Graves bouquet, the flavour quite rich and certainly attractive and it finished nicely. In spite of its youth already enjoyable and will of course continue to improve.
1967 La Mission-Haut-Brion	A dark colour, sweet charming bouquet and it tasted equally well. 1967 was an irregular vintage, but this must be one of the better ones. If anything, the red Graves of 1967 appear to be more successful than the Médocs.
1964 La Mission-Haut-Brion	Dark colour, delightful bouquet, quite rich and full-bodied, fine quality.
1924 La Mission-Haut-Brion	Good colour, turning a little brown. An old but still sweet bouquet, heaps of fruit and flavour with a charming sweet finish. Still very good when most of its contemporaries gave up the struggle ages ago.

At supper that evening we tried the 1966 La Mission-Haut-Brion. A fine Graves bouquet, most of the tenacious 1966 tannin has disappeared, leaving nevertheless a firm wine with a distinctive Graves taste. This should continue to improve. At least that is what we all say of this 1966 vintage which has become a bit of a problem. It is hoped that this firmness, which is pretty well general, will not outlast the fruit.

Saint-Emilion
Thursday 16 October

The clerk of the weather is clearly doing his level best to destroy this vintage of 1980; it had rained steadily through the night and was to continue all day.

All picking of the grapes had been stopped when we arrived at Château Pavie in Saint-Emilion, a wonderful property on a steep hillside facing south and immediately across the valley from Château Ausone. In a way it is similar to Ausone because the fine cellar hewn into the rock, where the young wine is housed, was also a medieval quarry, whence the stone had been used to build the ancient town and ramparts of Saint-Emilion. The temperature in these old quarries is of course ideal for the maturing of young wine in barrel.

On account of its geographical configuration, this fine vineyard can be divided into parts, for it lies virtually on three levels. The best area, the plateau on top and the upper part of the steep hillside, is where the *merlot* vines are planted and the lower level, but still on the slope, is mainly devoted to *cabernet franc* and *cabernet sauvignon* vines. The proportion of vines planted corresponds to the classic admixture for the great vineyards of the district of Saint-Emilion, namely 55 per cent *merlot*, 25 per cent *cabernet franc* and 20 per cent *cabernet sauvignon*. From these vines there is an average annual production of some 14,000 cases.

The first records of vines on the hillsides of Ausone and Pavie date back as far as the fourth century and these it seems were the first vineyards to be planted in the area. Apart from the cellar in the old stone quarry already mentioned, there is the main building where the wine is fermented etc. and another for the storage of stock in bottle. It was in the main building that the proprietor, Jean Paul Valette, had set out his wine for the tasting in which I was joined by Patrick Danglade and Jean-François Moueix.

Château Pavie

Wine	Characteristics	My points
1979	Very dark, almost purple colour, the delightful bouquet which seems special to this vintage and a nice mouthful of flavour, rounded and easy to taste, should make an attractive bottle.	18/20
1978	Dark colour, a fine fairly rich bouquet, complete and well made, but seems to lack some of the 'fat' of the 1979.	16/20
1977	Medium colour, quite a pleasant bouquet, but of course lighter and thinner than the 1978; not bad though for its year.	15/20
1976	Quite a dark colour, an attractive bouquet, full, round and quite rich flavour, some tannin still to lose, nevertheless beginning to show well, a good wine here.	18.5/20
1975	Dark colour, a fine rich bouquet, still closed up but quite a powerful wine with heaps of fruit. Probably needs another five or more years to develop.	18/20
1971	Dark colour and a delightful bouquet already well developed. A big rich wine with a lovely finish and very easy to drink. Excellent now and will continue to improve, a fine example of Saint-Emilion.	19/20
1970	Dark colour, but with a tinge of brown, a pleasant rich nose, powerful but still closed up and at the moment lacking charm.	16/20
1967	Good colour, also touched with brown. Rich well developed bouquet, complete with plenty of flavour, typical of its year.	16/20
1966	Dark colour, good Saint-Emilion bouquet. As with most 1966s still firm and closed up, but it has lost its tannin and aggressiveness. Full, round and complete and should continue to improve.	16/20
1964	Good colour and a nice nose. Not a big wine but quite well made. Our host told us it had been matured for too long in old oak casks, i.e. for three years. *Note.* The use of new oak casks began on this estate with the 1964 vintage.	15/20
1961	Dark colour, a fairly rich bouquet, a powerful wine but one which should be drunk now. A good 1961, but not one of the great ones!	18/20

We enjoyed some of the above with our lunch which as usual at time of the year was the same as that of the *vendangeurs*. Proprietors have to put their best foot forward with the food they provide at harvest time. Picking the grapes is strenuous work and the pickers can be discriminating, to the extent that they are inclined to sell their labour where the meals are best!

In a succinct summing up of the vintages we had tasted, Jean François Moueix pointed out how noticeable was the general improvement in quality since the 1970 vintage (i.e. when Jean Paul Valette had assumed the responsibility of the vineyard). Indeed, the improvement from 1971 onwards highlighted the importance of the man in charge of any vineyard and especially so in the case of a leading one such as this.

Happily this tasting had not been at all tiring, so we were well prepared for the remarkable evening which lay before us at Domaine de Chevalier in Léognan as the guests of Claude and Monique Ricard. Claude is a gifted pianist and had intended to make music his career until he inherited this splendid property; it must have been very difficult to decide which career to follow, that of music or that of wine! To put us in the right receptive mood for the meal he played for us just before we went in for dinner.

It is all a matter of opinion, but generally accepted, that apart from the delicious white Haut-Brion of which so little is made (in consequence one seldom has an opportunity to enjoy it), the two finest vineyards available to the general public for white Bordeaux are those whose produce we were about to taste – the Domaine de Chevalier and Laville Haut-Brion.

Wine	Characteristics
1978 Domaine de Chevalier	Very pale colour, tremendous finesse both of bouquet and taste, truly *un grand seigneur*.
1978 Laville Haut-Brion	Very pale colour, a more perfumed bouquet, more honeyed and easier to taste than the slightly more backward, consequently more reserved, Domaine de Chevalier.
1976 Domaine de Chevalier	Pale colour, a fuller nose and body, than the 1978, clean, dry and aristocratic.
1976 Laville Haut-Brion	The colour a little more golden, a fuller bouquet with a splendid fragrant flavour.
1975 Domaine de Chevalier	A very pale colour, a fine distinguished bouquet, very dry and of great quality, the epitome of elegance and finesse.
1975 Laville Haut-Brion	Colour a pale golden, the bouquet richer and full of honey, although dry, a seemingly richer and sweeter, if one can so describe a dry wine.
1971 Domaine de Chevalier	Pale colour, not a pronounced bouquet, just a little honeyed perhaps. Quite dry, but definitely a little richer than the 1975 and the 1978 from this vineyard. There was a query over this particular bottle, the case having been purchased from a source where the storage may have been suspect.
1971 Laville Haut-Brion	Light golden colour, with a much more mature bouquet, richer in style but very dry in fact, with the delightful honeyed flavour so typical of this vineyard. A wine of considerable breeding.

Here is further evidence that the white Graves take longer than generally imagined to develop and the notes on this visit alone demonstrate how well they will keep.

The comparison of several vintages of these two very fine white Bordeaux proved both instructive and agreeable and, although of equal status, the two were totally different. It is no wonder there are such firm protagonists among the *cognoscenti* for each of these vineyards.

The difference could perhaps be summed up thus: the Domaine de Chevalier, which tends to keep its very pale colour, is perhaps a little more severe, nevertheless a true example of both elegance and breeding. It is no disparagement to say the colour of the Laville Haut-Brion is inclined to turn more golden as the wine ages. Its style is fuller and slightly richer with that hint of honey both on the bouquet and on the palate.

The cause of this difference between the style of these two examples of the finest white wine of Bordeaux may not lie so much in the difference of *communes*, although that may count to a certain extent for Talence is some distance away from Léognan and the soil must be different, but in the mix of the vines in the two vineyards. At Laville Haut-Brion there are some 60 per cent of *sémillon* vines and 40 per cent of *sauvignon blanc*. The complete reverse is the case at Domaine de Chevalier where the proportion is 60 per cent *sauvignon blanc* and 40 per cent *sémillon*! Perhaps the larger proportion of *sauvignon blanc* in Domaine de Chevalier accounts for its retaining its pale colour as it ages in bottle.

It was now the turn of the red wines. Although it does not occur frequently there are years when the quality and style of the wine made in the Graves district differs from that made in the Médoc. Admittedly it is a long time ago now but the most striking example occurred with the two good vintages of 1952 and 1953. The 1952s of the Médoc, with heaps of fruit, had excessive tannin and for years refused to develop and in fact only recently have they been fulfilling their early promise. As mentioned earlier on, I sold all my Latour 1952 despairing of its ever coming round and now of course it is magnificent! Whereas, from the very beginning, the 1953s of the Médoc were utterly charming but their span of life has been relatively brief. There are, of course, some attractive 1953 Médocs still around, but for this writer at any rate most of them have lost that magic so evident in their youth.

Strangely enough the reverse was the case with the red Graves, where the 1953s have outlived the 1952s.

Apart from the 1974 vintage, there were no noticeable differences during the seventies. But in the decade of the sixties 1969, 1967, and especially 1964, were more successful vintages for the red Graves – in fact 1964 was something rather special. We were now to see for ourselves how good two of these red Graves were.

Wine	Characteristics
1964 Domaine de Chevalier	Very good colour, still with a hint of purple, a delightful sweet bouquet, and a charming sweet wine which should continue to improve.
1964 La Mission-Haut-Brion	Dark colour, powerful Graves bouquet, a fine robust powerful wine, packed with fruit but which has by no means yet reached its best.

The generosity of our host was unlimited for there were still two red wines to follow, but both alas suffering from *anno domini*. Before the war the 1924 Haut-Brion had a tremendous reputation and was much sought after, but that bottle, at any rate, was dead and gone. The other, the 1921 Cos d'Estournel, the same wine we had enjoyed with Bruno Prats on the first day of this visit to Bordeaux, while good was not so splendid a bottle. In this case, with increasing age, the original sweetness and charm had clearly slipped away.

The following day we set off on our journey home and after two weeks of bad weather it was difficult not to feel apprehensive concerning the quality of this very late vintage. Fortunately the weather was to improve immediately after our departure and the rest of the crop was gathered in under quite good conditions. Indeed a vineyard proprietor in Saint-Emilion, who had delayed the picking of his grapes until the fine weather finally arrived, later on indicated he had been agreeably surprised by the quality of his new wine. Generally speaking though, it would be unwise to be unduly optimistic over this small crop harvested so late and not under the best of conditions.

After all that rain it is a wonder there was not widespread *pourriture* among the vines. The avoidance of disaster can be ascribed, at least to a certain extent, to the new mixture the growers had been using on their vines. One I know, who at first had viewed it with some scepticism, had to admit he was delighted with the result.

Possibly the salient point of this particular visit was the favourable manner in which, at a year old, the 1979 vintage was presenting itself. While the Médocs and red Graves of 1978 may have more depth or substance, as well as firmness, than the 1979s, there were definitely a few growers who preferred their 1979 vintage. In addition, the lesser Médocs of 1979 are certainly more regular than their equivalents of 1978, many of which are distinctly disappointing.

Already in these notes it has been mentioned that, although the finer vineyards among the red Graves of 1978 were successful, the selection of the lesser ones has to be treated with some caution. On the other hand, 1979 appears to be a much more regular all-round vintage for this district.

These are early days for prediction, but the greatest success of 1979 may lie beyond the river Dordogne where the 1979 Saint-Emilions, and particularly the Pomerols, undoubtedly have a better colour and more depth than they had in 1978. Indeed at the moment it looks as though the district of Pomerol will be flying the standard for the 1979 vintage. Whatever happens, with these two satisfactory vintages of 1978 and 1979, it would appear that this decade of the seventies has ended on a reasonably high note.

Tasting of fine Bordeaux wines at the Ritz Hotel, London. From left, Bruno Prats (Ch.-Cos d'Estournel), Emma Cazes (Ch.-Lynch-Bages), H. W., Claude Rickard (Domaine de Chevalier), Emma Broadbent, Thierry Manoncourt (Ch.-Figeac). Alastair MacKenzie in foreground.

XII Burgundy, February 1981

At Heathrow Airport there was a four hour delay on our Air France plane to Paris, and so, instead of reaching Burgundy that evening, we spent the night at the Hotel Paris et Poste in Sens, just south of Paris. All was not lost though because in view of the lateness of our arrival, we had telephoned ahead and an excellent platter of cold food was set out in our bedrooms together with a bottle of 1980 Beaujolais, the latter better than expected! I have visited this hotel a number of times and have never been disappointed.

As advisor to the Annabel Group, I was travelling with Jonathan Goedhuis who manages what must surely be one of the most attractive wine shops in the country, Birley & Goedhuis in the Fulham Road. The rest of the group includes the famous Annabel's in Berkeley Square, Mark's Club in Charles Street, W.1, and Harry's Bar in South Audley Street – all under the chairmanship of Mark Birley.

Under normal circumstances on such journeys one has to look mainly for the less expensive wines, but on this occasion we were to search for better quality to suit the demand of the above outlets. Even more unusual, we wanted mature wine ready to drink, and that made it all the more interesting.

The weather can be very cold in Burgundy at this time of the year and so it was, with snow all around. Luckily the sun was shining brightly so after an early start we were able to make up for lost time and keep our first appointment as planned with Monsieur Robert Ampeau in Meursault. The latter is a noted grower especially of white wine; but since owing to tax problems, he did not wish to sell his younger vintages, this suited us well.

Wine	Characteristics
Red Wine Auxey-Duresses 1972	Being on the light side the colour was not inspiring and in spite of a fairly rich bouquet, the wine was a little disappointing.
Volnay-Santenots 1973	Good colour, a fine bouquet, plenty of fruit and body and of first rate quality. A wine to buy.
White Wine Puligny-Montrachet les Combettes 1973	A delightful bouquet and flavour with a fine finish, excellent quality.
Meursault-Charmes 1973	Good colour and a very good bouquet, good fruit but still somewhat backward. Good quality all the same.
Meursault 1972	Attractive bouquet, still very young with some acidity to lose, needs three to four years.

Meursault-Charmes 1972	Heaps of character on both the nose and flavour. Lots of style here, but also too much acidity, this too needs time to develop.
Puligny-Montrachet les Combettes 1972	Another fine bouquet, good depth of flavour but still has some acidity to lose. Good quality nevertheless.
Meursault-Perrières 1972	Another fine bouquet, full-bodied, but also needs time to develop. *Note.* It is extraordinary how these 1972s have retained their youth and freshness, probably on account of their acidity. Most of them need several years yet to be at their best.
Meursault 1971	A fragrant bouquet, a good full-bodied wine which is ready now.
Meursault-Charmes 1971	A bouquet with far more distinction, a delightful taste too, outstanding quality and worthy of the finest restaurant wine list.

The white burgundies of 1973 and 1971 appear to be showing remarkably well at the moment.

Our next call was on the *négociant*, Bichot, in Beaune where Gilles de Courcel had prepared an interesting tasting for us. Besides their own wines Bichot now handle the Lupé-Cholet range as well as that of the Domaine Clos Frantin.

Also in front of us were several examples of fine Chablis from Long Depaquit. My memory goes back a long way with the latter. Although totally blind the late Monsieur Long Depaquit was an important owner as well as a splendid wine maker. It was he who actually owned the vines of Chablis Moutonne in the heart of the very best part of the whole district.

Unfortunately we were too late to taste all that had been laid out for us, but here are some notes.

Wine	*Characteristics*
White Wine	
Chablis, Les Lys 1979	Pleasant bouquet, good fruit and flavour, easy to drink.
Chablis, Vaudésir 1979	Very good bouquet, a well bred wine of fine quality.
Red Wine	
Château Gris, Nuits St.-Georges 1978 *Lupé-Cholet*	A deep colour, fine bouquet, a delightful flavour and altogether distinguished. Incidentally Château Gris is one of the finest vineyards of the *commune* of Nuits Saint-Georges.
Domaine Clos Frantin, Corton 1978	Good colour with some depth of flavour. Not so great perhaps as might be expected from this name.
Vosne-Romanée, Malconsorts 1978	Good colour and a well bred bouquet. Medium body but has an attractive flavour, should make a good bottle.
Chambertin 1978	Marvellous colour, a fine rich nose, a huge wine of great quality. It makes one realise how good these red 1978s are.

Ines and Lily de Lupé joined us for lunch at the Hotel Côte d'Or in Nuits St.-Georges, which well deserves its rosette in the Guide Michelin. With excellent *belon* oysters we greatly enjoyed the 1978 Petit Chablis of Lupé-Cholet. With such a relatively humble label, this wine is always unexpectedly good. Ines explained they have bought this particular wine for many years from a small grower and take his entire production.

Although pretty firm and immature, the 1976 Château Gris went wonderfully well with my sweetbreads and *girolles* in a cream sauce. A fine full-bodied wine which in a magnum really needs a good five or more years to show at its best. Yet another proof there is more tannin in the 1976 vintage than for many years.

Later on in the afternoon we called on Tim Marshall, an Englishman who a number of years ago now courageously established himself here as a wine broker. With him, we tasted the following.

Wine	Characteristics
1978 Macon-Villages Uchizy *Domaine Talmad*	Heaps of bouquet, a full wine with a pronounced flavour, rather good.
1979 St.-Véran *Jean Germain*	Nice bouquet, easy to taste, perhaps a little flabby.
1978 St.-Véran *Jean Germain*	Good full bouquet, still backward, but should be good in say 1982.
1979 Bourgogne Blanc (chardonnay) *Domaine Darnat*	Clean nose, fresh with a trace of acidity.
1978 Bourgogne Blanc *Domaine Darnat*	Good nose, more depth of flavour, much better.
Rhône Valley Côtes-de-Rhône	Good colour, plenty of flavour, quite good.
Domaine la Seraphine 1978 *Pascal*	Good colour, plenty of flavour, quite good.
Domaine de la Brune 1978 *Pascal*	Good colour, a nice nose, full-bodied, a really big wine, even better than La Seraphine.
Gigondas 1978 *Augustin Peyrouse*	Dark colour, a rich bouquet, a big rich wine, one to buy.

Then Tim took us to a firm new to me, Marchard Gramont, established some six years ago with an up-to-date plant which is rapidly acquiring some fine vineyards of its own.

Wine	Characteristics
1980 Bourgogne Rouge	A light wine but quite pleasant.
1980 Clos-de-Vougeot 11.3°	An unexpectedly dark colour for its year, good fruit too but with a slight bitterness at the finish of the taste.

In view of all the rain last year, the owner told us how pleased he had been to save his 1980 vintage from *pourriture*; he had used the new spray, a mixture of half Ronilau and half Sumisclex. His first spraying had been just before the flowering, the second as soon as the grapes were big enough to start touching one another, the third as they began to turn red and the fourth three weeks before the date of harvesting.

This treatment must surely be the greatest breakthrough in vine growing or viticulture of this century, as important perhaps as the introduction of grafted vines had been at the time of the phylloxera. When used correctly, it seems it avoids rotten grapes which can seriously damage any crop in unsettled weather. Grapes are particularly susceptible after rain followed by spells of hot sunshine. Those terrible years of 1963, 1965 and 1968 bore evidence of the damage which can be caused by rotten grapes.

Although this treatment appears to have been used here and there during the past two or three years, the 1980 vintage was the first time it has come to my personal notice; in fact I had heard people talking about it while in Bordeaux in October 1980. It was noticeable there was little or no *pourriture* after all that rain during the two weeks immediately preceding the picking, and I could not understand why this was so and imagined it was on account of the lack of spells of warm sunshine which noticeably had been few and far between.

Wine	Characteristics
1978 Pommard les Bertins	Made from 50 year-old vines. A lovely deep colour, a fine fruity bouquet and a splendid deep flavour. This was so good I promptly ordered some cases for myself!
1977 Pommard les Bertins	Good colour and bouquet, reminiscent of a fine tobacco, plenty of fruit and body, but a trace of bitterness.
1976 Pommard les Bertins	Very dark colour, distinguished bouquet, a big full-bodied wine with almost excessive tannin. This will need at least five years to develop properly. One is accustomed to considerable tannin in the wines of Bordeaux, but seldom does one encounter it to this extent in Burgundy. The 1976 vintage here is good all the same, but tasting the two vintages on the spot I am coming to the conclusion I prefer the 1978s which are so well balanced.

Johnnie and I were staying at the excellent hotel Lameloise in Chagny which now has three rosettes in the Guide Michelin. It must be 30 years since I first came here, when it was a modest place with very ordinary decoration, totally different from today; but even then the great attraction was the excellent cooking of Monsieur Lameloise as well as *le bon accueil* of his able wife.

The irony is that after all the tasting of the day as well as a good lunch, it is not so easy for those in the wine business to appreciate properly the splendid cooking at the Lameloise! All the same my *coquilles St. Jacques* tasted as superb as they looked and were accompanied by a very good 1978 Rully.

As I explained to Johnnie, I had never heard of this particular wine until my first visit to Burgundy in 1939, nor I think was it known much on the English market. In those days, so I am informed, it was not sold under its own label but was used chiefly for blending with better known white Burgundies in order to give them more substance. Anyway, I ordered a cask to be shipped to Block, Grey & Block in London and it arrived just before all shipments ended on the outbreak of war. It proved both inexpensive and very popular but I was in the army by then and never tasted it again.

Tuesday, 24 February

Another fine day, but still very cold. Our first call was upon Jean Pierre Naigeon, a prominent wine grower who lives in Gevrey-Chambertin. His wine is sold under the name Domaine de Varoilles, a word difficult for my English tongue to pronounce. While discussing the 1977 vintage, our host admitted it was more successful for white wine, but considered the reds were turning out better than he had expected. I was not sure I shared his enthusiasm.

Wine	*Characteristics*
Domaine de Varoilles	
1977 Gevrey-Chambertin, tastevinérm	Medium colour, not much bouquet, light to medium body. Nothing great but had quite a pleasant finish.
1977 Gevrey-Chambertin Clos Prieur, tasteviné	Medium colour, a well bred nose, quite good fruit and flavour, made from 45–50 year old vines, but obviously rather unripe grapes, hence the slightly bitter finish.

In view of the poor quality of the 1977 vintage, Monsieur Naigeon has, as it were, declassified the produce of some of his better vineyards and was selling it under the label of Gevrey-Chambertin and had done likewise with his 1979 vintage.

Wine	*Characteristics*
1977 Clos Vougeot	Medium colour, pretty bouquet, good fruit and flavour and a much better finish. Thirty to forty year old vines.
1977 Bonnes-Mares	Quite a good colour, a fragrant bouquet, quite a big wine but still some acidity.

All of the above bore the *Chevaliers du Tastevin* label, which shows they should be ostensibly better quality than many of their category.

Wine	*Charactersitics*
1976 Gevrey-Chambertin	Medium colour, a nice bouquet and body and a pleasant finish, but nothing very special.
1976 Gevrey-Chambertin, Clos Prieur	A better colour, fairly full bouquet, good body and lots of tannin as well as an unexpected trace of bitterness. At the moment the excessive tannin covers much of the fruit.
1976 Gevrey-Chambertin, La Romanée	Medium colour, attractive bouquet, a fairly light wine but with elegance and more forward than the Clos Prieur. This vineyard is situated on the uppermost part of the hillside near the trees.

1976 Gevrey-Chambertin, Clos des Varoilles	Medium colour, a delightful bouquet and a much fuller wine with more depth than the others and more character. Excellent quality. A wine I would like to buy.
1976 Bonnes-Mares	Medium colour, distinguished bouquet, good fruit and flavour. Made from 35 to 40 year old vines. Well bred, but somehow I had expected more from a Bonnes-Mares of this vintage.
1976 Clos Vougeo	Medium colour, delightful bouquet; although still undeveloped a splendid depth of flavour.

1978 Vintage

1978 Gevrey-Chambertin	Medium colour, interesting bouquet, good fruit and preferable to the 1976 vintage of same wine.
1978 Gevrey-Chambertin, Clos Prieur	Medium colour, a fine bouquet, not a big wine but has a nice taste. Also prefer this to the 1976.
1978 Gevrey-Chambertin, La Romanée	Medium colour, attractive bouquet, light, elegant and rather nice.
1978 Gevrey-Chambertin, Clos des Varoilles	Medium colour, a fine full bouquet, lots of fruit, well balanced and a nice finish. Made from old vines. Another wine to buy.
1978 Clos Vougeot	Quite a good colour, a fine scented bouquet, a lovely rounded wine with a very good finish. Prefer this even to the good 1976 Clos Vougeot. Excellent.

Later on that morning with Henri Thomas of Moillard we tasted the following:

Wine	Characteristics
1977 Chassagne-Montrachet, Blanc	Nice nose, not a big wine but pleasant.
1978 Meursault, Genevrières	Good bouquet, has a good depth of flavour too, fine quality.
1974 Nuits St.-Georges, tasteviné	Quite a nice nose, a firm masculine wine which has a good flavour. (In fact this was the Château Gris.)
1974 Volnay, Champans	Attractive bouquet, good fruit with plenty of body, *un vin solide*.
1973 Chambolle-Musigny	Good nose, medium body, lots of charm and ready now.
1978 Clos Vougeot	Fine bouquet, with an equally good flavour.
1978 Bonnes-Mares	A full attractive nose, a fine big wine.
1976 Nuits St.-Georges	Very good bouquet, has plenty of fruit and of course a lot of tannin.
1972 Corton, Clos des Vergennes	An attractive bouquet, delightful flavour, has both style and balance.
1969 Vosne-Romanée, Les Malconsorts	A lovely bouquet, a well bred mouthful of wine.
1973 Nuits Grandes Vignes	Attractive bouquet, delightful flavour with an excellent finish.

A Burgundian cellar

[191]

1972 Nuits Thorey	Fine bouquet, fine flavour.
1971 Nuits Thorey	Lovely bouquet, superb flavour, a splendid wine.

There were some first rate wines among this selection, the best among the reds at least in my view being: 1978 Clos Vougeot, 1978 Bonnes-Mares, 1976 Nuits St.-Georges, 1974 Volnay, Champans, 1973 Nuits Grandes Vignes, 1972 Corton, Clos des Vergennes, 1972 Nuits Thorey and especially 1971 Nuits Thorey.

Later on in the afternoon we called on Monsieur Clair Dau.

Wine	Characteristics
Rosé de Marsannay 1978	A pale colour of course, a pleasant bouquet, quite sweet and easy to taste. (*Note* Monsieur Dau enjoys a considerable success with this *rosé*.)
1974 Gevrey-Chambertin, Clos St.-Jacques	Medium body, well bred but not exceptional.
1974 Bonnes-Mares	Good nose, lots of fruit and flavour, but could have more charm. Perhaps it is the vintage!
1973 Gevrey-Chambertin, Clos St.-Jacques, tasteviné	Rather pale colour, medium body, very good bouquet, elegant and of fine quality.
1973 Bonnes-Mares, tasteviné	A delightful bouquet, not a big wine but has a lovely flavour.

Thursday 26 February

The first call was on Roland Thevenin in Puligny-Montrachet. There is a plaque on his house which says that Napoleon's mother, Letitia Bonaparte, stayed there in 1815 on her way to Italy.

In the post-war period it was still a penance to taste in the cellar on a cold morning such as this, but nowadays the cellars are heated sufficiently to get the malolactic fermentation over as quickly as possible, so there was no hardship. Our hosts were Monsieur Galet of the firm of Poulet in Beaune and Ronnie Thompson, an Englishman and a director of an Anglo-Swiss firm, Alesia, which has just taken over both Thevenin and Poulet.

Usually so soon after the vintage most white wines are still cloudy, but the first, an exceedingly dry 1980 Bourgogne Blanc, was clear of all fermentation. We tried three other 1980s, the Puligny-Montrachet, Les Rechaux was still fermenting, but the other two, a Meursault *premier cru* and a Puligny-Montrachet, Les Folatières, in spite of their vintage showed some promise. It would appear the white 1980s are going to be more successful than the reds.

Wine	Characteristics
1979 Puligny-Montrachet, Les Folatières	An attractive bouquet, very good flavour and plenty of quality, a wine to buy.
1979 Puligny-Montrachet, Clos de la Garenne	A fine distinguished bouquet with an equally attractive taste. Even better than Les Folatières. Also a wine to buy.

Later on Madame Thevenin and her son invited us into the house to taste their excellent 1978 Clos de la Garenne. It had a lovely full flavour and appeared every bit as good as it did when I bought some for my own cellar in England.

It is difficult to keep on schedule when tasting so we were late in arriving at Joseph Drouhin. However we were not too late to taste some of Robert Drouhin's 1979 white and 1978 reds – the general quality was impressive. In fact this particular visit to Burgundy has done quite a lot to diminish some of my disillusion which has been building up over the years. A number of *négociants* and growers appear to be more aware of the ground they have lost both in the U.S. and Britain.

White wines

Wine	Characteristics
1979 Chablis	Quite a full bouquet, on dry side but with a pleasant flavour.
1979 Chablis, *premier cru*	A rounder bouquet, a fuller wine with an attractive taste.
1979 Chablis, Les Clos	A delightful scented bouquet with a lovely continuing range of flavours. Needs about two years. Robert told us he has been increasing his ownership of vineyards in Chablis and in future will have a fairly broad range of the famous names.
1979 Meursault	Nice nose, good fruit and flavour.
1979 Beaune, Clos des Mouches	A fuller bouquet than the Meursault, quite full-bodied too with an attractive honeyed flavour. Robert explained that recently he had changed the method of vinification of this particular wine, giving it more finesse than hitherto. We were to notice this later on when we compared it with the 1969 vintage. Although a fine full flavoured wine, the 1969 did not have the elegance and distinction of the 1979 so the change is clearly for the better.

Red wines

Wine	Characteristics
1978 Vosne-Romanée, Les Beaumonts	Good colour, a delightful bouquet, lovely taste with a fine finish, a nice 'long' wine and one to buy.
1978 Chorey les Beaune	A pretty bouquet, not a big wine but packed with charm. Unfortunately this name is not well known, but this should make a delightful bottle before too long. A wine to buy.
1978 Griottes-Chambertin	Dark colour, excellent bouquet, a really good flavour, another one to buy!

Later on in the afternoon we called at the Domaine Jacques Prieur situated on the outskirts of Meursault. Formerly the production had been under contract to Calvet in Beaune; indeed on my last visit I had been shown around by Pierre Poupon, a son-in-law of the late Jacques Prieur and himself an authority and author of several important books on the wine of Burgundy.

Our present host, Jean Prieur, explained that the contract was now coming to an end and the family was already entitled to sell half the crop themselves.

The demand it appears is brisk especially for export, and the entire 1978 stock, both red and white, was already sold.

The 1980 white wines were still fermenting, but we tried the 1980 Beaune Clos de la Feguine, a vineyard which is entirely owned by the family. A few good wines are always made in a poor vintage, but on the whole 1980 is of little importance for red wine, although not too bad for white. Surprisingly the colour of this 1980 Clos de la Feguine was fairly dark and although very young it appeared to be quite good. We then tried the 1979 vintage from the same vineyard and it was of course considerably fuller and better. This family also owns vines in Chambertin, Chambertin Clos-de-Bèze, Chambolle-Musigny and Volnay, but is better known for its white wine.

Wine	Characteristics
1979 Meursault, Clos de la Mazeray	An elegant bouquet with a fine flavour.
1979 Meursault-Perrières	A fuller deeper bouquet, a fine fairly full-bodied wine.
1979 Puligny-Montrachet, Les Combettes	An attractive well bred bouquet, plenty of fruit but a more 'earthy' flavour.
1979 Chevalier-Montrachet	A fine bouquet, a wine with lots of style and breeding, at the moment though appeared on the light side with some acidity to lose.
1979 Montrachet	A much fuller richer bouquet, a fine full-flavoured wine, still some acidity to lose though.

All of the above had only been bottled a month before and clearly had not yet had time to settle down; no doubt they will all be showing much better later on this year.

With Patrick Javillier in Meursault.

Wine	Characteristics
1979 Bourgogne Blanc	Clean but very dry.
1979 Chablis	A nice fresh dry wine.
1979 Meursault, Les Tillets	(from his own vines). Attractive nose, good flavour and plenty of character.
1979 Meursault, Clos du Cromin	(also his own vines). A good bouquet, a rounder wine with more depth than Les Tillets.
1979 Chassagne-Montrachet	Good bouquet, full flavoured and quite good.
1979 Meursault-Charmes	Nice nose, plenty of body, but it tailed off at the finish.

The reds which had been set out for us were really too light in style and too expensive for our market, rather typical of much modern red burgundy and it is not surprising the demand has dropped both in Britain and America. It is just as well some of the *négociants* like Robert Drouhin and Moillard as well as a number of the growers have realised this fact and are taking steps to rectify an obvious weakness. The world demand for red burgundy is well in excess of supply, and the temptation to over-produce must have been difficult to resist. In many cases the result has been expensive pale coloured rather thin stuff, ready to drink early and unworthy of the famous vineyard concerned. So far, there is nowhere in the world where *pinot noir* can touch the potential of burgundy, so surely it is better to concentrate on quality rather than quantity.

Patrick confirmed that the white 1979s are more flattering at the moment and more commercial than the probably finer 1978s, but the latter will keep better and should be finer in the long run.

We then set off southwards to drive to the Beaujolais where we had booked rooms at the Chapon Fin in Thoisey. It was Paul Blanc, the proprietor who, 30 years ago, introduced me to the late Eugène Dessalle and he opened my eyes to the possibility of genuine Beaujolais. At that time the British bought their Beaujolais in Beaune and Nuits and few if any came as far south as the district itself. The wine they purchased had mostly been suitably blended for the English market. The growers I met at that time told me I was the first English merchant to buy wine straight from them and were so pleased they asked me to form a chapter of the Compagnons du Beaujolais in London so that at least a few people in England would know what genuine Beaujolais tasted like. All the same, while the method of purchase is altogether better nowadays and the wine more authentic, I have a feeling that the general standard has dropped somewhat with many growers concentrating more on the quick turnover of the Beaujolais Nouveau, in my opinion a much over-rated commodity.

<table>
<tr><td>*Friday 27 February*</td><td>The fine weather had left us but since this was Johnnie's first visit to the district we drove through the fog along the Route du Beaujolais in order to show him what a beautiful country it is.</td></tr>
</table>

At Belleville-sur-Sâone we called on Robert Felizzato who manages Les Caves de Champclos, where we tasted a nice Macon Blanc as well as a Pouilly-Fuissé of 1979. Most of his best 1979s had already been sold, and he told us the 1980s were so poor he was not going to buy any. Even so, later on while visiting Georges Duboeuf we did try some of his 1980s, but they were very pale in colour, very light and must surely be short-lived. His 1979s were infinitely more serious.

During the week we had been collecting samples of Bourgogne Rouge, so before departure we arranged a blind tasting and of the dozen bottles, those which came out best were from Moillard, Marchard Gramont and Lupé-Cholet.

To sum up, this seems to have been an unusually good moment to visit Burgundy. Perhaps it is unwise to be too dogmatic but for red wine, 1978 could prove one of the finest vintages for many years, even better perhaps than 1971. Apart from their charm and obvious quality, the 1978s seem to be extremely well balanced. The 1976s are also good if not quite in the same class; their balance is not so regular as that of the 1978s and they have a large percentage of the tannin, caused no doubt by that hot summer in 1976.

The white wines are equally exciting; the 1979s are full of charm and should prove to be very commercial although they may not have a long life. The 1978s on the other hand are still closed up and backward. These firm well-made wines should turn out really well, as well perhaps as the 1971s. It should therefore be possible to drink the attractive 1979s first and give the finer 1978s sufficient time to show their true worth.

St. Etienne la Varenne

Château de Corton

The inauguration of the Paris chapter of Les Amis du Vin

M.T.S. Daphne: Harry and Prue on the vintage cruise

The enthronement of the Mayor of Bristol as a Compagnon de Beaujolais

Index

Acknowledgements

The author and publishers wish to thank the following for kind permission to reproduce the illustrations on the pages quoted: 55, Hank Case; 96 and 97, Michael Kennedy; 151, 155, 191, 196, Food from France; 175, Lord Snowdon; 184, Doug McKenzie; 73, 131, 149, Alan Gagney. We would also like to thank Alison Stanford and Edmund Penning-Rowsell for reading the proofs.